NO FREE SPEECH FOR FASCISTS

No Free Speech for Fascists explores the choice of anti-fascist protesters to demand that the opportunities for fascists to speak in public places are rescinded, as a question of history, law, and politics. It explains how the demand to no platform fascists emerged in 1970s Britain, as a limited exception to a left-wing tradition of support for free speech.

The book shows how no platform was intended to be applied narrowly, only to a right-wing politics that threatened everyone else. It contrasts the rival idea of opposition to hate speech that also emerged at the same time and is now embodied in European and British anti-discrimination laws. Both no platform and hate speech reject the American First Amendment tradition of free speech, but the ways in which they reject it are different. Behind no platform is not merely a limited range of political targets but a much greater scepticism about the role of the state. The book argues for an idea of no platform which takes on the electronic channels on which so much speech now takes place. It shows where a fascist element can be recognised within the much wider category of far-right speech.

This book will be of interest to activists and to those studying and researching political history, law, free speech, the far right, and anti-fascism. It sets out a philosophy of anti-fascism for a social media age.

David Renton is a British historian and barrister. His other books include *Labour's Antisemitism Crisis: What Should the Left Have Done?* (Routledge 2022) and *Never Again: Rock Against Racism and the Anti-Nazi League 1976–1982* (Routledge 2019).

Routledge Studies in Fascism and the Far Right
Series editors

Nigel Copsey, Teesside University, UK and Graham Macklin, Center for Research on Extremism (C-REX), University of Oslo, Norway.

This new book series focuses upon fascist, far right and right-wing politics primarily within a historical context but also drawing on insights from other disciplinary perspectives. Its scope also includes radical-right populism, cultural manifestations of the far right and points of convergence and exchange with the mainstream and traditional right.

Titles include:

The Rise of the Dutch New Right
An Intellectual History of the Rightward Shift in Dutch Politics
Merijn Oudenampsen

Anti-fascism in a Global Perspective
Transnational Networks, Exile Communities and Radical Internationalism
Edited by Kasper Braskén, Nigel Copsey and David Featherstone

British Fascism After the Holocaust
From the Birth of Denial to the Notting Hill Riots 1939–1958
Joe Mulhall

Fascism, Nazism and the Holocaust
Challenging Histories
Dan Stone

France's Purveyors of Hatred
Aspects of the French Extreme Right and its Influence, 1918–1945
Richard Griffiths

Conservatives and Right Radicals in Interwar Europe
Edited by Marco Bresciani

Radical Right Populism in Germany
AfD, Pegida, and the Identitarian Movement
Ralf Havertz

No Free Speech for Fascists
Exploring 'No Platform' in History, Law and Politics
David Renton

Global Resurgence of the Right
Conceptual and Regional Perspectives
Edited by Gisela Pereyra Doval and Gastón Souroujon

For more information about this series, please visit: www.routledge.com/
Routledge-Studies-in-Fascism-and-the-Far-Right/book-series/FFR

NO FREE SPEECH FOR FASCISTS

Exploring 'No Platform' in History, Law and Politics

David Renton

LONDON AND NEW YORK

First published 2021
by Routledge
2 Park Square, Milton Park, Abingdon, Oxon, OX14 4RN

and by Routledge
605 Third Avenue, New York, NY 10158

Routledge is an imprint of the Taylor & Francis Group, an informa business

© 2021 David Renton

The right of David Renton to be identified as author of this work has been asserted by him in accordance with sections 77 and 78 of the Copyright, Designs and Patents Act 1988.

British Library Cataloguing-in-Publication Data
A catalogue record for this book is available from the British Library

Library of Congress Cataloging-in-Publication Data
A catalog record has been requested for this book

ISBN: 978-0-367-72219-7 (hbk)
ISBN: 978-0-367-72062-9 (pbk)
ISBN: 978-1-003-15393-1 (ebk)

Typeset in Bembo
by Deanta Global Publishing Services, Chennai, India

CONTENTS

1

INTRODUCTION

The purpose of this book is to help readers decide whether fascists should be allowed to speak.[1] The scenario it envisages is as follows. The leaders of a political party share with interwar fascism a taste for violence, an insistence that the nation is under threat and that their country can only be restored to greatness if democracy is limited and the party's many critics silenced. One of those leaders has been offered a platform: a chance to give a televised talk, or an election meeting, or a lecture at a university. Anti-fascists insist that if the fascist is permitted to speak the rights of everyone else will be diminished. They call on the organisers to rescind the fascist's invitation to speak. Are the anti-fascists correct to demand that the fascist meeting is cancelled?

There are other books which also address this question. Most of their authors say that restricting free speech in this way is always and unequivocally wrong (i.e. that free speech must take precedence),[2] or that it is usually wrong (i.e. that free speech is an absolute priority until the point at which a speaker advocates violence against their opponents or physically intimidates them, in which case a prohibition is justified).[3] You can characterise these both as free speech positions, albeit that one is absolute while the other is conditional.

The theme of this book is whether speech can legitimately be restricted even in circumstances where violence is only a latent rather than an immediate threat. Fifty years ago, parts of the British left worked out a sophisticated answer to this question: no platform. Since then, the phrase "no platform" has become common across the English-speaking world, as has the related but different idea of "deplatforming."[4] The way these terms have been used is less specific than in the 1970s and includes actions (for example, the restriction of access to social media sites) which were inconceivable 50 years ago. The original idea of no platform was to deny opportunities to speak to fascists because they were fascists. The tradition of Mussolini and Hitler believed in silencing Communists, conservatives, liberals, feminists, indeed *everyone* except for themselves. Refusing to let their speech go unanswered was not about reducing the number of people speaking; rather, it was a means of protecting the number of people who could be heard.

The distinctiveness of no platform lay not only in answer to the question of who should be refused a platform (i.e. fascists, and fascists only). The theory also had an idea as to who should decide whether a speech was curtailed. The subject of no platform was a mass movement, whether of radical trade unionists, rebellious students, or advocates of black power or of women's liberation. The supporters of no platform were not asking for the state to side with them. Rather, they assumed that an insurgent people needed to take back power both from the authoritarian wing of the state and from its allies, among whom the fascists could be counted.

Often, advocates of free speech warn of what they call the "taboo ratchet."[5] It is impossible, they argue, to limit one category of unwanted speech without causing others to say that they too have unwanted opponents whose chances to speak should be limited. If you would oppose fascists, they ask, who else would you ban?[6] In response, no platform gives a simple answer. Fascism is qualitatively different from all other forms of politics, including right-wing or even far-right politics. Unlike them, it seeks to create a dictatorship and one in which all rival forms of speech would be curtailed. It is a politics of unlimited censorship.[7] Its threat enables anti-fascists to refuse speaking rights to fascists only. The right-wing landscape of the 1970s was no less complex than our own, with each of the following prominent in public discussions – economic monetarists, anti-abortion campaigners, supporters of the death penalty – and many other kinds of right-wing politics beside them. Advocates of no platform criticised each of these trends, might have attended their meetings and heckled them, but held back from stopping their speech altogether.

Alongside that approach, there were ideas about the role of fascism in relation to other right-wing movements. Anti-abortion or anti-immigration protesters might ally, during an election, in support for a Conservative or Republican candidate. But fascism was not just a single-issue politics. It was a total theory of life. It saw itself as the "Spearhead" for the advance of inegalitarian ideas.[8] Fascism was capable of breaking through in moments of crisis, and when it did it taught its supporters to absorb reactionary answers to every social question.

The uniqueness of fascism lies not merely in its dictatorial ambitions, nor in the way it offers its supporters a total theory of reactionary politics. The other way in which fascism is distinctive is that it has employed violence against a wide range of opponents at every stage of its development: the model of fascism which contemporary far-right parties seek to emulate is not merely that of Hitler's racial dictatorship, but also the Mussolini of 1921–1922, who encouraged his support-ers to attack and burn socialist buildings and kill their occupants. There is no rupture in the history of fascism; no moment of innocence after which a healthy political development was driven off course. Rather it has used violence against its racial and political opponents continuously: as a minority within a wider milieu of disgruntled ex-soldiers, then as a political party, as one large enough to contest for power, as a faction governing in coalition with others, and as a dictatorship. In all these different stages of its history, fascism's violence was extensive.

As well as the part they played in the murder of six million Jews, Hitler and Mussolini were also supporters of genocide against the Roma and Sinti, advocates of a sped-up and ultra-aggressive form of colonial racism, of the subordination of women, of the destructions of unions and the murder of Communists. Each of these plans reinforced one another. This totalising dynamic made fascism a uniquely destructive enemy.

Fifty years ago, the collective memory of the 1920s and 1930s was clearer than it is today. The interwar years were seen as a time of economic crisis, in which fascists had been able to grow quickly. Both in Italy and Germany, they had begun as factions of a large anti-political milieu with barely a few dozen supporters. From there, the fascists acquired members to the point where they were hegemonic on the right and non-fascists were required to bend to them. Anti-fascists in the late 1970s did not expect that they were facing the same immediate danger, but if there was any possibility that fascism might enjoy a similar dynamic of explosive growth, the prudent approach was to organise against fascists when their supporters were few.

No platform as a range of behaviours

So far, no platform has been described as if it was a single thing: a group of campaigners co-operating to do all they can to have a fascist's invitation rescinded. This is however a simplification. No platform has been a spectrum of tactics. At its most moderate, no platform takes in (for example) the Labour candidates, who in the 1990s sought to curb the rise of the British National Party by refusing to share a platform with members of that party. In so doing, they helped to isolate the BNP and deny it the legitimacy it craved.

At the other end of the scale, no platform included militant anti-fascists who attempted to disrupt far-right meetings. So, to take another example from Britain, in the 1940s anti-fascists would try to occupy public speaking places which otherwise would be taken by supporters of Oswald Mosley's Union Movement. Such activity could be time-consuming, even exhausting. When supporters of the Union Movement saw what anti-fascists were doing, they responded by coming earlier to the same sites until both groups were having to sleep overnight in order to hold the best "pitches." Those who occupied these spaces bore every risk of physical attack, in the dark, or when they were asleep. Often enough, anti-fascists would not try to occupy a space pre-emptively but capture ground which was being held by fascists. Anti-fascists' memories of this period include being attacked by fascists armed with knives, knuckledusters, and razorblades.

Between these two extremes, there were all sorts of behaviours. Near the minimal end of commitment, no platform might involve researching a venue where a talk was due to take place and phoning the owner and inviting them to reconsider the booking; or organising a petition to the managers of a meeting-space to demand that a talk was cancelled.

Closer to the militant end, anti-fascists took part in intelligence gathering, posing as members of far-right groups, collecting lists of names – and this was never an activity which could be done without a physical risk to those who volunteered for it.[9]

For the purposes of this book, "no platform" is treated as a shared frame of reference, but no one should imagine that beneath this slogan there has ever been a consensus as to how exactly fascism should be stopped. Even amongst those who have agreed in seeing fascism as a uniquely threatening enemy, and even among those who emphasised self-activity over petitioning the state, the debates have continued as to which speakers to target and how best to defeat them.

No platform and hate speech

Although the term "no platform" was used repeatedly by different left-wing activists in the 1970s, it emerged alongside other approaches for answering racism or fascism and its ideas must be disentangled from theirs. Since the 1970s, no platform has given way to a similar seeming but in fact different argument that freedom of expression should be rescinded when a speaker is likely to offend a significant part of his or her audience. Its approach to the scenario with which this book opened is on the surface the same no platform: if a speaker would treat a group of people as less than human, if the speaker would offend and humiliate them, it is right to rescind the speaker's invitation. This position is often assumed to be identical to no platform, but the rationale for rejecting hate speech is radically different. A hate speech approach insists that speech must be limited whenever it would be hateful to those who would be humiliated by it.

Although a hate speech politics can co-operate with no platform, the former has a different underlying philosophy and leads to different conclusions. It gives a different answer to the question: who else would you condemn, other than fascists? In the early 1970s, its supporters answered: only other racists. But soon other justice campaigns demanded – and plausibly – that they too required protection. There never has been a convincing argument for saying that racism is a unique evil and should be condemned, while sexist or homophobic speech can be tolerated.

A further distinction between the strategies of no platform and hate speech is that the advocates of the latter rarely distinguish between strategies to stop fascism from above or below. Their priority is to stop demeaning language and only unusually do those involved consider whether hate speech should be stopped (as it was in the 1970s) by pickets and demonstrations, or (more often these days) by complaints to social media companies, university administrators, or the police. While there has been a range of opinion within no platform, and indeed within those who sought to prevent hate speech, in general, no platform has given much more care to the question of who is doing the banning, and how fascists are to be stopped (Table 1.1).

TABLE 1.1 Hate speech v no platform

	Hate speech	No platform
Who can be banned	Fascists, the far right, racists, sexists, homophobes, transphobes, anyone who uses discriminatory language in any form	Fascists
Who applies the ban	A judge, a police officer, university managers, the owner of a business (including, often, a media business)	An insurgent people: workers, students, members of an oppressed community

The hate speech approach typically requires a good faith response from others with greater political power than those who initiate the original anti-fascist protest. A weak, top-down protest movement might require media companies or university administrators to do all the work for them. Even a more confident protest movement hopes that the managers who have acquired a taste for banning will stop there and will not proceed to silence the left, Muslims, LGBT activists, etc. The greater the power of the interceding authority, the harder it is for protest movements to influence it. Part of the purpose of this book is to argue that, in justifying the limitation of meetings by invoking the risk of hate speech, the left has made a misstep. This approach has widened the radical objection to free speech too far and lost sight of who enforces it.

Structure

The early chapters of this book describe how the left and right have approached the wider question of censorship. The left has until recently supported free speech in almost all contexts other than fascism. The starting assumption that speech should be free is, surely, the correct one. It fits comfortably with left-wing ideas both of negative freedom (a weakening of the state in favour of ordinary people), and of positive freedom (a future in which people are at absolute freedom to say, read, or do whatever they like). The emergence of no platform in 1970s Britain is placed within the left-wing milieu in which it was born, and a time when the right and left repeatedly clashed in the streets. There were millions of people watching who had no great love for either the Front or its opponents. With each new act of NF violence, however, more and more people came to accept that the Front were not just another party but a threat to almost everyone.

Yet, from the mid-1980s onwards, the far right has grown, beginning with the breakthrough of Jean-Marie Le Pen in France, through a series of clashes in which free speech arguments played a part. The right has become more experienced at claiming victimhood and has used the threat posed to its entitlement to speak as a means to win recruits.

The far right's support for free speech has remained partial and limited. So, for example, the far-right platform Gab calls itself: "A social network that champions free speech, individual liberty and the free flow of information online."[10] Yet it hosts any number of people who are militantly opposed to free speech, who are planning to remove all rights to speak from their racially defined opponents, including Muslims and Jews. In October 2018, one of Gab's members, Robert Bowers, boasted of his willingness to carry out a mass murder. Condemning other rightists as cowards, he posted, "Screw your optics, I'm going in," before driving to the Tree of Life synagogue in Pittsburgh and shooting and killing 11 of the Jewish worshipers.[11] How could free expression be achieved by allowing innocent people to be shot and making their voices permanently silent? Yet, narrow and partisan as its support for free speech has been, the association of the far right with the principle of free expression has been to its advantage.

The middle chapters of the book are dedicated to explaining why hate speech is an insecure basis on which to oppose fascist speech – or any form of hurtful speech. Those who oppose unwanted speech on the grounds that it is immiserating argue that there is a credible distinction to be drawn between benign and hateful speech. To qualify as sufficiently offensive to be hate speech, such language must not be merely unpleasant, it must also derive some of its effect from the subordinate status of the people at which it is aimed: a member of an oppressed group.

One difficulty with this approach comes when you take seriously the relationship between hateful speech and the subaltern character of the people it targets. This is a more complex point than many opponents of hate speech realise. For, as a consequence of the partial success of previous struggles, we live with a rightly expanding vocabulary of concepts, all of which capture some aspects of social power and powerlessness: race, sex, disability, sexual orientation, age, religion, or belief … Almost everyone is in a subordinate position on one of these axes. In recent years the far right has learned to pose itself as the defender of certain powerless groups who are defined in opposition to other members of the oppressed: in Holland 20 years ago as the champion of gay men against migrants, or in Britain in recent years as the hero of women and children against the imagined voracious sexuality of Muslim men.

The middle chapters of this book set out in more detail the logic of hate speech, drawing on the writings of one of its most sophisticated advocates, Jeremy Waldron,[12] and showing how that idea is reflected in UK and EU anti-harassment law. These chapters explore the difficulties that the courts – meaning the Supreme Court in the United States, the European Court of Human Rights, and civil courts in the UK – have had in following social activists' distinction between powerful groups and powerless minorities, or in applying their insistence that the militant supporters of the powerful only should be denied their right to speak.

Politics increasingly takes place online, on competing network media whose underlying business model is based on advertising and audience competition. Part of the right's recent appeal has been the success it has had in presenting its supporters as victims. People who were not previously supporters of the far right have felt that in their own lives they were prevented from speaking and have seen the far right as allies. By campaigning against hate speech, left-wing radicals (against all our intentions) have equipped the right with a moral claim of self-defence.

The final chapters of this book examine the politics of no platform and hate speech in relation to the crisis of the past five years. A further complexity is explored: the increasing ideological diversity of the far right and the relative subordination of fascism. This, again, poses a challenge for those who would restrict fascist speech. Are there any fascists left, or do all our opponents belong to the more amorphous category of the far right? Where, within the far right, should the line be drawn? Is it appropriate to call for removal of speech rights from people who accept the rules of democratic politics? This book argues that in focussing on the style of fascism, in particular its ideological debt to the 1930s and its use of violence, it is still possible to distinguish between fascism and other far-right traditions and for anti-fascists to resist the former group. But this approach requires sophistication and a knowledge of your enemy to be effective.

Where a speaker belongs to a clearly non-fascist far right, this book argues, the starting point should be to challenge the speaker's views rather than to deny them a platform. This book gives examples of activists succeeding in disrupting and mocking far-right speeches, without needing to have their invitation to speak altogether rescinded.

In most books which address the issue of free speech for the far right, the answer of whether a fascist should be permitted to speak or not is treated as a straightforward one, delivering a quick and easy answer. That is not the approach of this book. It understands that being principled is difficult; and that living by a political code requires you to constantly reassess your assumptions and to consider the risk that you are mistaken. Anti-fascists can get this wrong: either by allowing destructive forms of politics a chance to organise without opposition, or by extending the category of unwanted speech so widely that our opponents can claim a fake mantle of victimhood.

In short, this book argues in defence of no platform, not as a universal approach to be adopted in response to all far-right politics, but as a necessary and limited incursion to free speech, a means of resisting groups which stand recognisably in a fascist tradition.

Notes

1 My thanks to Craig Fowlie, Sadie Fulton, Graham Macklin, Shelley Mack, Gary McNally, Evan Smith, Jeff Sparrow, Gavan Titley, and Alyx Zauderer for their comments on drafts of this manuscript, and to the many other friends, in person and online, with whom I have shared parts of this book. My love above all to Anne, Sam, and Ben with whom I have discussed the ideas more keenly than anyone.
2 N. Strossen, *Hate: Why We Should Resist It with Free Speech* (Oxford: Oxford University Press, 2018); M. Hume, *Trigger Warning: Is the Fear of Being Offensive Killing Free Speech* (London: Collins, 2015); A. Neier, *Defending My Enemy: American Nazis, the Skokie Case, and the Risks of Freedom of Speech* (New York: International Debate Education

Association, 2012 edn); K. S. Stern, *The Conflict over the Conflict: The Israel/Palestine Campus Debate* (Toronto: New Jewish Press, 2020).

3 T. Garton Ash, *Free Speech: Ten Principles for a Connected World* (New Haven, CT: Yale University Press, 2016).

4 E. Smith, *No Platform: A History of Anti-Fascism, Universities, and the Limits of Free Speech* (London: Routledge, 2020).

5 Garton Ash, *Free Speech*, pp. 159, 249.

6 A. Brown and A. Sinclair, *The Politics of Hate Speech Laws* (London: Routledge, 2020), pp. 220–240.

7 There is a popular internet meme which captures this point. In the left-hand column it set outs 14 groups of people who are hated by fascists, including disabled people, feminists, socialists, Jews, trade unionists, and many others. In the right-hand column, it lists the sole group hated by anti-fascists: "fascists."

8 The title of a magazine edited between 1964 and 2005 by John Tyndall, the sometime chairman of the (British) National Front.

9 See the discussion of the life in Wendy Turner in D. Renton, 'We Fight Fascists,' *Lives Running*, 23 October 2020.

10 Accessed 20 July 2020.

11 J. Sparrow, *Fascists Among Us: Online Hate and the Christchurch Massacre* (London: Scribe, 2019), p. 60.

12 J. Waldron, *The Harm in Hate Speech* (Cambridge, MA: Harvard University Press, 2012).

PART I

History

2

FREE SPEECH C. 1640–C. 1972

The idea of no platform was first drawn up by small groups of socialists in Britain in the early 1970s. The people who applied the theory were left-wingers and some were the veterans of free speech campaigns, in which they had been the people threatened with censorship by an over-mighty state. The people whose platforms they sought to restrict, i.e. fascists, were in all other contexts the enemies of free expression. No platform was intended to be a strict, limited exception to a general approach of free speech.

It is not possible to grasp both sides of no platform, i.e. both its willingness to curtail fascist speech and its unwillingness to extend that prohibition further, without fully contextualising it and locating it in a longer tradition of left-wing thinking.

The theme of this chapter is that for most of the past four centuries, and up to 1972 when no platform was formulated, the left has been on the side of maximum public expression. Free speech was an "active partisan signifier," i.e. a programme associated with the left and a way that the left distinguished itself from the right. In the last 40 years, as writers such as Stanley Fish (*There's No Such Thing as Free Speech*),[1] or P. E. Moskowitz (*The Case Against Free Speech*)[2] observe, the term has been broken out of that context. Free speech has been repackaged first as a universal imperative to which no rational person might object, and then as a banner behind which an electoral right and a street far right could ally.

Later chapters of this book describe how that change happened and how the mainstream right took up a demand which it had not previously supported. This chapter is concerned with what free speech meant in European and American politics between 1640 or so (i.e. during the first steps of the political and social revolution that would lead to the execution of King Charles in England) and around 1970 (i.e. when the centre-right grasped that it needed to reach a compromise with the post-war left around free expression and which was the prelude to today's backlash).

During the three centuries in which free speech was a left-wing cause, the left chose the side which best reflected its values – of equality for all, and especially for groups such as workers or the poor who faced the greatest risk of being silenced.

The right gave little or no support to campaigns for free speech. Often, it actively supported censorship. At other times, it was indifferent to the issue, arguing for the toleration of its own programme and speakers, and blithe to the suppression of people it disagreed with. Where censorship ran at 90 degrees to party politics – where it concerned obscenity – major thinkers of the right and the right's senior politicians either supported censorship or were untroubled by it.

For hundreds of years, the different approaches to free speech were never simply a matter of politics, but nor was the division between left and right ever far from sight. Those who wished to weaken the monarchy and aristocracy opposed censorship, while those who wanted the old rulers to remain in power unchallenged opposed greater free speech. In the words of one historian of seventeenth century Britain, Sheila Lambert:

> Attitudes to censorship have always been to some extent a matter of personal and political predilection … Writers who wish to champion the underdog and take the side of those who strive against authority find censorship everywhere, while those who prefer law, order and a quiet life are inclined to belittle the importance of occasional instances of repression, however ferocious those are shown to be.[3]

The left and the right in revolutions

Our modern categories of left and right go back to the events of the English and French Revolutions of 1649 and 1789. In both cases, there was a party of change and a party of restoration. During the French Revolution, the advocates of maintained royal power stood in the National Assembly on the right side of the assembly's president, while those who held most firmly to the revolution stood to his left.[4] It is at this moment that the left and right were born.

In England, the pre-revolutionary rules of Queen Elizabeth, and Kings James and Charles practised censorship routinely. Since the practice was pervasive and uncontroversial, ministers barely had a language for it. Certainly, there was no equivalent of our modern idea of defending free speech from authority. Such courts as the High Commission and the Star Chamber heard complaints against single-sheet pamphlets, books and printed ballads which disturbed the peace, libelled the monarch, or which denounced the behaviour of his supporters (the aristocracy, the clergy, etc.). In France both the monarchy and the Church practised censorship, with the latter publishing indices of banned books, starting in 1559 and continuing until recent times.

In terms of understanding left defences of free speech, a key figure is the poet John Milton whose 1644 address to Parliament, *Areopagitica*, contrasts the tradition of freedom to that of censorship. "Who kills a Man kills a reasonable creature, Gods Image," he argued, "but hee who destroyes a good Booke, kills reason it selfe, kills the Image of God, as it were in the eye." Tailoring his argument to the reform-minded and patriotic instincts of his listeners, Milton contrasted life in Protestant England with its culture of reverence for the written word with Catholic Europe, where values of authoritarianism and censorship flourished:

> I could recount what I have seen and heard in other Countries, where this kind of inquisition tyrannizes; when I have sat among their lerned men, for that honor I had, and bin counted happy to be born in such a place of Philosophic freedom, as they suppos'd England was, while themselvs did nothing but bemoan the servil condition into which lerning amongst them was brought.[5]

Today, Milton is often read as the prophet of universal tolerance. But he was also a revolutionary; he supported a military uprising against absolute monarchy. While allowing the principle that Royalists should have access to print, he wanted to see their armies defeated in the field. When looking at the right, he drew a distinction between those of his enemies who advocated a return to the King's rule (much though he disagreed with them, he would not deny access to their writings), and those who would bring the methods of the Inquisition to Britain. It was in this context that he allowed one exception to the rule that all voices should be heard. If a party advocated general censorship ("suppression") and if the plans of that party had any real prospects of success, then their views and theirs alone no longer deserved wide circulation: "[I]t would be no unequall distribution in the first place to suppresse the suppressors themselves."[6]

The nearest the Anglophone right has to a defence of censorship is in the writing of Edmund Burke, the founder of the modern conservative tradition, whose 1790 book *Reflections on the Revolution in France* made the case that the people are incapable of governing themselves, but must always require a ruler to protect them. While Burke was chiefly concerned with the defence of the existing sovereign and of property, his idea of popular rights (which are few) and responsibilities (which are many) created the space for a defence of censorship. The publication of books, Burke argued, gave rise to both desirable and undesirable outcomes, to learning and to libel. In pre-revolutionary Europe, books were published in the defence of the existing order and, as such, there was no good reason to limit their publication or to censor them:

> Learning paid back what it received to nobility and to priesthood, and paid it with usury, by enlarging their ideas and by furnishing their minds. Happy if they had all continued to know their indissoluble union and their

proper place! Happy if learning, not debauched by ambition, had been sat-
isfied to continue the instructor, and not aspired to be the master![7]

Once learning had ceased to protect property, however, then it became libel,
and the appropriate place for its author was in jail. In France, before 1789, error
had gone unpunished. "The desultory and faint persecution carried on against
them, more from compliance with form and decency than with serious resent-
ment, neither weakened their strength nor relaxed their efforts." A relaxation of
censorship in England might prove fatal. Burke made this point through a discussion of the eighteenth-century radical Lord George Gordon, who had been
jailed following riots in 1780:

> We have rebuilt Newgate and tenanted the mansion. We have rebuilt pris-
> ons also as strong as the Bastille, for those who dare to libel the queens of
> France. In this spiritual retreat, let the noble libeller remain.[8]

This passage was aimed at a single instance of irresponsible speech: Gordon's
followers had criticised the crown, demanded the suppression of Catholicism
(which was assumed to be the ideological pillar of absolutist monarchy) and taken
to the streets where they set fire to the Bank of England. It indicated Burke's
general approach, in which politics was always seen from the perspective of the
interests of the state and, beneath that, rights of the propertied. So that if anyone
was foolish enough to say that the wealth of the rich should be shared among the
poor, this opinion ("libel") was so obviously wrong and contemptible that its
speaker should be imprisoned.

Twenty years later, a young Prince Metternich, the Henry Kissinger of nine-
teenth-century Europe, set out a vision of how to turn the back the tide on revolutionary sentiment, which seemed to be on the rise throughout Europe. Crucial
to the re-establishment of the old monarchies, he argued, was the censorship of
the liberal press, and of the "pamphleteers" at its left edge:

> [The French] have the game to themselves; they have only occupied an
> empty place by seizing the desks of the journalists, and no one can reproach
> them with silence; they have taken up the weapon we have disdained to
> make use of, and they are now employing it against ourselves
>
>   Public opinion is the most powerful of all means; like religion, it pen-
> etrates the most hidden recesses, where administrative measures have no
> influence. To despise public opinion is as dangerous as to despise moral
> principles; and if the latter will rise up even when they have been almost
> stifled, it is not so with opinion; it requires peculiar cultivation, a contin-
> ued and sustained perseverance. Posterity will hardly believe that we have
> regarded silence as an efficacious weapon to oppose to the clamours of our
> opponents, and in a century of words!
>
>   Who can blame us if we will not allow the public to be supplied with
> lies about us? The newspapers are worth to Napoleon an army of three

hundred thousand men, for such a force would not overlook the interior better, or frighten foreign Powers more, than half a dozen of his paid pamphleteers.[9]

One of the main demands of the radicals of the nineteenth century was for free speech. In the words of Karl Marx, "You cannot enjoy the advantages of a free press without putting up with its inconveniences. You cannot pluck the rose without its thorns."[10]

Fifty years of free speech and censorship

In the early years of the twentieth century, there was already a left and a right recognisably similar to today's, with the former in favour of increased rights including social redistribution, and the weakening of the repressive powers of the state, while the right called for more soldiers, police officers, and censors. In France, Charles Maurras' Action Française was founded in 1899 on a programme of defending the old institutions of France from secularism, from the threats posed by the idea of the rights of man, and from the far left. Action Française's street wing, the *Camelots du Roi*, was launched in 1908 after a lecturer Amédée Thalamas published a book describing Joan of Arc as a "legend." Challenged by a student who insisted that Joan had been a saint, Thalamas answered, "miracles have nothing to do with history." Right-wing students drowned Thalamas out when he attempted to speak. When the lecturers resumed, Action Française was able to mobilise a group of students who overwhelmed the podium and beat the lecturer.[11]

In Britain in 1918, the far left still included a number of people who had participated in the last wave of free speech struggles, protests at Trafalgar Square, including the deaths of John Dimmock, William Curner, and Alfred Linnell, which had established central London as a space where mass meetings were tolerated. Numerous veterans of that struggle could still be found on the left, including Edward Carpenter, the former clergyman turned mystic who was Britain's best-known advocate of the rights of gay men and lesbians.[12]

Advocates of censorship either supported the right from the outset or headed in that direction because of the logic of their demand to silence speech. Part of the right's critique of the left was that it would tolerate any opinion no matter how shocking. So Radclyffe Hall's novel *The Well of Loneliness* (1928) – whose protagonist Stephen Gordon is attracted to other women – was prosecuted for obscenity. The most senior politician to argue for the charge was Conservative Home Secretary William Joynson-Hicks, who had organised the government's resistance to the General Strike two years earlier, an authoritarian and anti-semite known to his contemporaries as Mussolini Minor. James Douglas, the editor of the right-wing *Sunday Express*, wrote of Hall's book, "I would rather give a healthy girl a phial of prussic acid than this novel. Poison kills the body, but moral poison kills the soul." The Director of Public Prosecutions Sir George

Stephenson asked the poet of British Imperialism, Rudyard Kipling, to be a prosecution witness. Meanwhile the novelists E. M. Forster and Virginia Woolf told the socialist paper, the *Daily Herald*, that they were willing to speak on Hall's behalf. The National Union of Railwaymen and the South Wales Miners' Federation sent letters of support for Hall opposing the prosecution.[13]

When socialist and syndicalist ideas became a mass force in the United States, between 1905 and 1914, they did so through countless speech acts, each of which was criminalised. So, one of the first of many arrests in the long activist career of the "Rebel Girl" Elizabeth Gurley Flynn began with a speech she gave in August 1906 beneath a red flag with the word "Unity" on it. Gurley Flynn was arrested and accused of promoting anarchism.[14]

Between 1907 and 1916, the Industrial Workers of the World (the organisation with which Gurley Flynn was associated) conducted 30 major free speech fights, campaigning to defend their right to organise against various state bans. An early example took place at Spokane, Washington, in 1909. The Wobblies objected to the use of employment agencies to force down the average rate of pay. Flynn was one of hundreds of soap-box orators arrested as part of this fight. The city balked at spending $1,000 a night on repressing leftists. Members of the IWW violated censorship laws by holding rallies, filling the jails with hundreds of prisoners until the local press and even mainstream liberal civic groups had no choice but to rally to the Wobblies' cause. In response to this campaign, the centre-right and far right insisted on using the state to suppress unwanted speech. The Espionage Act of 1917 and Sedition Act of 1918 were created to defeat left-wing organising. In 1917, Socialist Party presidential candidate Eugene Debs was convicted under the Espionage Act for speaking out against the war and was sentenced to ten years in prison.[15]

The left were opponents of censorship: they had to be. But this instinct went beyond mere self-interest. So, for example, the first versions of James Joyce's *Ulysses* to appear in the United States were extracts published in Margaret Anderson and Jane Heap's magazine, *The Little Review*, from 1918 where they jostled for readers' interest with pieces praising the anarchist Emma Goldman, and Thomas Mooney and Warren Billings, two trade unionists who had been wrongly accused of planting bombs in San Francisco. The serialisation of *Ulysses* continued until 1921 when the Post Office seized copies of *The Little Review* which was then prosecuted for obscenity, making it impossible for the extracts to continue.[16]

The Supreme Court, and exceptions to the First Amendment

At first sight, the use of state power against Joyce's modernist fiction may be surprising. For in the United States, the First Amendment makes free speech a constitutional principle. The common assumption is that American law must always have been quite as tolerant as it is today. What has happened in reality is that over the past 50 years our collective memory has sought to push back in time a history which only began at the end of the 1960s, and to make such post-First World War judges as Oliver Wendell Holmes Jr or Louis Brandeis the champions of free speech, especially during the years 1917–1927, when laws prohibiting left-wing speech and outlawing obscenity were applied as harshly in the United States as they were anywhere else in the world.

One of the reasons why it is possible to believe that America has a continuous history of support for free speech, is that after the First World War a small group of appellate judges chose, while limiting speech as tightly as they could, to couch their decisions in a language of virtuous commitment to liberal principles. A story of the continuous American attachment to liberty can be constructed, in other words, by selective quotation from such celebrated opinions of the Supreme Court as *Schenck v United States*, *Abrams v United States*, or *Whitney v California*.

Each of these three decisions contained dicta paying lip-service to the importance of free speech, and if they are read simply as political literature, parts of those opinions are compelling. Indeed, these Supreme Court rulings are used to manufacture a narrative that American judges have for decades distinguished themselves from their European counterparts by the consistency with which they upheld the universal principle of free speech.

What is usually forgotten, however, is that each of these cases ended in decisions subordinating free speech. In *Schenck*, for example, the Supreme Court held that distributing leaflets opposing the compulsory draft of citizens into the Army (and titled, ironically, "Long Live the Constitution of the United States") was a criminal act. This was the unanimous decision of the entire Court, and Justice Holmes himself penned the Court's opinion.[17]

Charles T. Schenck was General Secretary of the Socialist Party. His party published a leaflet calling on its readers to "obstruct the recruiting or enlistment service," which the Supreme Court treated as a conspiracy not merely to prevent volunteering but to obstruct the draft, in violation of the Espionage Act. Writing for the Court, Justice Holmes accepted that the defendants may have been within their constitutional rights in distributing the leaflets "in ordinary times."[18] He held, however, that the First Amendment protected free speech only until the point where "words [were] used ... in such circumstances ... as to create a clear and present danger."[19] America in 1917, when the leaflet was published, had been at war. Accordingly, Justice Holmes concluded that an interference with free speech was legitimate.

> When a nation is at war many things that might be said in time of peace are such a hindrance to its effort that their utterance will not be endured so long as men fight and that no Court could regard them as protected by any constitutional right.[20]

Abrams was a 7–2 majority decision of the court, upholding a 20-year prison sentence for protesters who had leafleted against the sending of American troops to attack Soviet Russia. Dissenting in *Abrams*, Justice Homes held that it was better to leave such words unpunished and rely instead on "the competition of the market" to defeat them, bequeathing to successive generations the notion of a "marketplace of ideas."[21] He wrote that:

> [The right to free speech] is an experiment, as all life is an experiment. Every year if not every day we have to wager our salvation upon some prophecy based upon imperfect knowledge. While that experiment is part of our system, I think we should be eternally vigilant against attempts to check the expression of opinions we loathe and believe to be fraught with death, unless they so imminently threaten interference with the lawful and pressing purposes of the law that an immediate check is required to save the country.[22]

While previous cases had concerned leaflets published while the nation was at war, *Abrams* concerned leaflets handed out in August 1919, after the war had ended. Therefore, the route followed by the Court in *Schenck* – that free speech ends once war is declared – was no longer available. In an expansion of the rationale endorsed in *Schenck*, while still dissenting from the majority in *Abrams*, Holmes suggested that the notion of "danger" sufficient to warrant limiting free speech might apply not merely in the context of an active war, but when any immediate threat of interference "with the lawful and pressing purposes of the law" presented itself.[23]

The third of these cases, *Whitney*, was a unanimous decision affirming a sentence of 14 years imprisonment for Charlotte Anita Whitney, a member of the Communist Labour Party. Ms Whitney had attended a 1919 congress of that party and was in the room as other members approved motions advocating the desirability of a workers' revolution. As it happened, Whitney had spoken against those motions and moved a counter-proposal that the party take a slower approach to the transformation of the country ("We again urge the workers who are possessed of the right of franchise to cast their votes for the party which represents their immediate and final interest ... at all elections"),[24] but, for the majority of Justices, that was no defence; merely by being with her comrades Whitney had associated herself with other speakers' insurgent words sufficiently to give rise to liability under the California Criminal Syndicalism Act.

Justice Brandeis wrote separately in concurrence with the majority opinion. Long passages from his concurring opinion in *Whitney* are routinely republished in the US press as a sign of the country's commitment to free speech. They are treated with the same reverence as Lincoln's Gettysburg's Address, or Martin Luther King's speech during the March on Washington:

> Those who won our independence believed that the final end of the State was to make men free to develop their faculties, and that, in its government, the deliberative forces should prevail over the arbitrary. They valued liberty both as an end, and as a means. They believed liberty to be the

secret of happiness, and courage to be the secret of liberty. They believed that freedom to think as you will and to speak what you think are means indispensable to the discovery and spread of political truth; that without free speech and assembly discussion would be futile; that, with them, discussion affords ordinarily adequate protection against the dissemination of noxious doctrine.[25]

In so writing, Brandeis was inventing a tradition, i.e. constructing a narrative in which ever since the founding fathers ("those who won our independence … "), the law of the land had always held that there should be no limit to the principle of free expression.

Yet those who take Justice Brandeis's lofty dicta in concurrence in *Whitney* at face value are not reading the opinion closely enough. For Brandeis was explaining why he had voted to *uphold* a 14-year jail sentence for someone expressing the opinion that socialists should stand for office. The justifications for censorship are themselves embedded in the last two dozen words of the above quotation and in the idea that widespread public discussion will "ordinarily" provide sufficient protection against noxious ideas (i.e. Communism). *Whitney* turns, in other words, on the same question as the one posed by Holmes' dissent in *Abrams*. What unusual conditions need to exist before free speech may be constitutionally restricted?

"Only an emergency can justify repression," Brandeis wrote.[26] Consistent with previous decisions of the Court, he reasoned that free speech must be allowed until the point at which it creates a clear and present danger. Brandeis acknowledged the vagueness of this test.

> This court has not yet fixed the standard by which to determine when a danger shall be deemed clear; how remote the danger may be and yet be deemed present; and what degree of evil shall be deemed sufficiently substantial to justify resort to abridgment of free speech.[27]

This lack of clarity gave Brandeis the chance to uphold Ms Whitney's conviction.

The Supreme Court of the 1920s was not the custodian of absolute free speech rights that today's journalists and lawyers want the Justices to have been. But was their caution nonetheless defensible; were Justices Wendell Holmes or Brandeis the philosophical inheritors of Milton, carving out an exception to free speech only "to suppress the suppressors"?

We can see this question playing itself out in *Abrams* and the decision to uphold the jailing of anti-war protesters. Justice Homes' tacitly assumed in his dissenting opinion that pacifist ideas were always wrong. That is why his dissent refers to people handing out leaflets calling on soldiers not to shoot as "opinions we loathe and believe to be fraught with death." American soldiers invading Russia were, in his eyes, fighting for life. Anyone objecting represented "death." But people handing out anti-militarist leaflets were not – in actuality or in embryo – a state machine of universal oppression. They were seeking only and legitimately to prevent another war.

As for Anita Whitney, Justice Brandeis accepted that the prospect of a Communist dictatorship in the United States was distant and could not satisfy the court's test of a clear and present danger.

> I am unable to assent to the suggestion in the opinion of the Court that assembling with a political party, formed to advocate the desirability of a proletarian revolution by mass action *at some date necessarily far in the future*, is not a right within the protection of the Fourteenth Amendment.[28] (emphasis added)

Accordingly, he justified her imprisonment on other grounds:

> [T]here was other testimony which tended to establish the existence of a conspiracy, on the part of members of the International Workers of the World, to commit present serious crimes, and likewise to show that such a conspiracy would be furthered by the activity of the society of which Miss Whitney was a member. Under these circumstances, the judgment of the state court cannot be disturbed.[29]

This is where the American Supreme Court of the 1920s had the worse of the argument and Milton the better of it. His idea of protecting free speech for everyone save the suppressors was a narrow incursion into free speech rights and one which tended to support greater speech both as a short-term goal and as a long-term ambition. It protected all speech save that of a violent and intolerant minority. It limited their speech only to protect the right of the majority to speak in the future. The Supreme Court's alternative was to make free speech available to those who agreed with the country's existing social arrangements. If strikes or protests were banned by law, then speech associated with them could be prohibited. The Justices saw the question of free speech through the eyes of law enforcement officers who had been tasked with supressing Communism and gave them a broad discretion to criminalise radical speech.

Fascism and censorship

The best-known example of the right's approval of censorship remains its sustained use in the 1920s and 1930s by the fascist states. Following Mussolini's seizure of power in October 1922, rival political parties and their periodicals were outlawed in 1926, when the Socialist, Communist, and People's Parties were banned, and their MPs arrested. From 1925–1926, papers came under the control of Mussolini's brother Arnaldo Mussolini, who headed a High Commission (i.e. press court) with the power to dismiss journalists or editors who published stories at odds with the interest of the regime. Italy's highest-circulation newspaper, the *Corriere della Sera*, was taken over and converted into a pro-fascist publication. Censorship notices were served on the privately owned press at the rate of up to 4,000 a year. Films could only be shown if approved by an Office for Cinematography. The active support of the industry meanwhile was guaranteed by a system of film credits, where companies could apply to have up to a third of the expenses of a pro-fascist film paid in advance by the regime. Radio programmes were controlled by the Italian Radiophonic Union which had monopoly control over broadcasting.[30]

Fascism in Germany was able to reshape the state much more quickly than in Italy. Within four weeks of Adolf Hitler being appointed Chancellor on 30 January 1933, his government suspended article 118 of the Weimar Constitution which protected the right of every German to freedom of speech ("Every German has the right, within the limits of the general laws, to express his opinion freely by word, in writing, in print, in picture form, or in any other way … ").[31]

Hitler tended not to say directly that Nazi rule would lead to the suppression of all other voices. Rather he spoke of the pleasure of obedience. He pointed to the risk of economic collapse and warned that this danger could be averted only by national unity. His government, he said, would "regard it as its first and supreme task to restore to the German people unity of mind and will." Germany was at war with itself, and he would bring peace. "In place of our turbulent instincts," his government would "make national discipline govern our life."[32]

On 6 March 1933, the German Communist Party was banned. The moderate Social Democratic Party followed on 22 June. By the middle of that summer, all other political parties in Germany, their meetings banned and harassed by Hitler's supporters, had also agreed to disband themselves. In April 1933, Hitler's party took control of the journalists' association. In June, the newspaper publishers' association was required to purge any members who did not support the new regime. On 4 October, the government passed a law requiring editors to "keep out of the newspapers everything … which is calculated to weaken the strength of the German Reich abroad or at home."[33] That autumn saw the passage of a Reich Propaganda Law, giving the state control over literature, press, radio, theatre, and music. In a briefing note written by Rolf Reinhardt of the Newsprint Allocation Office, the tasks facing the press under Nazi rule were explained as follows: "The National Socialist world-view sees in the press a means of educating the people for National Socialism. In consequence the press is an instrument of the National Socialist State. The National Socialist world-view demands total acceptance."[34]

On 10 May 1933, the German Students' Association occupied Franz Joseph Platz in central Berlin. The students stood opposite the university, adjacent to St Hedwig's Cathedral and the Berlin State Opera House. In the presence of Reich Propaganda Minister Joseph Goebbels, they set fire to left-wing books. As each new consignment was added to flames, they were instructed to shout out slogans. As Karl Marx's writings were burned, they recited: "Against class struggle and materialism. For the national community and an idealistic outlook."

When it was the turn of the novelist Erich Maria Remarque, the author of the anti-war classic *All Quiet on the Western Front*, the fascists chanted, "Against literary betrayal of the soldiers of the World War. For the education of the nation in the spirit of military preparedness." Then came the works of the satirist Kurt Tucholsky, who had warned of the brutality of the police, the ruthlessness of the rich, and the brutality of Hitler's party. The students proclaimed, "Against arrogance and presumption. For veneration and respect for the immortal German national spirit."[35] More than 20,000 books were burned in Berlin, including the autobiography of the American disability rights campaigner Helen Keller, the modernist plays of Bertolt Brecht, and the domestic comedies of the gay Irish dramatist Oscar Wilde. Similar fires were lit that evening outside 90 other universities and libraries.

By the end of 1938, the Nazi state held an index of banned books. In addition to the categories you might expect to find (Germans who had fled Nazi rule, anti-fascists, Jews, and others of the Nazi racial enemies), there was also included Christian literature, anything which encouraged pacifism or liberalism, anything which admitted the existence of state euthanasia policies, or which advocated abortion or birth control.

The difference between the right in this period, with its defence of censorship, and the left, with its assumption of publication, is illustrated by the translation of Hitler's memoir *Mein Kampf* into English. By 1933, there were translations of the book available in both Britain and the US, but the American translation was short (one-third of the length of the original) and criticised for leaving out the passages which showed Hitler's anti-semitism. The publishing house Reynal & Hitchcock approached New York's New School for Social Research, proposing that a team of German refugees compile an unabridged translation. Another anti-fascist, Alan Cranston, brought out a further edition in 1939 with the costs of translation supported by the Anti-Defamation League and with publicity to the effect that not one penny in royalties would be paid to Hitler.[36]

The same decision was taken in 1934 when German exiles in Paris founded a "German Freedom Library." Among the 20,000 books they collected were not just the works of prominent anti-fascists, and copies of every book burned in Berlin, but also key Nazi texts. For a while the fascists sought to destroy every trace of their enemy, anti-fascists were determined to study their antagonist, reasoning that to expose fascists you needed access to their words.[37]

Meanwhile, the pro-fascist military regimes in Spain and Portugal and much of Eastern Europe were little different from the actual fascist states. The first act of General Franco's regime on securing its victory at the end of the Civil War was the internment of its opponents. Around half a million people were placed in camps: 50,000 anti-fascists were put to death. A Press Law was passed giving the regime full control of the country's press. For more than two decades afterwards, there was no independent journalism in Spain. Rather, civil servants were tasked with informing the population of the activities of government, just as other civil servants planned the building of new roads or collected the taxes. Reports in the

Nazi press commended Franco on the extent of censorship: "Every house, every flat, every office is kept under constant observation and supervision," one paper reported. "The Marxist parties are being destroyed and exterminated down to the very last cell far more drastically even than here in Germany."[38]

Under fascism, any ideas were banned which stood in opposition to that tradition's insistence on the inequality of human beings. But the restriction of speech went even further than this. It was not enough that prominent non-fascists were silenced; rather, they were required to speak in support of Hitler, at the risk of death if they kept quiet.

Free speech campaigns: 1945–1972

After 1945, politics was complicated by the existence of not just one state (the Soviet Union) but a whole series of them (the Eastern bloc, China, Vietnam ...) which were both authoritarian and of left-wing origin. Plainly, this distorted the politics of free speech and not merely in the obvious sense that these were one-party regimes where expression was limited, but also in a second sense that a number of the best-known leaders of the Western left idealised these regimes, apologised for them, or developed ideas of what a future socialist society should be like which borrowed from key elements of this model of "really existing socialism."

A further complicating factor was the role played by colonialism. For nearly 50 years parties of the left had supported free speech at home while doing little to protect its growth in European colonies abroad. After 1945, this contradiction became almost unbearable: so, in 1956, when French Communists voted in support of special powers to prohibit the spread of pro-independence groups in Algeria, they were in turn denounced by figures to their left such as the philosopher Jean-Paul Sartre for betraying socialist principles.[39]

In the West, overall, the picture remained broadly the same after 1945 as before: the right supported censorship. Most of the left stood for the rights of free expression and assembly. The same processes could be seen in the United States and in most countries in Western Europe. Between about 1960 and 1980, many of the richest countries in the world saw an extraordinary increase in free expression. The left was at the forefront of these struggles. But the conclusion of these struggles also provides the immediate context for the reversal of positions we have seen since 1970, i.e. the moves by the right to accept free speech and then to use it factionally.

The best-known example of post-war censorship was McCarthyism in the United States, in which 10,000 people were driven out of jobs in education, public service, and the media. Directives instructed public servants to hunt through the 200 or so overseas libraries administered by US embassies, for fear that they might contain works written by Communists, former Communists, or those who had spoken out against McCarthyism. At the centrepiece of the system were the hearings of the House Un-American Activities Committee, which writers, actors, and civil servants were compelled to attend. They were quizzed on their trade union activities, their homosexuality, or anything else which might prove their actual or latent Communism.

In addition to such official censorship, countless employers acted pre-emptively, reducing the risk of investigation by announcing that they would not employ leftists or allow them a platform. The Motion Picture Association of America operated a blacklist, while right-wing magazines published lists of actors, writers, musicians, and journalists suspected of Communism. Even Frank Capra (the director of *It's a Wonderful Life*) found himself having to defend his creation from the complaints of the FBI's review team (assisted by right-wing novelist Ayn Rand) who found in the movie: "a rather obvious attempt to discredit bankers."[40]

If censorship in the 1930s and 1940s Italy and Germany is blamed on fascism, McCarthyism was the product of something different – a recognisably non-fascist far-right with deep roots in American conservatism and in the institutions of the centre-right. Joseph McCarthy was not a fascist, he was a Republican senator. During the Second World War, he served in the American Marine Corps. In the 1950s, his key allies were fellow Republican politicians, including the President, Dwight Eisenhower, and the head of the FBI, J. Edgar Hoover. FBI agents spent hundreds of hours scouring through Bureau files to provide crucial details of information which the Senator might use.[41] Bureau staff wrote speeches for McCarthy and taught him how to place stories in the press. McCarthy emerged from within the existing state, and was championed by such mainstream conservatives as William F. Buckley Jr., editor of the *National Review*, who insisted that the Senator proposed nothing more troubling than that Communists should be excluded from "positions of public trust and popular esteem."[42] Long after McCarthy's fall, the instinct of the American right to demand censorship remained intact.

Part of McCarthy's success, moreover, was that he told American politicians of the centre-right what they wanted to hear, namely that recent Democratic (Roosevelt and Truman) administrations had drawn up their foreign policy with the express purpose of making it easier for the Communists to spread their empire into Eastern Europe and China. McCarthy did not expose only a few left-wing artists and film-makers, he described General George C. Marshall, one of the country's most senior military commanders, as a dupe of the Communists, he invited Secretary of State Dean Acheson to seek asylum in the Soviet Union, and he sought to persuade his audience that the 1952 presidential candidate Adlai Stevenson was an ally of Soviet spy Alger Hiss.

In almost every town in the United States there were people who were willing to run their own censorship campaigns, following in the footsteps of McCarthy. The *Boston Post* campaigned against the city's libraries claiming they held "thousands" of books written by Communists or fellow travellers. School students in Brooksville, Florida, noticed that copies of the *Communist Manifesto* were freely available in local libraries. Members of the library board kept the books on the shelves but insisted that they were stamped, "Propaganda." Catholic colleges and universities placed texts by Marx and Engels in restricted access. When students at Marquette University applied to read them, their names were passed on to their Archbishop.[43]

This instinct of censorship was not extended merely to such foreign doctrines as Soviet Communism, but to any writer speaking honestly about injustices in the US. When Richard Wright's novel *Black Boy* was published, with its sympathetic portrayal of a black man who flees from the South before settling in Chicago, it was banned in Mississippi. Senator Theodore Bilbo (a right-wing southern Democrat) defended its censorship:

> *Black Boy* should be taken off the shelves of stores, sales should be stopped; it was a damnable lie, from beginning to end; it built fabulous lies about the South. The purpose of the book was to plant seeds of hate and devilment in the minds of every American. It was the dirtiest, filthiest, most obscene [book], filthy and dirty, and came from a Negro from whom one could not expect better.[44]

Similarly, the John Birch Society demanded that George Orwell's anti-Stalinist parable *Animal Farm* was removed from libraries. As late as the 1960s, many New York schools still refused to teach it. The most frequent reason given was that "Orwell was a Communist."[45]

As the 1960s wore on, however, America saw numerous attempts to demand freedom of expression, including the Free Speech Movement at U.C. Berkeley, a campaign which began in September 1964. The university had long observed a policy, Rule 17, permitting political or religious speakers on the college's property only if permission had been obtained in advance for them to speak. Students operated in response a free speech area on Sproul Plaza just outside Sather Gate, one of the main entrances to campus. In September 1964, under police instruction, the university authorities rescinded the students' permission to hold meetings there.

On 1 October, Jack Weinberg was arrested for hosting an information table on campus and soliciting donations for the Congress of Racial Equality (CORE), a civil rights campaign. Students blocked the police car and occupied the road. In the words of one participant, Jerry Rubin, "We demanded his release in exchange for their release. The cops would have to drive their car over our bodies to take out brother to jail."[46] Weinberg remained locked in the car for 32 hours, while police sought to take him away, and up to 3,000 students protested at a time.

Time magazine detected behind the upsurge old enemies, warning that, "A few known Communists have been spotted at Berkeley and probably have contact with the FSM leadership." The institution's President Clark Kerr warned that unless pro-civil rights campaigners were restricted, Berkeley would become "a sanctuary for fugitives from the police."[47]

Once again, free speech was a dividing point between left and right. On the left, student leader Mario Savio was later an election candidate for the Peace and Freedom Party. He and his allies were widely accused of Communism. State Senator Burns headed the Senate's Fact-Finding Subcommittee on Un-American Activities and demanded that the demonstrating students be investigated and expelled. Conservatives made jokes that their enemy was a Filthy Speech Movement, telling themselves that the students supported unfathomable causes: not just civil rights but access to birth control literature and pornography. When Ronald Reagan ran for the Governorship of California in 1966, he promised to "clean up the mess at Berkeley."[48]

One activist from the 1960s, the lawyer Kenneth Stern, conveys the common sense of his generation, that freedom of expression was the means to achieve social revolution:

> Free speech was a necessary precondition for positive social change. This wasn't only about burning draft cards or the ability to wear clothing that said, "Fuck the Draft," but about challenging a power system that denied American equal rights. Rosa Parks' refusal to move to the back of the bus wasn't only a question of public accommodation, it was a protest, and an act of expression, an assertion of an idea.[49]

The demand for free speech was felt beyond the borders of the US. In February 1965, for example, the University of Cambridge hosted a televised debate on whether the American dream was at the expense of the American Negro. The event set the black novelist James Baldwin against William F. Buckley Jr., the right-wing journalist and defender of white privilege in the Southern states. Buckley put the case for the existing order, Baldwin for civil rights. Buckley warned that behind Baldwin's defence of equality, there stood a Communist politics which could never be allowed to flourish. The majority of Americans, he promised, would fight another civil war, and would kill, rather than permit such ideas to be heard:

> [I]f it does finally come to a confrontation, a radical confrontation, between giving up what we understand to be the best features of the American way of life, which at that level is indistinguishable, so far as I can see, from the European way of life, then we will fight the issue, and we will fight the issue not only in the Cambridge Union, but we will fight it as you were once recently called to do on beaches and on hills, on mountains and on landing grounds.[50]

Buckley has gone down in history as a "gatekeeper" on the right (i.e. some-one who built up the mainstream and excluded interlopers from far right).[51] Yet being in the mainstream did not prevent him from justifying violence. For Buckley, force was needed to protect a way of life. Therefore, if that violence took the form of the lynching of black (or indeed white leftist) supporters of civil rights – then such killings were both necessary and desirable.

Another incident which was followed closely by free speech advocates abroad was the Chicago conspiracy trial, in 1969–1970, when eight prominent activists of the American left, including Bobby Seale, Abbie Hoffman, Jerry Rubin, and Tom Hayden, faced charges of crossing state lines to incite a riot, following protests outside the Democratic National Convention in Chicago. The defendants responded by doing all they could to bring out the political character of the trial: blowing kisses at the Judge, unfurling Vietcong flags, dressing in black judicial robes beneath which were hidden police uniforms. Their attorneys submitted 54 questions to facilitate juror challenges including, "Do you know who Janis Joplin and Jimi Hendrix are?", "Would you let your son or daughter marry a Yippie?" Judge Hoffman only allowed one; whether the prospective jurors had relatives or friends who were connected to law enforcement.[52]

One defendant, the Black Panther Bobby Seale, was knocked to the ground on the order of the judge and beaten. Seale sat in court, his legs and hands cuffed to the leg of his chair, and with a gag in his mouth tied behind his ear.[53] After protests, a second judicial order to beat Seale, and several days during which the gag remained in place,[54] Judge Hoffman finally agreed to declare Seale's hearing a mistrial, and the trial continued with the remaining seven defendants.

The recent history of post-war America was, according to those on trial, merely the continuation of habits of censorship perfected in Nazi Germany. One defendant, the veteran pacifist David Dellinger, told the Judge, "You wanted us to be like good Germans, supporting the evils of our decade … now you want us to be like good Jews going quietly and politely to the concentration camps while this court suppresses freedom."[55] Defence attorney Bill Kunstler echoed this idea that the choice was between free speech and fascism:

> I am not one who believes we have, at this moment, a fascist state in the United States. But I am one who believes that there is handwriting on the wall … the faint outline of the swastika … If we fail here [in Chicago], I'm not saying this is the end of fairness and the sweet life of free expression but I say that if we fail here that the shadow on the wall will be darker … because this case was deliberately designed to put dissent on trial … The state is attempting to silence hundreds and thousands of others through these eight.[56]

It was this context, with the civil rights movement of the early 1960s giving way to the insurgent left-wing underground that saw the consolidation of free speech doctrine and its adoption by the Supreme Court. Politically, the Trial of the Chicago Seven was the key moment in this transformation, for it seemed to reveal to everyone – and especially those who wanted to keep American capitalism going and its people quiet – that clamping down on political speech was counterproductive. There was no way of putting the left-wing underground on trial without giving its leaders a chance to speak. In the words of one defendant, Lee Weiner:

> We wanted to present political arguments to the jury, and more importantly, to the broader public, that would convince people to condemn the government, its war, and its efforts to crush dissent ... The newspapers loved it. We are about as famous as you could be before the internet, Twitter, Facebook, and Instagram.[57]

Legally, the crucial case was *Brandenburg v Ohio*. It concerned a KKK leader in rural Ohio Clarence Brandenburg, who was filmed with his supporters standing around a burning cross, wearing KKK gowns and hoods. "We're not a revengent organisation," Brandenburg declared, "but if our President, our Congress, our Supreme Court, continues to suppress the White Caucasian race, it's possible there might have to be some revengeance taken."[58] He called for the expulsion of blacks and Jews from the US.[59] Brandenburg was prosecuted under post-First World War legislation prohibiting criminal syndicalism (i.e. Communist activities) which were defined as any speech "advocating ... the propriety of ... violence ... as a means of accomplishing industrial or political reform." The *Brandenburg* Court understood this was a time when popular protest was becoming pervasive and was conscious of the need to accommodate it. Justice Douglas (joined by Justice Black, who also wrote separately in concurrence), spoke of the post-war anti-Communist loyalty tests as "the most blatant violations of the First Amendment we have ever known."[60] Justice Douglas suggested that all free speech acts should in principle be excluded from the criminal law, save where speech is "brigaded with action."[61] In other words, speech should only be restricted where the speaker urged others to take action to resist the law, and where lawlessness was both imminent and likely. Justices Black and Douglas were both Democrats and New Deal era appointees to the Court. Although the *Brandenburg* decision served to protect the rights of white racists, it simultaneously invalidated a speech-based conviction under anti-Communist legislation (the Ohio Criminal Syndicalism Act) and was widely seen as a victory for the left.

In France, censorship remained common into the 1960s. Laws prohibited mention of "banditry," lies, theft, or debauchery in books for children. The novelist Henry Miller's publishers were convicted of pornography. In October 1961, a peaceful march through Paris of 30,000 demonstrators calling for freedom for the people of Algeria, who were living under curfew, was attacked by the police, who killed at least 120 people, leaving the streets in Simone de Beauvoir's words, "full of autumn leaves and blood."[62] Eyewitness accounts were kept out of the next-day's papers while films covering the event were censored. Meetings to protest the killings were banned.

The abolition of theatre censorship, and reform of the law on homosexuality were also introduced in most European countries in the 1960s and early 1970s.

The liberation of press censorship in Ireland can be dated to the Censorship of Publications Act 1967, which provided that any past decision that a book was obscene would expire naturally after just 12 years. Denmark decriminalised pornography in the late 1960s. Portugal and Spain too chose the path of liberalisation, on the deaths of their dictators in 1974 and 1975. Other liberalising measures followed, including the liberalisation of abortion and divorce.

In Britain, the free speech conflicts of the post-war years repeatedly placed the left and the right on opposite sides. At the start of the 1960s, the British Library still held a "Private Case" of 4,000 books considered so offensive that even serious researchers were refused access to them. The rule was that if a reader accurately requested a book with the correct shelf-mark, then the book had to be delivered to his or her desk. But, to prevent this from happening, the shelf-marks of these proscribed books were kept hidden from the public and away from the Library's General Catalogue. To enable the private reading of these banned books, one collector, Alfred Rose, privately printed a list of all known books in the Library's Private Case, and donated a book containing this list to another institution, the private-subscription London Library. In that way, diligent readers willing to walk the mile and a half which separated these two libraries were able to access such banned books as William Burroughs' *Naked Lunch* or Anne Cécile Desclos' *Story of O*. Among the writers who revealed the existence of this Private Case, and thus compelled the Library to grant readers unfettered access to its contents, was Peter Fryer,[63] a dissident Communist, supporter of the 1956 uprising in Hungary, and historian of black immigration to Britain.

In 1960, Penguin, the publisher of D. H. Lawrence's novel *Lady Chatterley's Lover* was prosecuted under the Obscene Publications Act 1959, which prohibited publications whose "effect [was] if taken as a whole, such as to tend to deprave and corrupt persons who are likely … to read [it]." This strained language assumed both a class of people who were incapable of corruption (judges, politicians) and another class of people who were likely to become depraved should they be given unsuitable books. Prosecution counsel Mervyn Griffith-Jones explained this distinction in his opening speech by asking the jurors: "Is it a book you would wish to have lying around in your own house? Is it a book that you would wish even your wife or your servants to read?"[64]

The prosecution was proposed by the Attorney General in the Conservative government, Reginald Manningham-Buller. Lawrence's wrongdoing was to imagine an affair between an educated woman and a servant, her gamekeeper. The Defence called 35 witnesses including John Robinson, the liberal Bishop of Woolwich and Richard Hoggart, a left-wing sociologist and authority on working-class popular culture. The Crown had real difficulty in finding experts to match them. The jury's decision to acquit encouraged the liberalisation of British life: in the same year, gambling was legalised, shortly afterwards the censorship of plays by the Lord Chamberlain was scrapped, and swearwords were permitted to be spoken on the BBC.[65]

In the 50 years since the trial, literary views of Lawrence have changed dramatically; beginning with Kate Millett's book *Sexual Politics* (1970).[66] Scholars shaped by the politics of women's liberation have reread the novel with rather more care than the prosecution in the trial with its blunt calculation that X number of one swearword or Y of another would persuade a jury that the book was obscene. The 1960s beliefs that Lawrence stood in an uncomplicated way for the right of working-class people for respect, and of sex to be free, no longer seem as clearly true as they once did. But the trial belongs in its own historical context. It was not about Lawrence (who was long dead) or even the sexual practices of his protagonists. Those who prosecuted him chose to fight on the terrain that literature representing sex between middle- and working-class people always required censorship. The political right instigated the trial and lost it in the jury-room and beyond along generational, class, and gender lines.

The British left in the epoch of no platform

If *Lady Chatterley* established the defence of literary merit, where did that leave obscene works without that quality? The issue was posed in the 1971 trial of *Oz* magazine, a magazine of the hippie "underground," which placed witty left-wing journalism (written by the likes of Richard Neville and Germaine Greer) alongside soft pornographic images of women without their clothes on, of multiracial couples, and occasionally of gay men. In 1970, the editors had invited their young readers to edit a special "Schoolkids Oz"; a follow-up to previous special issues ("Hippy Atrocities *Oz*," "Acid *Oz*," and so on). The contents included an article criticising the left's dependence on demonstrations ("How many of us know our oppressed brother?") as well as pieces cautioning against the use of drugs. Fifteen-year-old Vivian Berger tweaked a cartoon by Robert Crumb to show a tumescent Rupert the Bear penetrating Gipsy Granny. No-one could pretend that this image was high art. The kindest plausible description was from *Oz*'s Marsha Rowe (later the founder of feminist magazine *Spare Rib*) who admitted it was "puerile"[67] but denied that it justified jailing her editors. The best justification of it came from Berger himself, nominally a prosecution witness but rooting for the defence. He did not dispute that the scene portrayed in the cartoon was obscene but insisted that the mere reproduction of offensive material did not make an image obscene. War was obscene, but its reporting not necessarily so.

Oz's opponents came from the right: from senior civil servants and the police. *Oz*'s allies were on the radical left, with the likes of John Lennon and Yoko Ono attending protest marches and recording a single for the magazine's defence fund. Leading defence counsel was the novelist John Mortimer, a former Communist and now a vocal supporter of Labour.

On the right, the *Oz* trial was attended by censorship advocates Lady Birdwood and Mary Whitehouse. Since the 1950s, Birdwood had campaigned for the rights of Ukrainian anti-Soviet exiles, many of whom were former supporters of Hitler. In 1970, she brought a blasphemy prosecution against the actor John Bird for his play *The Council of Love*. As the decade wore on, she was a speaker at meetings of the Conservative Monday Club, the National Front, and the British chapter of the World Anti-Communist League.[68]

Mary Whitehouse, the former senior mistress at Madeley School for Girls in Shropshire, had joined the campaign for censorship in 1964, when she launched Clean-Up TV (later the National Viewers and Listeners' Association). Whitehouse objected to the repeated use of the word "bloody" on *Till Death us Do Part* (but not to the racism which accompanied it), the swearing on the Rolling Stones' album *Exile on Mean Street*, the appearance of "obscene vegetable matter" on Doctor Who, and (with grim predictability) the sexual content of the BBC series *Casanova*.[69] Six years after the *Oz* trial ended she returned to court, bringing a private blasphemy prosecution against *Gay News* for a poem presenting a Roman centurion's attraction to the dying Christ. Various left-wing campaigns demonstrated their opposition to the prosecution, including *Socialist Worker* and *Socialist Challenge*, by reprinting the poem.[70]

One young Marxist, David Widgery, was the Mackenzie friend to Richard Neville the editor of *Oz* (i.e. a non-lawyer, with whom Neville could discuss legal arguments in court). Widgery kept hold of the defendants' copy of the jury list. He was aware of the significance jury challenges had played in the trial of the Chicago Eight since *Oz* had reported on the Chicago trial and raised money for the defendants. Widgery succeeded in eliminating 26 potential jurors, anyone with a suit or tie, who could be assumed to support the prosecution.

Widgery is an important figure in the next chapter of this book: he would go on to play a key role in the history of British anti-fascism. Writing in 1973, he presented the *Oz* trial as merely a small part of a general offensive of the state against dissident opinion:

> Those liberals still left can take comfort from the Appeal Court's reluctant modification of the sentence, radicals are more likely to agree with Richard Neville's assessment that "if Judge Argyle had been a little brighter, we'd all still be in jail"; and the revolutionaries will add it to the lengthening list of political prosecutions brought under the "law and order" rubric, tighten their political belts and stroke up their anger. And somewhere in the Forest of Wyre, equipped with her teasmade, bedside Bible and daily help ("a very nice woman who seems to sense that I have a lot on my mind and gets on with the job") Mary Whitehouse is picking up her phone to make another complaint.[71]

Yet for all the fireworks of Widgery's prose, he was more wrong than right in arguing that revolutionaries needed to tighten their political belts – i.e. prepare for a further wave of state persecution. In fact, *Oz* marked the end of a series of prosecutions, the sign of a new period in which those who sought to protect the state would have to find new strategies for keeping the peace without being able to rely on simply jailing leftist authors.

The task of promoting censorship would increasingly fall to those outside the state, right-wing outliers such as Whitehouse. Something similar would happen to racism, with the rise of racist parties providing the opportunity for politicians to tighten border controls; not out of their own choice, they would say, but because the people demanded it.

The last issue of *Oz* published in winter 1973 carried an article by the journalist Duncan Campbell warning of the rise of the National Front and of the revolt on the centre-right which stood behind it. The ultra-right groups, Campbell concluded, were encouraged by a much widespread authoritarianism. It was "the latent fascism, the hidden element, that is more dangerous … the bus conductor who tells a Pakistani woman he's full up when he's not, the Lord who tells the House that *parents* of muggers ought to be flogged."[72]

As the far right grew during the late 1970s, the generation which had campaigned for universal free speech found itself increasingly having to choose whether it really did support absolute freedom of expression – if that included the people who would happily see the left in jail, its bookshops on fire, and its magazines closed down.

Notes

1 Oxford: Oxford University Press, 1995.
2 New York: Bold Times, 2019.
3 S. Lambert, 'State Control of the Press in Theory and Practice: The Role of the Stationers' Company before 1640', in R. Myers and W. Harris (eds), *Censorship & the Control of Print: In England and France 1600–1910* (Winchester: St. Paul's Bibliographies, 1992), pp. 1–32, 1.
4 N. Bobbio, *The Left and the Right: The Significance of a Political Distinction* (Cambridge: Polity, 1996).
5 J. Milton, *Areopagitica* (Oakland: Octavo, 1988 edn), pp. 4, 19.
6 Milton, *Areopagitica*, p. 67.
7 E. Burke, *Reflections on the Revolution in France* (London: Penguin Books, 1986 edn), p. 173.
8 Burke, *Reflections*, p. 161.
9 R. Metternich, *Memoirs of Prince Metternich 1830–5 vol V* (New York: Charles Scribner's Sons, 1880–1882), p. 225.
10 E. Ford, 'Winning the Battle,' *Weekly Worker*, 15 October 2020.
11 E. Nolte, *Three Faces of Fascism: Action Française. Italian Fascism. National Socialism* (London: Weidenfeld & Nicolson, 1965), pp. 101, 120.
12 S. Rowbotham, *Edward Carpenter: A Life of Liberty and Love* (London: Verso, 2008).
13 M. Fellion and K. Inglis, *Censored: A Literary History of Subversion and Control* (London: British Library, 2017), pp. 157–169.
14 *New York Times*, 23 August 1906; *New York Globe*, 23 August 1906; *New York Herald*, 23 August 1906; K. Kelly, 'Free Speech Fights Have Historically Targeted the Left,' *TeenVogue*, 4 August 2020.
15 D. Renton, *Classical Marxism: Socialist Theory and the Second International* (Cheltenham: New Clarion Press, 2002), pp. 113–128.
16 N. J. Karolides, M. Bald, and D. B. Sova, *120 Banned Books* (New York: Checkmarks Books, 2005), pp. 390–393.

17 *Schenck v United States* 249 US 47 (1919).
18 249 US at 52.
19 249 US at 52.
20 249 US at 52.
21 *Abrams v United States* 250 US 616 (1919).
22 250 US at 630.
23 250 US at 630
24 *Whitney v California* 274 US 357 (1927).
25 274 US at 376–77.
26 274 US at 376–77.
27 274 US at 376–77.
28 274 US at 379.
29 274 US at 374.
30 D. Mack Smith, *Mussolini* (London: Orion, 1994), pp. 123–124.
31 'The Constitution of the German Empire of 11 August 1919,' *German History in Documents and Images.*
32 J. Noakes and G. Pridham, *Nazism 1919–1945, Volume 1: The Rise to Power 1919–1934* (Exeter: University of Essex: 1983), pp. 131–134.
33 J. Noakes and G. Pridham, *Nazism 1919–1945, Volume 2: State, Economy and Society 1933–1939* (Exeter: University of Essex: 1984), pp. 388–389.
34 Noakes and Pridham, *Nazism, Volume 2*, p. 391.
35 Noakes and Pridham, *Nazism, Volume 2*, p. 402; R. Ovenden, *Burning the Books: A History of Knowledge under Attack* (London: John Murray, 2020), p. 1.
36 D. Lankiewicz, '*Mein Kampf* in America: How Hitler Came to Be published Inside the United States,' *Printing History* (2016), pp. 3–28.
37 Ovenden, *Burning*, p. 126.
38 M. Richards, *A Time of Silence: Civil War and the Culture of Repression in Franco's Spain* (Cambridge: Cambridge University Press, 1998), p. 35.
39 'Jacques Duclos Explains the Communist Vote in Favour of the Government,' *Marxists .org*, J.-P. Sartre, 'Preface to Frantz Fanon's "Wretched of the Earth",' *Marxists.org.*
40 Z. M. Seward, 'The FBI Considered *It's a Wonderful Life* to Be Communist Propaganda,' *The Atlantic*, 24 December 2013.
41 C. Gentry, *J. Edgar Hoover: The Man and the Secrets* (New York: W. W. Norton and Co., 1961), p. 379.
42 D. M. Oshinsky, *A Conspiracy So Immense: The World of Joe McCarthy* (Oxford: Oxford University Press, 2005), pp. 473, 478.
43 Karolides, Bald, and Sova, *120 Banned Books*, pp. 118–126.
44 Karolides, Bald, and Sova, *120 Banned Books*, pp. 20–29.
45 Karolides, Bald, and Sova, *120 Banned Books*, pp. 137–142.
46 J. Rubin, *Do It! Scenarios of the Revolution* (New York: Simon and Schuster, 1970), p. 21.
47 'Campus Agitation vs. Education,' *Time*, 29 January 1965.
48 J. Kahn, 'Ronald Reagan Launched Political Career Using the Berkeley Campus as a Target,' *UC Berkeley News*, 8 June 2004.
49 K. S. Stern, *The Conflict over the Conflict: The Israel/Palestine Campus Debate* (Toronto: New Jewish Press, 2020), p. 63.
50 N. Buccola, *The Fire is Upon Us: James Baldwin, William F. Buckley Jr., and the Debate over Race in America* (Princeton: Princeton University Press, 2019), p. 398.
51 A. Felzenberg, 'How William F. Buckley Became the Gatekeeper of the Conservative Movement,' *National Review*, 19 June 2017; A. Marantz, *Antisocial: How Online Extremists Broke America* (London: Picador, 2020 edn), p. 118.
52 R. Neville, *Hippie Hippie Shake: The Dreams, the Trips, the Trials, the Love ins, the Screw Ups … The Sixties* (London: Bloomsbury, 1995), p. 178.
53 M. L. Levine et al (eds), *The Trial of the Chicago 7* (New York: Simon & Schuster, 2020), p. 74.

54 L. Weiner, *Conspiracy to Riot: The Life and Times of One of the Chicago 7* (Cleveland, OH: Belt Publishing, 2020), pp. 95–96.

55 J. C. Tucker, *Trial and Error: The Education of a Courtroom Lawyer* (New York: Avalon Travel Publishing, 2003), p. 191.

56 J. Hoffman and D. Simon, *Run Run Run: The Lives of Abbie Hoffman* (New York: Seven Stories Press, 2019), pp. 29–30.

57 Weiner, *Conspiracy to Riot*, pp. 74, 85.

58 *Brandenburg v Ohio* 395 US 444 (1969) at 446; P. Strum, *When the Nazis Came to Skokie: Freedom for Speech We Hate* (Lawrence, Kansas: University Press of Kansas, 1999), pp. 40–41.

59 395 US at 447.

60 395 US at 456.

61 395 US at 454 (Douglas, J., concurring).

62 D. Gordon, *Immigrants and Intellectuals: May '68 and the Rise of Anti-Racism in France* (London: Merlin Press, 2012), pp. 25–26.

63 P. Fryer, *Mrs Grundy: Studies in English Prudery* (London: Denis Dobson, 1963) pp.16–17.

64 Fellion and Inglis, *Censored*, p. 191.

65 Fellion and Inglis, *Censored*, pp. 191–201.

66 New York: Doubleday and Co.

67 Neville, *Hippie*, p. 358.

68 N. Fountain, 'The Dowager Lady Birdwood,' *Guardian*, 30 June 2000.

69 D. Sandbrook, *State of Emergency: The Way We Were: Britain 1970–1974* (London: Allen Lane, 2010), pp. 461–466.

70 D. Sandbrook, *Seasons in the Sun: The Battle for Britain 1974–1979* (London: Penguin, 2013), pp. 410–413.

71 D. Widgery, *Preserving Disorder* (London: Preserving Disorder, 1998), pp. 131–134.

72 D. Campbell, 'The Suede Jackboot,' *Oz*, November 1973.

3

THE EXCEPTION

Fascism and anti-fascism

If the left was historically the party of free speech, a partial exception was always made for its response to fascism. The left fought the fascists from the 1920s onwards, with most socialists arguing that if fascism took power the result would be the creation of a state in which all rival parties were banned. That assessment was part of the left's thinking, in the 1930s, in the 1940s, and later in the drawing up of no platform. The focus of this chapter is on Britain, since it was here that no platform was first set down in writing, although the events I describe – support for fascism in the 1930s, physical resistance to it, a period of isolation for the far right after the end of the Second World War – had their counterparts in the US and throughout Europe.

In the 1930s, anti-fascist protests were largely restricted to the far left. At Olympia in 1934, socialists, Communists, and others forged tickets to a fascist rally, managed to get in, and heckled the British fascist leader Sir Oswald Mosley from inside his meeting. As the anti-fascists heckled, Mosley stopped speaking, and his supporters shone spotlights on the hecklers so that they could be beaten. In the meeting's aftermath, Mosley was widely denounced in the public press, and his wealthiest domestic backers abandoned him. Two years later, at the Battle of Cable Street, a crowd of 150,000 socialists and British Jews, summoned onto the streets by East End Communists, confronted Mosley and the police, and prevented him from marching through the East End.

The conflict between left and right was violent, with fascists boasting of the beatings they inflicted on their opponents, and the left being unafraid of using force in its defence. Unsurprisingly, therefore, when you read fascist accounts of these struggles, the references to free speech are few and shallow. In February 1933, Oswald Mosley told readers of *The Blackshirt* that anti-fascist protests meant that "we have reached a point in this country in which free speech is a thing of the past." This was stated briefly, in a matter-of-fact manner and with little suggestion of regret. The real purpose of invoking free speech was to advertise the fact that a "Fascist Defence Force has been organised to protect free speech." It had already "often met and defeated 'Red' violence."[1] Mosley had in fact been operating a private militia for two years by this point, explaining in a message to its members that they would be "an iron core in [our] organisation around which every element for the preservation of England will rally when a crisis ... comes."[2]

On the other side of the barricades, the discussion of free speech was more intense. In 1937, the poet Nancy Cunard wrote to 148 of her fellow writers asking them their opinion of the Spanish Civil War. "I am for the legal Government [in Spain]," the literary critic Lascelles Abercrombie wrote, "and true nationalism inspired by social justice and free culture." A victory for fascism, the poet W. H. Auden argued, "would create an atmosphere in which the creative artist and all who care for justice, liberty and culture would find it impossible to work." Should Franco triumph, wrote the novelist Gerald Bullett, it would "mark the end of freedom and civilisation in Europe." Short story writer Thomas Burke characterised fascism as "the regimentation of the People." Being for "freedom of opinion," he found it contemptible. "Civilisation," the novelist Storm Jamieson maintained, is incompatible with fascism, "this doctrine which exalts violence and uses incendiary bombs to fight ideas." "Fascism suppresses truth," agreed the philosopher C. E. M. Joad. "Two things make the future real," the journalist John Langdon-Davies wrote, "the artist's imagination and the worker's hope. Fascism destroys both." Being for free speech, each of these writers insisted, meant opposing those who would turn Europe into a giant prison.[3]

In the 1970s, references to this earlier period of left-wing struggle were ubiquitous. But the end of the 1930s also saw fascists being prevented from organising, and not by a popular movement this time but by the state.

Prevented from organising – by the government

From 1939, Britain was at war with Germany. Until then, the British fascists had always been able to present themselves as a force of British patriots, cutting with the grain of widespread ideas about the state, the monarchy, and the army. After the declaration of war, however, these claims ran increasingly hollow. The Second World War was an ideological conflict in which democratic Britain and France fought fascist Italy and Germany. Oswald Mosley's principal political activity was now to campaign for peace with the two fascist states, from which he had received (as civil servants had identified) tens of thousands of pounds of financial subsidy. On 9 April 1940, Britain's ally Norway was invaded by the German army. On the same day, Vidkun Quisling, the leader of the Nasjonal Samling Party, proclaimed himself prime minister. The German ambassador demanded that the Norwegian king recognise Quisling in this role. Ten days later, politicians in Britain's governing Conservative Party met to consider the risks posed by a Fifth Column. In the public mind, Mosley was the prime candidate to play the role of Quisling in Britain.

From 22 May 1940, the authorities began to intern prominent fascists under Defence Regulation 18B. More than 750 supporters of Oswald Mosley were eventually detained. Almost all the leading fascists were held in custody.

In war-time conditions, the state became more important, while the left had limited means to influence the decisions taken by leading politicians, civil servants, or judges. Up until this point, all measures to restrict fascist organisation had tended to fall as hard on the left as they had on the right. The Public Order Act 1936 prohibited uniforms and empowered the police to ban political protests. The prohibition on marches was mainly against left-wing protests. In the words of Phil Piratin, later the Communist Member of Parliament for Stepney, Mile End in East London: "the people ... learned that if law and order were to be maintained they would have to do it themselves."[4] But the decision to ban Mosley was not the people doing it for themselves. Rather, it was the state taking into its own hands additional powers to stifle free expression which it had not been permitted for many years. Those powers could just as easily be turned on the left. Hence, when other radicals of this generation were asked whether they wanted the state to ban fascists, a principled minority argued against.[5]

Moreover, the internment of several hundred British fascists came at a time when the state was closely monitoring Communist and other left-wing meeting meetings. In spring 1940, the Soviet Union was still in a pact with Germany, and Communist publications criticised the war using a pacifist language little different from Mosley's. Plainly the expansion of state power raised the possibility that the British Communists would be next on the state's list. Indeed, their *Daily Worker* newspaper was suppressed just six months later.

In these circumstances, you might have expected a certain nervousness in the Communists' response to the internment of British fascists. Instead, and especially from summer 1941 onwards (i.e. after Hitler's declaration of war on the Soviet Union), the Communist Party sought to position itself as the keenest exponent of the continued internment of Mosley's followers. In 1943, the barrister and Communist fellow-traveller, D. N. Pritt, drafted legislation to make fascism unlawful. It would have created six offences: the advocacy of fascist doctrines, the veneration of fascist leaders dead or alive, the display of fascist symbols, the advocacy of racial hatred, printing of literature for any of these purposes, or the membership of a proscribed party.[6]

In November of the same year, Oswald Mosley was released. Reports gathered by the Home Office showed indignation storming across the country. The Communist Party organised a series of demonstrations against his release, especially in factories engaged in war production. Deputations of workers marched down Whitehall. Petitions came from the Communists' industrial base in the engineers', rail-workers', electricians', and miners' trade unions.[7]

Champions of free expression often argue that measures to limit speech are counterproductive, that they only serve to radicalise the unwanted minority, sending it underground, encouraging its supporters into ever-more violent acts. Others argue that when the state intervenes against a party it can destroy the latter's capacity to organise and deal it a shattering blow from which that movement never recovers.

The psychological damage of internment caused British fascists to exhibit both of these reactions at once. Plenty of them simply gave up on far-right politics. Nellie Driver, who had led the BUF in Nelson in Lancashire, exchanged fascism for Catholicism. Alec Miles, one of the BUF's industrial organisers, left the movement and reinvented himself as a left-Labour councillor in Westminster. The novelist Henry Williamson begged his fellow fascists to renounce politics. "[Mosley] was news," Williamson wrote, "but bad news."[8]

Others, meanwhile, saw themselves as having been unjustly martyred and used their anger at repression to justify increased activity. Fascists who had been minor characters in the interwar years played much more prominent parts in the post-war fascist movement, including Mosley's future lieutenant Jeffrey Hamm. Some exchanged relatively moderate forms of fascism for more extreme forms, including James Larratt Battersby, the Stockport hat maker and BUF member, who became increasingly convinced that Hitler had been a "divine spirit" sent to free the world of evil. A barrister William Barlow donated Battersby a specially built altar, guarded by a pair of mastiffs, on which he and around 20 friends in a self-declared Christian Herald commune held midnight services praying to God and to Hitler his messenger.[9]

Kicking over the platforms

After the war ended, various attempts were made to revive the British Union of Fascists. These efforts reached their peak in summer 1947, with a succession of different fascist groups holding street meetings at up to 20 different locations on Saturdays. Events in Palestine helped Britain's Fascists. Following the bomb attack on the King David Hotel, and the killing of two British sergeants at Netanya, there were large anti-Jewish riots in August 1947, in Liverpool, Eccles, Salford and Manchester, and smaller incidents in Plymouth, Bristol, Birmingham, Cardiff, Swansea, Devonport, and Newcastle. These anti-Jewish riots gave Mosely's supporters a national profile. The *Daily Mail* reported the fascists' weekly meetings under the regular title: "The Battle of Ridley Road." Mosley's supporters across London were required to attend these meetings, which for a period of 2 months had a regular audience of around 2,000–3,000 people.

Given that one of the themes of this book is the distinction between no platform and hate speech approaches, it is worth acknowledging that for the antifascists of the 1940s, there was no basis on which this distinction could sensibly have been drawn. Mosley's supporters were fascists, anti-black, and anti-Jewish. Their speech was both fascist and hate speech. The new recruits to Mosley's party were attracted to his cause by racism; inside Mosley's party their racism was deepened, so that it ceased to be a casual belief and became the organising concept which explained everything else. Speaking about events in Palestine, one fascist Bertram Duke Pile said,

Hundreds of our lads have been maimed and killed by these murderers. Why have [sentences of imprisonment] not been carried out? I will tell you. The reason is because the government of today is rotten and controlled by the Shylock moneylenders of New York and the world.[10]

And many other fascists gave speeches of the same sort.

Different left-wing and anti-racist groups were involved in the struggle against fascism in the 1940s, including members of the Communist and Labour Parties, Commonwealth, and supporters of the Association of Jewish Ex-Servicemen. Anti-fascist journalists published articles warning of the growing strength of Mosley's movement. In recent years, the best-known anti-fascist organisation from this period has been the 43 Group, a body of around 500 young Jewish men and women, many of whom had recently served in the British army during the war.

The 43 Group had its own newspaper, *On Guard*, which sought to both report on events in Britain and give coverage to anti-fascists elsewhere. The singer Paul Roberson gave an interview. Other articles criticised the first sitting of the House Un-American Activities Committee, recognising the threat it posed to free speech.

Much of what the 43 Group did was the sort of campaigning that anti-fascist groups have done in Britain and elsewhere both before and since. Spies were sent to infiltrate fascist meetings. Speakers were teased and heckled ("Hello, Clark Gable ... Take his photograph. Mussolini used to stand like that").[11] If members of the 43 Group could defeat Mosley's supporters peacefully – for example, by claiming a local speaker's corner before the fascists did, they would.

The distinctive tactic of the 43 Group, in 1946 and 1947, was to form its members into what was termed a flying wedge, a group of about 15 people who would charge a fascist speaking platform, knocking it over and sending the speaker flying.

One member of the 43 Group, Morris Beckman, conveys the extent to which their activities focussed narrowly on turning over speaker's platforms. By summer 1946,

> Between six and ten fascist meetings per week were being attacked by the Group ... A rough estimate showed that one third were ended by the speakers' platform being knocked over, another third were closed down by the police to keep the peace, and the remaining third or so continue to the finish due to too heavy a presence of police or stewards.[12]

This was a time before television, when most people would get their news from the radio, the press, or cinema. Entry to these strategic media was closed off to the far right, as indeed to the far left and to religious minorities, but particularly to the right because this was after a war in which hundreds of thousands of British people had died fighting fascism. Beneath the public world of high political debate, there was a busy tradition of informal discussion, with dozens of town and urban markets in which people would stand on a wooden box and speak.

While no one had yet formulated the phrase no platform nor would for many years, the day-to-day political work of the 43 Group was a practical application of that tactic. It was a narrow and specific method, limited to fascists. It was intelligence-driven: the 43 Group had infiltrators within the circles of Oswald Mosley's most senior supporters, and relied on them to provide credible accounts of when a fascist assembly was due to start.

It was based in certain contexts: not the universities (although these have been much more important in recent times), nor elections, nor new media, but an older forum – street meetings. When thinking of "platforms," Beckman and his comrades meant them literally. The members of the 43 Group wanted to close off any possible means by which fascism might win new recruits. The tactic emerged in a Britain where, if it was possible to turn over 20 platforms in a single afternoon, then Mosley's route to his audience would be closed off entirely.

Notes

1 E. Smith, *No Platform: A History of Anti-Fascism, Universities, and the Limits of Free Speech* (London: Routledge, 2020), pp. 44–47.

2 S. Dorrril, *Blackshirt: Sir Oswald Mosley and British Fascism* (London: Viking, 2006), pp. 229–230.

3 *Authors Take Sides on the Spanish Civil War* (London: Left Review, 1937), pp. 6, 8, 12, 14.

4 P. Piratin, *Our Flag Stays Red* (London: Lawrence & Wishart, 1948), p. 16.

5 For example, in October 1939, the Russian Revolutionary Leon Trotsky was invited to testify as a witness before the House Un-American Activities Committee. He agreed to attend, but a visa was refused. He wrote that he intended to oppose the banning of the American Nazi Party, on the grounds that "The outlawing of fascist groups would inevitably have a fictitious character: as reactionary organisations they can easily change colour and adapt themselves to any kind of organisational form since the influential sections of the ruling class and of the governmental apparatus sympathize considerably with them and these sympathies inevitably increase during times of political crisis." L. Trotsky, 'Why I consented to appear before the Dies Committee,' *Socialist Appeal*, 30 December 1939.

6 D. N. Pritt, *The Autobiography of D. N. Pritt: Part Two: Brasshats and Bureaucrats* (London: Lawrence and Wishart, 1966), pp. 52–54.

7 D. Renton, 'Not Just Economics but Politics as Well: Trade Unions, Labour Movement Activists and Anti-Fascist Protests 1945-1951,' *Labour History Review* 65/2 (2000), pp. 166–180.

8 D. Renton, *Fascism, Anti-Fascism and Britain in the 1940s* (Houndmills: Palgrave, 2000), p. 30.

9 G. Macklin, *Very Deeply Dyed in Black: Sir Oswald Mosley and the Resurrection of British Fascism and 1945* (London: I. B. Tauris, 2007), pp. 14–15.

10 D. Sonabend, *We Fight Fascists: The 43 Group and Their Forgotten Battle for Post-war Britain* (London: Verso, 2019), p. 107.

11 Renton, *Fascism, Anti-Fascism*, p. 98.

12 Smith, *No Platform*, p. 50.

4

NO PLATFORM IN THE UK 1972–1979

As the historian Evan Smith has shown in his book *No Platform*, the history of no platform can be traced back to a single source: a front-page article in *Red Mole* magazine, the newspaper of the International Marxist Group, published on 18 September 1972: "No platform for Racists." Written by the IMG's John Clayton, the piece began, "Up and down the country, fascist activities are organising racist agitation on a scale not since the 1930s." The piece was clear about the problem, which was the National Front and its allies, described by Clayton as "fascist organisations" and "the extreme right." The piece was vague though about the answer: "the pernicious activity of the extreme right must be knocked on the head." An unsigned editorial accompanied the piece, arguing that fascist meetings should be broken up. The editorial was titled "Free Speech for Racists?" As in the mid-1940s, supporters of fascism should be denied a chance to speak. This time, it was not so much that their platforms should be knocked off. Rather, non-fascist organisations (unions, schools, universities) should refuse a platform to them.[1]

At its spring conference in May 1974, the National Union of Students, through the intervention of its National Secretary Steve Parry, passed a motion committing the NUS to a policy of no platform for racists and fascists.

> Conference recognises the need to refuse any assistance (financial or otherwise) to openly racist or fascist organisations or societ[ies] (e.g. Monday Club, National Front, Action Party/Union Movement, National Democratic Party) and to deny them a platform.
>
> However, conference believes that in order to counter these groups, it is also necessary to prevent any member of these organisations or individuals known to espouse similar views from speaking in colleges whatever means are necessary (including disruption of the meeting).[2]

Student unions with 204,618 members approved of the motion. Others representing 187,760 students opposed it. Except for brief moments when the policy was reversed only to be immediately restored, no platform has remained the policy of the NUS ever since.

Looking at the wording of the motion, certain factors stand out. First, this was directed at student unions, and written at a time when meetings of student unions were mass affairs in which every member of the student body was entitled to vote on what happened to union resources (buildings, canteens, student union money for different societies), to the point where the members of an engaged student body were entitled to express an opinion on who was invited to speak. It was not a case of several hundred students voting with their feet whether to attend as consumers a talk given by one or another speaker, nor of deferring decisions to a (hopefully) representative student council meeting. Rather, students felt entitled to say, and did say repeatedly, that these were their institutions, and they had control over what took place in them.

The list of groups prohibited under the motion contained three instances of clear fascist parties, and only one example of something that was clearly not. The Union Movement was Oswald Mosley's successor to his pre-war British Union of Fascists. The National Front was a merger of three far-right parties in 1967, its early leaders included former full-timers for Mosley's party (A. K. Chesterton) and others who had been repeatedly in the press for their support of a National Socialist milieu that was even further to Mosley's right (John Tyndall). The National Democratic Party was a tiny group which had been excluded from the negotiations which led to the launching of the Front and had been in merger negotiations with that party more recently.

The Monday Club was something different. Previously a faction within the Conservative Party, it had been operating for some time with independent membership lists and in 1971–1973 it repeatedly collaborated with the Front; for example, by holding rallies against immigration which were taken over by members of the NF. One member of the Club, John Ormowe, told an undercover *Mirror* journalist in 1971 that he was an admirer of Hitler, saying, "If you read *Mein Kampf*, you will see it has been wrongly derided."[3] Another supporter of the Monday Club, the future Conservative MP Neil Hamilton, attended the 1972 Conference of the neo-fascist MSI in Italy. In February 1973, the leader of the Front John Tyndall was invited to address a Monday Club meeting at Chelmsford. From 1973 onwards, however, supporters of the Conservative Party had been pushing back against the Club. They demanded it break its links with the NF, which it did.[4]

The phrase "racist organisations" had a more specific meaning than might be apparent. The National Union of Students was not saying that all racist speech was prohibited. If the drafters of the motion had wanted the NUS to use it to oppose racism in all its forms, they would have begun with the police, immigration officers, and the courts. They might have objected to the main television channels in Britain, which up to this point were still running numerous shows

(*Mind Your Language, Love Thy Neighbour, Till Death Us Do Part* …) whose central joke was the strangeness and stupidity of foreigners, as opposed to the calm of the British. They could alternatively have called for a ban on such mass-circulation newspapers as the *Sun*, the *Mirror*, and the *Express*, who responded to mini-waves of migration to Britain by Kenyan, Ugandan, and Malawian Asians, by running stories that refugees were being housed in four-star hotels and by exaggerating the number of potential migrants. When the arrivals came from Malawi, a country whose Asian minority included no more than 200 British passport holders, the *Sun* warned that 4,000 people would immigrate; the *Express* predicted 145,000.[5]

The reason the no platform motion ignored such instances of institutional racism is that the target of the drafters was not racism but fascism. The primary justification for the motion was not the racism of the National Front but the risk it posed to democracy and free speech. Shortly after the motion was passed, the National Union of Students brought out a leaflet explaining its new position to affiliated student unions:

> To turn the problem of "free speech" from a practical into an abstract question is to jeopardise the position of the labour movement and its defence of democratic rights, and to allow fascists and racists to shelter under the democratic freedoms when their ultimate aim is to destroy such freedoms.[6]

If it is right that the object of no platform was, in reality, fascism and not racism, then why did its earliest expressions, in *Red Mole* and the 1974 motion, demand action against racist or fascist organisations, when they might with greater economy have chosen only the latter?

Part of the answer is that the people campaigning for no platform mainly had in mind the National Front, and this was a complex and unstable enemy. It was clearly and unambiguously racist; it was not unequivocally fascist. The popular memory of the National Front is that it was a party of fascists or even Nazis (hence the title of the group set up to fight it, the Anti-Nazi League), led by men such as John Tyndall, with their roots in the neo-Nazi subculture of the early 1960s. But this memory is the product of a successful campaign that was waged in the second half of the 1970s to stigmatise the Front. The early National Front had in fact rather more in common with the hybrid far right of our own era. The organisation was set up with a model of achieving power through winning elections and of de-toxifying the far right. Its first leader, A. K. Chesterton, had been selected because in 1939–1945 he, unlike most fascists of his generation, had fought for Britain. Rather than being invited into membership, let alone leadership of the NF, John Tyndall was originally excluded, and later permitted to join only because Chesterton was persuaded that he had renounced his earlier pro-Nazi views. One early critic, the left-wing journalist and some-time *Oz* contributor Nigel Fountain, writing in *New Society* in 1969, called the National Front "a formative fascist party,"[7] and the phrase is exact – the Front was a mix of different politics, inside which the fascist element only slowly came to dominate.

The most common method used by anti-fascists to discredit the Front, once Tyndall became the Front's Chairman, was to reproduce photographs of him in the neo-Nazi uniforms he had worn a decade earlier; but this image did not become pervasive until after the two general elections in 1974, after NUS's no platform motion. In autumn 1974, Tyndall was even briefly removed from leadership of the party, by a wing that wanted to see the Front develop in a non-fascist direction (the "Populists") and he did not return to the leadership until 1976.[8]

The demand to no platform both racists and fascists was ambiguous; and this ambiguity was necessary; it reflected the complex nature of the far right at the time.

So far, this book has characterised no platform as a single source of opinion, capable of being distinguished from opposition to hate speech. Yet no platform and other justifications for restricting free speech emerged alongside each other, with many people switching from one rationale to another without noticing that they had. To see this, we need to look closely at the literature of the student left, parts of which were just on the verge of leading an anti-fascist movement of hundreds of thousands of people.

From the start, there were in fact two distinct justifications given for no platform. In the first of these approaches, no platform was a tactic to be employed strictly against fascists. It was based on what can be called "the anti-fascist wager,"[9] i.e. an analysis that fascism had greater potential for rapid growth and for violence than other kinds of right-wing politics, and that unless the fascists were deprived of a chance to organise there was a risk that they would triumph, and would remove free speech rights for everyone else.

An instance of this first variant of no platform can be found in the writings of the International Socialists' group at the London School of Economics and their magazine *Red Agitator*, which in the aftermath of the NUS motion, produced a Special Issue on the subject of "No platform for Fascists." It was illustrated with the photograph of a 1930s Nazi rally (designed by Andrew Milner, later a historian and sociologist of literature), and an ironic speech bubble, "Personally, I don't agree with what he says, but I defend his right to say it."[10]

The (unsigned) *Red Agitator* piece argued that the NUS motion had been wrong to treat "fascism and racism" as identical, "for the tactics we use will differ in some cases." The authors supported limits on the free speech of fascists; they were cautious about any wider ban:

> It is because we are determined to prevent [the] growth [of fascism] that we want to put forward the arguments to support the ban on their speakers. The fascists and racists are not in their sordid business to win debates – they want action.[11]

Around a decade later, one of the authors of the *Red Agitator* piece, the anti-war and socialist activist Lindsey German, wrote a second piece, "Free speech for all?" There, she went even further in distinguishing between no platform for fascists and free speech for everyone else. She insisted that her generation had been right to see the National Front as fascists:

> The experience of fascism in Germany demonstrated … that [they would] suppress all forms of political opposition … It was therefore argued that … they had to be prevented from gaining a platform to propagate their ideas.[12]

The same approach did not apply, however, to other political forces on the right, which did not share with fascism the same desire to suppress all dissident voices:

> To some extent this is true of Tory ministers and MPs. They have horrible racist and sexist ideas and are responsible for all sorts of anti-working-class measures. But again, their ideas can be defeated politically, and many Tory students can be won to seeing that those ideas are wrong – if socialists know how to argue with them … Racists and sexists should not go unchallenged in union meetings. But the way we challenge again has to be sensitive and not just a blanket ban.[13]

There was in addition a second variant of no platform, akin to today's hate speech arguments. In this approach, no platform was a tactic to be used against any racist. It was based on the idea that racism was a kind of politics which asserted the superior moral worth of one individual over another, that it was hurtful and caused suffering, and that the closing down of racist speech was necessary in order to make universities a space in which everyone could flourish.

One IMG pamphlet was titled, "Fascists and Racists: free speech will not stop them." Its targets included the Conservative MP, Enoch Powell, who had been in the news repeatedly since 1968 for his calls to limit black migration to Britain and to start "voluntary" repatriation. "When any racist agitates," the author of the document wrote, "he may or may not be aware of the fact that he is encouraging the state to crush black people through more vicious legal means or the fascists through illegal means."[14] All racism was, in this approach, equally wrong.

Advocates of an approach to no platform which focussed on fascism also believed that racism should be opposed, and indeed both groups had supported the NUS motion. The strict anti-fascists were clear however that more moderate tactics were needed for the fight against racists with non-fascist politics: they could be heckled and embarrassed, but their opponents should go no further than that. They did not call for the likes of Enoch Powell to be banned from speaking.

The explanation for this reticence is that these two different kinds of right-wing politics had a different relationship to the state. The National Front believed in a complete transformation of the British state: the increase of its military function, and of state surveillance, the replacement of a form of political democracy with one-party rule, the submission of the people to a single leader. Enoch Powell may have been a racist, but his political programme was for the continuation of Parliament as it stood, the maintenance of political competition between parties, and the toleration of views which were not his own. He was arrogant, pompous, and uninterested in those who disagreed with him, but he never seriously called for a system of mass censorship, or the creation in Britain of a 1930s-style dictatorship with a monopoly of speech.

Steve Parry, the President of the National Union of Students in 1974, came from a different ideological background to either the IS or the IMG. The latter based their politics on a rejection of the authoritarian regimes of Eastern Europe, while Parry was a Communist and had been an enthusiastic participant in the Eastern Bloc's World Youth Festivals. As the leading figure within the students' union, Parry was the focus of press demands that someone come forward to justify the union's new position. In calling on delegates to pass the resolution, Parry's language was close to the purely anti-fascist version of no platform: he pointed to the activity of prominent British fascists, and the alliance they made with similar groups abroad:

> Did reasoned argument stop the fascists led by Mosley in the East End in the 1930s? Of course, it did not. Had reasoned argument stopped Colin Jordan and his cronies in the Union Movement having armed camps in the Britain and working with ex-Nazis in Germany? Had reasoned argument stopped the junta in Chile killing thousands of people?[15]

Another article written by Parry for the Communist's *Labour Monthly* in June 1974 however portrayed the no platform tactic as something of much wider applicability. The National Front and other groups were wrong, Parry argued, because they were racists. The rights of black students to be heard overrode the entitlement of racists to speak:

> To deny racists and fascists a platform is to "limit freedom of speech" but one cannot see this freedom as something which exists in the abstract ... [T]he NUS is fighting for ... [the] freedom to live without discrimination on the basis of race.[16]

Parry was speaking in the middle of a fast-moving debate. It is only with the advantage of hindsight that we can see that he and other speakers were in fact making different sorts of arguments: some which would treat no platform as a strict exception to the principle of free speech, and others which would see it as a tactic that could be applied to most situations of ordinary political conflict.

No platform: From student politics to mass movement

Over the next six years, anti-fascists in Britain organised one of the largest anti-racist and anti-fascist movements Europe or America have seen. It began with the launch of Rock Against Racism in winter 1976–1977. Over the five years of its existence, RAR organised more than 500 gigs and around a dozen carnivals (300 of the former in 1978 alone). Its 2 London Carnivals in 1978 saw roughly 80,000 and then 100,000 attend joyful, free, anti-racist events. If you add together all the people who took part, whether in attending demonstrations, handing out leaflets or painting out graffiti, the total number who passed through the campaign is probably half a million people. RAR was joined in 1977 by the Anti-Nazi League, which had 50,000 members at its peak, sold some 750,000 badges, and distributed 9,000,000 anti-fascist leaflets. Both campaigns grew in response to a sharp rise of racism following the press reporting of the arrival of Malawian Asians to Britain. Rock Against Racism set out to challenge the echo of that racism in popular music. The Anti-Nazi League, by contrast, was a one-purpose campaign, to stop the National Front, which in 1976–1977 seemed capable of displacing the Liberals as the third main party of British politics.

The ANL set itself the goal of closing every National Front talk and of disrupting every Front paper sale. The members of the League set out to make it impossible for the Front to grow again. The justification for this incursion on free speech principles was a theory of fascism in which that movement carried the threat of destroying both social democracy and democracy itself.

Central to the activities of the Anti-Nazi League was the task of proving that the National Front were fascists. So, a mass-circulation ANL leaflet, *Why You Should Oppose the National Front*, began by asking, "The National Front says it is just an ordinary political party. Is it?" There followed numerous quotes from the Front's Chairman John Tyndall and its National Organiser expressing their support for Adolf Hitler and *Mein Kampf* and descriptions of themselves as a "well-oiled Nazi machine." Readers were reminded that Tyndall had boasted, "When we get to power, our opponents will be swept aside like flies" and said, "We should restore 'real' freedom of press. We wouldn't allow anything seditious or slanderous or subversive."[17]

For a member of the 43 Group, as we have seen, the defining act of everyday anti-fascism was confronting a fascist speaker and seeking to knock over their platform. For a member of the Anti-Nazi League, the equivalent act was protesting outside a National Front election meeting or seeking to block a Front demonstration.

So, for example, in April 1978 around a thousand anti-fascists in Leeds stood outside a Martin Webster election meeting, chanting anti-Front slogans, and seeking to drown out the speakers. Meanwhile, inside the hall, Webster told his supporters that their opponents were "raucous beer can-throwing stinking animals ... an insult to the animal kingdom" and claimed that the anti-fascists were led and controlled by Jews.[18]

In the run-up to the 1979 general election, so common were the protests that the owners of large venues refused to allow the Front to hold meetings. According to the Front's Tony Simms, "The trouble we had booking rooms for meetings was unbelievable ... We had to lie about who we were."[19] Labour-controlled local authorities such as Newham insisted that halls should not be made available to the NF. Labour's National Executive Committee endorsed this policy in September 1978, and in the same document instructed its candidates not to appear on platforms or radio or TV broadcasts with members of the National Front. On occasion the Front was able to have these bans overturned, but only after costly and protracted litigation.[20]

One union which supported no platform was the ANL-affiliated technicians' union ACTT, which supported its members when they refused to air Front broadcasts. The *New Statesman*'s Francis Wheen rang Alan Sapper, general secretary of the ACTT, to ask if disruptive action would make martyrs of the Front. Sapper's response was typical of the no platform approach. "Democracy is threatened," Sapper told Wheen. "We don't need to bother with philosophical arguments. We can discuss democracy until the concentration camps come in."[21]

The Anti-Nazi League's main ally, Rock Against Racism had a different focus. Launched to respond to racist and pro-fascist quotes given by the musicians David Bowie (who retracted his remarks soon afterwards) and Eric Clapton (who did not withdraw his words until much later),[22] RAR was a movement of musicians and fans against all racism, not simply fascism.

One of the members of the RAR organising committee, and the author of its most important public statements was the doctor, journalist, and revolutionary socialist David Widgery who we encountered in the last chapter as one of the writers for *Oz magazine*, and a part of its defence team. In the first issue of RAR's magazine *Temporary Hoarding*, Widgery explained what the enemy was against which Rock Against Racism was fighting:

> The problem is not just the new fascists from the old slime, a master race whose idea of heroism is ambushing single blacks in darkened streets. These private attacks whose intention, to cow and brutalise, won't work if the community they seek to terrorise instead organises itself. But when the state backs up racialism, it's different. Outwardly respectable but inside fired with the same mentality and the same fears, the bigger danger is the racist magistrates with their cold sneering authority, the immigration men who mock an Asian mother as she gives birth to a dead child on their office floor, policemen for whom answering back is a crime.[23]

Because the target of RAR was institutional racism rather than fascism, its publications rarely if ever used the phrase "no platform." Nor was there much talk of preventing fascist speeches, let alone those of racists. Some of this can be put down to a division of labour in the movement: if a fascist meeting was called then it was up to the ANL, not RAR, to organise a response. Some of it can be explained also in terms of the much weaker position of anti-racists in relation to racism than anti-fascists in relation to the Front. As a mass movement with tens of thousands of members, the ANL could realistically set itself the ambition of defeating the National Front in elections and preventing its speakers from being heard. But what Widgery was calling for was the political defeat of the police and of the criminal system in which they worked. Plainly anti-racists were in no position to silence the police, the press, or the judges.

The logic of no platform was to distinguish between fascists whose platforms should be removed and racists who should be challenged but not prevented from speaking. Supporters of RAR were willing to put their own bodies on the line when it came to debating fascists, which they did in their own places (typically at anti-racist gigs) and on their own terms. So, RAR boasted of having recruited the band Sham 69, although Sham was popular with young skinheads, and despite the band's roadies including members of the neo-Nazi British Movement. Sham 69 gigs at Kingston University, the London School of Economics, and Middlesex Polytechnic ended in brawls. Security at RAR gigs was provided by the Royal Group of Docks shop stewards. RAR's Red Saunders recalls one of the dockers carrying a club hammer with a hole drilled through the end of it with a big leather strap, so that if the hammer was dropped in fighting it could be recovered and used again.[24] Such weapons were needed because RAR gigs were frequent targets for the far right, which sent hundreds of its supporters to attack them.

The worst of the fighting was seen at the Sham 69 gig at Middlesex Poly. As the evening went on, those in charge of security became increasingly worried. At the back of the hall, a chant could be heard echoing, "What we Got? Fuck All. National Front." At one desperate moment, National Front- and British Movement-supporting skinheads invaded the stage and were able to briefly grab the microphone, before they were repulsed, and the gig ended with black and white performers united on stage. RAR was criticised for having allowed supporters of the right into its gigs, but Saunders refused to apologise, "This is the fucking real world. This is Rock Against Racism. The white working class and a reggae band and we've brought them all together."[25]

Other RAR groups followed the same approach. In Birmingham, Sheryl Garratt recalls skinheads dancing to soul classic Liquidator, while chanting, "British Movement." Garratt confronted them, showed them the album with the Harry J. All Stars on its front and said, "Do you know what colour these people are?" The skinheads stopped chanting, remained, and at the end of the evening one of the organisers gave them a lift home. "They were National Front in the same way as I was left-wing. It was like a vague unease that things weren't right, and life wasn't fair."[26]

Rather than seeking to limit the group of people who could speak, RAR's focus was on increasing the number who were heard, and on expanding political discussion so that it took in songs, jokes, and art. In the words again of former *Oz* contributor David Widgery:

> The stakes are high. If we cede the difficult but necessary ground of the politic of everyday life – of the world of the cultural, the emotional and the sexual – it falls by default to the Right.

Over the last five years since the punk explosion and the international recognition of reggae music, beneath all the crap a surprisingly high proportion of the music has been aimed at educating rather than anaesthetising the senses – in illuminating rather than obscuring reality, in heightening awareness rather than promoting stupidity. It is music that has, both in the subjective and the objective, recorded social life at a particular stage, indicated possibilities and been a part of the future it predicted.[27]

RAR chose music as the nearest culture form through which its supporters could speak, could encourage others to speak, and could increase the number of people participating in a free-flowing and open political argument. RAR wanted the supporters of the far right to give up on that project. To win them over required a space in which the most vacillating of fascists could speak and be heard and be talked out of their opinions.

An article in RAR's magazine *Temporary Hoarding* reflected on the first year of the campaign. It described Rock Against Racism as if the movement's characteristic form was a paste table near some concert, and the people on the table were being overwhelmed by a constant to-and-fro of others, coming to talk and speak and debate:

Everyone wants stickers, everyone wants badges, everyone wants posters, everyone wants T-shirts, everyone wants to tell us about their experiences, their favourite local band, their ideas about how to fight racism, about their bigoted families, about mates beaten up, about anger and frustration, about their town, about racism in their street, their block of flats, about fear ... helplessness.[28]

You can read this passage as a discussion of what racism is or how to fight it, and the passage has a value. But it is still more interesting if you read it as a commentary on speech – as a description of the fast-moving conversations that surrounded a mass movement and enabled it to flourish.

There were occasions when Rock Against Racism worked together with the Anti-Nazi League in response to Front meeting or demonstrations. For the ANL, what was important was the outcome: fascists could not be permitted to organise or recruit. For RAR, by contrast, process and outcome were combined. While it was important that fascism suffered a setback, and therefore that all forms of racism were pushed back; it was equally important that anti-racist and anti-fascist struggles led to stronger black communities which were better capable of resisting all forms of institutional racism, not just the boot-boys of the Front.

Some of the ways in which these two different political approaches fitted together could be seen in April 1979, at Southall, as several thousand police officers confronted an anti-fascist protest outside the Town Hall. By the end of the evening, 64 people were receiving treatment for injuries at the hands of police officers. One anti-fascist demonstrator, a New Zealand-born schoolteacher, Blair Peach, was struck on the head by police and killed.[29]

The fighting at Southall took place after some 10,000 residents signed a petition calling for a ban on the National Front meeting taking place within the Town Hall. The council insisted however that the meeting should go ahead. The Anti-Nazi League was much more involved than Rock Against Racism in the planning of the demonstration and the political campaign to secure justice for Blair Peach. RAR worked mainly through musical networks. Angry and horrified as RAR supporters were after a police riot, they did not focus simply on Peach but gave equal attention to Clarence Baker, a black musician with the local reggae band Misty in Roots and a member of the RAR committee, who was also struck by a police officer, spent a week in a coma, and remained in hospital for weeks. Baker worked with a local youth campaign Peoples Unite Education, which had its headquarters in Southall, a building which also held literacy, numeracy, and drama and dance classes. On the night that the police killed Blair Peach and struck Clarence Baker, they also rioted through the People's Unite headquarters, breaking doors, walls, and plaster. The damage was so extensive that Ealing Council had to demolish the building.

Rock Against Racism was principally involved after the confrontations had ended, in putting on a huge concert raising money for the several hundred youngsters facing prosecution, with Aswad and Misty playing alongside The Clash and Pete Townshend of The Who, and in organising a series of further solidarity events as a "Dance and Defend" tour. In his book, *Beating Time*, David Widgery quotes the RAR solidarity leaflet for Southall:

> Southall is special. There have been police killings before. There will be police riots again. But on April 23rd the police behaved like never before. The tactics of the colonies had come back home to suburban back streets of West London with their rows of parked Morris Oxfords and their houses called Ivanhoe. To walk through the railway bridge that night was to walk through the valley of the wicked. Elders arrested coming home from the temple, kids rounded up back from football because the police had stopped the buses.
>
> The police were trying to kill our people. They were trying to get even with our culture … What free speech needs martial law? What public meeting requires 5,000 people to keep the public out?[30]

In these last two sentences, RAR was setting out – admittedly, in a brief form – a justification for the restriction of the free speech rights of the National Front. The campaigners were raising the possibility of a world in which all could speak freely, and all had the right to be heard. For the black community of Southall, that possibility could come about only if they were given an opportunity to talk, which until now they had been denied to them. RAR was arguing against a ritualised performance of free speech in which only fascist speech was allowed, and in favour of free speech and mass meetings. RAR wanted to hear a polyphony of voices: more talk, not less.

In the 1970s, no platform was an approach which came from below, not above; it required no politician, no judge, and no social media platform to implement it. The plan was to encourage popular control and increase speech, rather than limiting it.

Notes

1 *Red Mole*, 18 September 1972; E. Smith, *No Platform: A History of Anti-Fascism, Universities, and the Limits of Free Speech* (London: Routledge, 2020), pp. 91–92.
2 Smith, *No Platform*, p. 92.
3 D. Renton, *Never Again: Rock Against Racism and the Anti-Nazi League 1976–1982* (London: Routledge, 2018), pp. 21–22.
4 Renton, *Never Again*, pp. 35–36.
5 Renton, *Never Again*, p. 32.
6 S. Asquith, 'The Right and the Market Versus Free Speech on Campus,' *New Socialist*, 24 October 2017.
7 *New Society*, 3 April 1969.
8 Renton, *Never Again*, pp. 30–34.
9 D. Renton, *Fascism: History and Theory* (London: Pluto, 2020), pp. 1–5.
10 Red Agitator, *No Platform for Fascists* (London: LSE International Socialists, 1974).
11 Red Agitator, *No Platform*, pp. 1–2.
12 L. German, 'No Platform: Free Speech for All?' *Socialist Worker Review*, April 1986.
13 German, 'No Platform'.
14 Smith, *No Platform*, pp. 96–97.
15 Smith, *No Platform*, p. 93.
16 S. Parry, 'Students against Racism and Fascism,' *Labour Monthly*, June 1974.
17 *Why You Should Oppose the National Front* (London: Anti-Nazi League, 1978), pp. 1–2.
18 Renton, *Never Again*, p. 106.
19 T. Simms, *Match Day: Ulster Loyalism and the British Far-Right* (London: Create Space, 2016), p. 77.
20 *Martin Guy Webster and Richard Hugh Verrall (On Behalf of Themselves and the National Front) v Newham London Borough Council* (1980) 2 All ER 7.
21 F. Wheen, 'The National Front's Reptilian Aspects,' *New Statesman*, 22 September 1978.
22 For Clapton's 1976 speech, Renton, *Never Again*, p. 51. In recent years, Clapton has been asked repeatedly about these comments. As of early 2018, Clapton's explanation was that his mind was disturbed by excessive drug-taking, "I was so ashamed of who I was, a kind of semi-racist, which didn't make sense. Half of my friends were black." D. Sanderson, 'Drugs "Turned Eric Clapton Racist",' *Times*, 13 January 2018.
23 D. Widgery, 'What Is Racism?' *Temporary Hoarding* 1, spring 1977; J. Ash, N. Fountain, and D. Renton (eds), *David Widgery. Against Miserabilism: Writings 1968–1992* (Glasgow: Vagabond Voices, 2017), pp. 123–126.
24 Renton, *Never Again*, p. 104.
25 Renton, *Never Again*, p. 105.
26 Renton, *Never Again*, p. 64.

27 Widgery, *Preserving Disorder*, pp. 115–121.
28 *Temporary Hoarding* 4, winter 1977–1978.
29 D. Renton, 'The Killing of Blair Peach,' *London Review of Books*, 21 May 2014.
30 D. Widgery, *Beating Time: Riot 'n' Race 'n' Rock and Roll* (London: Chatto and Windus, 1986), p. 106.

5

A PATH NOT TAKEN

The United States 1977–1979

Often, when historians look back at a moment in the past, we set out to identify its longer-term historical causes. So, the rise of racism in Britain during the 1970s was shaped by the decline of Britain as an imperial power and the weakening of her industrial economy. Equally important was the memory of the Second World War – fascism still exerted a fascination, shaping the clothes that people wore, the music they listened to, even how they imagined good and evil. Faced with processes operating on this vast scale, it is tempting to assume that no platform, or something like it, was bound to emerge and that the likes of the Front were doomed to defeat from the start.

In the United States, however, anti-fascist organisers responded to similar events with different tactics. A proposed demonstration by fascists through the Chicago suburb of Skokie in 1977–1978, where many Holocaust survivors lived, received the support of the American Civil Liberties Union. This relationship began with a phone call from Frank Collin of the National Socialist Party of America (NSP) to David Goldberger, legal director of the Illinois ACLU, asking for the organisation's support in challenging a decision of the Skokie Park District that the NSP could march only if it first posted a bond for $350,000 as a guarantee there would be no disorder. Frank Collin explained that his supporters would march in full Nazi uniform: brown shirts, brown tie and swastika pin, black belts with buckles, dark brown trousers, and black engineer boots. Despite significant misgivings, the ACLU agreed to represent him.[1]

In Britain the ACLU's sister-organisation, the National Council of Civil Liberties, was on the side of anti-fascist demonstrators and monitored the police to ensure that anti-fascists' free speech rights were protected.[2] In the United States by contrast, the ACLU argued that the speech rights of the Nazi Party must have priority.

This decision was controversial within the American Civil Liberties Union, for the ACLU's roots were in reaction to the anti-Communist campaigns of the 1920, during which the ACLU had principally defended revolutionary trade unionists, conscientious objectors, and other left-wing protesters against a paranoid state – including Charlotte Anita Whitney, the member of the Communist Labour Party, whose case was described in a previous chapter. With one or two noteworthy exceptions[3] the ACLU had been supportive of civil rights campaigners ever since.

Of Skokie's 26 houses of worship, 9 were synagogues. Perhaps as many as 40 percent of the local population, or 30,000 people, were Jews. Among those demanding that the march be blocked were a number of Holocaust survivors. In pitching itself directly against the wishes of these residents, the ACLU made itself unpopular. "The reaction of those to whom we normally turn for support," Goldberger complained, "has become increasingly hysterical."[4] And this revulsion was felt far beyond Illinois. The union's membership fell from 270,000 in the early 1970s to just 185,000 after its public support for the right of Collin's National Socialists to march.[5]

The ACLU was successful in obtaining an order that city laws requiring permission for marches, prohibiting the dissemination of material which incited racial hatred, and preventing the National Socialists from marching in paramilitary uniforms were unlawful.[6] By a 6–1 majority decision, the Illinois Supreme Court approved both the right of the NSP to march and in particular their right to carry pins, armbands, and banners with swastikas on them:

> We do not doubt that the sight of this symbol is abhorrent to the Jewish citizens of Skokie, and that the survivors of the Nazi persecution, tormented by their recollections, may have strong feelings regarding its display. Yet it is entirely clear that this factor does not justify enjoining defendants' speech.[7]

Unlike in Britain, where the Front had up to 20,000 members, Chicago's National Socialists were capable of turning out barely two dozen people on their proposed march. Frank Collin, their Führer, was a "dull, inept, unimposing man," short and paunchy.[8] Born in Chicago in 1944, Collin's father Max was a Jewish survivor of the concentration camp at Dachau who had changed his name from Cohen to Collin two years after Frank's birth.

Collin claimed to have been converted to fascism by watching a television documentary, *The Twisted Cross* (1956). Uninterested in the film's intended anti-fascist politics, Collins was captivated by the images of Hitler speaking.

> When they would show a close-up of Adolf Hitler's face, I still remember my feeling – that here was a man who was saying something: whatever it was, he was deeply committed to it. He was feeling it deeply … I've loved Hitler ever since.[9]

In his memoir of the conflict, David Hamlin of the ACLU's Illinois office endorses the ACLU position that free speech rights were sacrosanct. What he also acknowledges however, to a greater extent than other ACLU authors who were further from the conflict, is the fury of Skokie's Jewish residents. The heart of Hamlin's narrative is the experience of going from school to synagogue, putting the case for free speech, only to have to face repeatedly the members of a Jewish community which was against them. In his account, the ACLU's stance, "was built on the premise that those who preach changes in constitutional law [i.e. a restriction of speech rights] are the enemy." The ACLU had equipped its full-timers, he explains, to think that they were akin to the Freedom Riders of the early 1960s spreading a gospel as virtuous as that of Civil Rights:

> The difficulty of that posture, we would discover a long time later, was that the Skokie controversy bore no resemblance whatsoever to the civil-rights confrontations of the sixties. There were no Bull Connors[10] in Skokie, no sheriffs with cattle prods.[11]

The task of ACLU officials was to compel a sullen and angry generation of elderly Holocaust survivors into accepting, against their better judgment, that it would be good for them if they were compelled to endure the sight of Nazis marching through their home town, with all the memories that would bring of their treatment in the Holocaust.

At the crux of the Skokie case was an issue which remains unresolved in US politics. The purpose of the First Amendment is to prevent the American *government* (i.e. both the legislature and the executive) from limiting speech. This can be seen from the Amendment's language, with its prohibition against limitation of speech by Congress and its guarantee of the rights of the people to assemble and to speak freely, and to petition the Government: "Congress shall make no law … abridging the freedom of speech, or … the right of the people peaceably to assemble, and to petition the Government for a redress of grievances." What should the courts do, however, if the opponents of fascist speech are not the government but people – an anti-fascist crowd?

The Jewish population of Skokie asked judges to treat them not as the government but as a group of people (the 30,000 Jews who lived in the city) seeking to restrict a protest on a truculent and unpleasant minority. But this the Judges would not – and could not – do. After all, the subject of the case was not whether Frank Collin should speak at all, or even whether his opponents could stop him, but whether the bond required by Skokie Park District was lawful. It was unquestionably a public law decision – an act of government, albeit local government.

This battle ended with a legal victory; the courts struck down the insurance requirement as unlawful. The ACLU's advocates triumphed in court. But the Union's membership list was diminished, the organisation was friendless, and a third of its local staff removed from their posts. It was a success, but not one that Hamlin was proud of:

> David [Goldberger] and I had long ago learned that no victory in this litigation would merit the language of celebration. We had seen first-hand more than enough of the anguish of Frank Collin's targets to applaud still more of it.[12]

Comments such as Hamlin's provide the context to one moment in popular culture which reflects the events at Skokie: Dan Aykroyd and John Belushi's film *The Blues Brothers* (1980). Elwood and Zee are driving through rural Illinois when they come across rival fascist and anti-fascist demonstrations, blocking a bridge and causing a tailback. The members of the American Socialist White People's Party pledge their allegiance to Hitler. "Those bums won their court case so they're marching today," a police officer says. "I hate Illinois Nazis," Zee answers. Elwood drives their car towards the Nazi march, sending its members leaping into a nearby stream.

The politics of Skokie continue: the 1970s era ACLU is celebrated by libertarians of the right and the left.[13] The ACLU has taken universities to court where they have introduced codes banning hate speech. The Union has succeeded in having such policies struck down at a number of universities, including Stanford University, the University of Michigan, and the University of Wisconsin. Similarly, at the Charlottesville protests in 2017, the ACLU provided free legal representation to Jason Kessler, the main organiser of the far-right march. The city wanted to move the Unite the Right event away from Emancipation Park, which held a statute of Robert E. Lee, the Confederate general whose future was the underlying source of the conflict. Taking Kessler's side, the ACLU argued that free speech required that the right should be entitled to assemble in Emancipation Park. "The First Amendment guarantees political speech, including protest, the highest level of protection," lawyers for the ACLU argued, "and the right to speak out is the most robust in traditional public fora, including public parks and streets."[14]

In the 40 years since Skokie, the ACLU has played a crucial role in persuading the public that free speech should have the totemic role that it plays within United States politics, as no longer merely a constitutional principle but *the* constitutional principle (the country's "First" Amendment) taking precedence over everything else.[15]

An anti-fascism indifferent to its audience

There is in addition a second way in which the protests in the United States in 1977–1979 point away from developments in Britain. Events at Skokie in 1977–1978 were followed in November 1979 by protests in Greensboro, North Carolina, at which a left-wing protest titled "Death to the Klan rally," ended in a shoot-out between Klansmen and anti-fascist protesters. Five of the latter were killed, four white men and one black woman, all by neo-Nazis, with the deaths recorded on camera and the facts incontrovertible. As the historian of these struggles Kathleen Belew shows in her book *Bring the War Home*, the Greensboro shootings came at the end of two years of conflicts between fascists and anti-fascists, after a run of incomplete victories for each side. In July 1979, for example, 100 members of the Workers Viewpoint Organisation (WVO), which later changed its name to the Communist Workers Party (CWP), attacked a community centre in China Grove at which members of the Klan had been watching *Birth of a Nation*, and successfully disrupted the viewing. Five months later at Greensboro, a camera caught American fascist Milano Caudle whispering, "China Grove," moments before the shooting began.[16]

Klan supporters and their allies from neo-Nazi and other groups prepared for the events in November by covering Greensboro with posters of a lynched black body and the slogan. "It's time for old-fashioned justice." Members of the CWP brought hard hats and clubs to the battle. Their opponents carried shotguns, nunchucks, hunting knives, tear gas and mace, three semi-automatic handguns and two rifles, one of them an AR-180 semi-automatic. Prominent neo-Nazis among the shooters included Green Berets who had served in Vietnam.

In Britain in 1978–1979, the death of a single left-wing protester, Blair Peach, was politicised by left-wing campaigners who drew on their support in the local black (Sikh Punjabi) community of Southall, and worked with the Labour Party, the unions and other mainstream figures to win an argument as to who had caused the violence – not anti-fascists, but the state.

At Greensboro, the right had much greater success in portraying themselves as the victims of outside agitators. Klansman Virgil Griffin declared, "I think every time a senator or a congressman walks by the Vietnam Wall, they ought to hang their damn heads in shame for allowing the Communist Party to be in this country." In the case that followed, an anti-Communist Cuban exile was selected as foreman of the jury, while afterwards other jurors praised the Klan.[17]

Meanwhile, the CWP played up to Cold War fantasies about them, marching to commemorate the dead with rifles and shotguns, inverting the reality of what had happened in November when minimally armed left-wing protesters had been gunned down. Members of the CWP refused to testify, even emptied skunk oil in court. Two criminal trials ended in acquittals. Only in a third, civil trial, was one of the killings recorded as unlawful, after a jury found the City of Greensboro liable for the death of Michael Nathan (he, unlike the other anti-fascists, had not been a member of the CWP). The City of Greensboro, not the killers, paid the settlement.

The Greensboro massacre took place at a dark time for the American far left. In the late 1960s, the example of leftist advance in China, Vietnam, and Cuba had been attractive, far more so in Britain (not least because the United States was in actual military contest with the second of these states – and losing). Through the 1970s such politics became less attractive. The countries concerned were now in conflict with each other, and one of them (China) was in alliance with the US. The jailing and murder of activists by the state encouraged burn-out and demoralisation and caused a rapid lurching between moderate and extreme forms of leftism.[18] The space to demand everything, and to be both principled and popular, was shrinking.

While the argument of this book is that no platform provides the best basis for restricting the free speech rights of fascists, this is not to say that the tactic should be invoked in every circumstance. No platform is a way of thinking about politics, a specific argument for closing fascist speech from below, rather than a general rule that all forms of right-wing opinion require harassment. The ordinary rules of effective politics (think before you act, build allies when you can, choose battles you can win) all continue to apply.

There is nothing automatic which says that anti-fascism in Britain should be more successful than anti-fascism in the United States. If activists in the UK tended to get most things right in the 1970s, the same could hardly be said of politics since 2016, when left and anti-fascist cultures have been more dynamic in the US than here. The reasons why anti-fascism prospered in 1970s Britain included that anti-fascist activists were alive to the value of unity on the left and used strategies for mobilisation which won over people with little interest in conventional politics. It was in that context that the practice of no platform flourished.

Notes

1 A. Neier, *Defending My Enemy: American Nazis, the Skokie Case, and the Risks of Freedom of Speech* (New York: International Debate Education Association, 2012 edn), p. 13.
2 National Council for Civil Liberties, *Southall 23 April 1979, Report of the Unofficial Committee of Inquiry* (London: NCCL, 1980).
3 Principally the active support given to McCarthyism by prominent figures within the ACLU, including its general counsel Morris Ernst and the director of its Washington office Irving Ferman, who actively contributed to the blacklist by sending the FBI and McCarthy's office details of ACLU affiliates who he suspected of Communism. C. Gentry, *J. Edgar Hoover: The Man and the Secrets* (New York: W. W. Norton and Co., 1961), pp. 438–440. This history only emerged in summer 1977, i.e. at about the same time that the ACLU took Frank Collin's case, Neier, *Defending*, p. 83.
4 P. Strum, *When the Nazis Came to Skokie: Freedom for Speech We Hate* (Lawrence, Kansas: University Press of Kansas, 1999), p. 82.
5 Neier estimates the number who left solely over Skokie as just 30,000 people. *Defending*, p. 90.
6 *Collin v Smith* 578 F.2d 1197 (7th Cir. 1978).
7 Neier, *Defending*, p. 64.
8 D. Hamlin, *The Nazi/Skokie Conflict: A Civil Liberties Battle* (Boston: Beacon Press, 1980), pp. 1–4, 179–180.
9 Strum, *When the Nazis Came to Skokie*, p. 4.
10 Connor was for two decades the Commissioner of Public Safety for the city of Birmingham, Alabama, and a vocal opponent of the Civil Rights Movement.
11 Hamlin, *The Nazi/Skokie Conflict*, p. 80.
12 Hamlin, *The Nazi/Skokie Conflict*, p. 144.

13 I. Glasser, 'The ACLU Would Not Take the Skokie Case Today,' *Spiked*, 14 February 2020.'

14 Moskowitz's *The Case*, p. 17.

15 While writing this book, signs emerged that the ACLU might be reconsidering its position, with the leaking of an internal discussion paper. One of the key proposals in the document was that the ACLU would no longer support legal challenges to rules prohibiting armed demonstrations. "The presence of weapons can be intimidating and inimical to the free exchange of ideas. They can chill speech and justify state suppression of protest. Accordingly, the ACLU generally will not represent protesters who seek to march while armed." 'Case Selection Guidelines: Conflicts Between Competing Values or Priorities,' *ACLU*, July 2020.

16 K. Belew, *Bring the War Home* (Cambridge, MA: Harvard University Press, 2018), pp. 62–74.

17 Belew, *Bring the War Home*, pp. 64–74.

18 M. Elbaum, *Revolution in the Air* (London: Verso, 2002).

6

THE RIGHT DEMANDS A RESPECTFUL AUDIENCE

The campaign of the British left against the National Front was eased by the lat-ter's unwillingness to pose as the victim or to invoke the language of free speech. On the face of it, this reticence was surprising. We like to think that the fasci-nation with the far right is a feature of the media in our time, but it was just as much a phenomenon of the 1970s. "The Front badly want publicity," noted the *Telegraph* journalist Sally Beauman. Its leaders "John Tyndall and Martin Webster will dismiss all journalists as liberals," but this was an affectation. "[The Front] seem fascinated by them; they know their names, the life-histories of those ... journalists who have reported their activities – they want to know if you know them too."[1]

This open-door approach even extended to those journalists who the leaders of the Front recognised as having a hostile agenda. Martin Walker combined writing about the National Front for the *Guardian*, with researching what would become a paperback expose of that movement. Between February and October 1974, he was granted interviews with Front leaders including John Tyndall, Martin Webster, Roy Painter and John Kingsley Read, Rosine de Bounevialle, Gordon Brown, and John O'Brien of the Front's ruling Directorate, as well as Colin Jordan of the British Movement. "I have been met with courtesy with a number of NF leaders," Walker wrote, "I have lunched, dined, drunk and talked to the small hours with some of them."[2]

The Front's leaders were aware of their isolation and impatient with it. The more time their party spent on the front pages, the happier they were.

On the other hand, the Front refrained from demanding the right to speak. NF publications insisted on treating every single encounter with anti-fascists as a military victory. When the scale of a defeat made that impossible, Front leaders refused to acknowledge their victimhood. By building up the threat posed by anti-fascists, the NF hoped to persuade the state to ban the left and force their oppressors underground. But the Front would not let anyone see the bruises on its members' faces, or the misery and hurt they suffered in defeat.

At the Battle of Lewisham in August 1977, for example, some 800 supporters of the Front were met by groups of anti-fascists who fought them at their assembly point at Clifton Rise, threw rocks and bricks at them, and charged the Front's marchers. The remnants of the Front reached central Lewisham but found it occupied by anti-fascists and had to be led away by the police.

Front Chairman John Tyndall was called on to make a speech to his supporters before they boarded the trains that would take them back to central London. He spoke for about ten minutes altogether – welcoming the fraternal support from the members of the Front National in France who had sent a contingent in support. In the final minute of his talk, Tyndall came close to presenting his group as free speech campaigners.

> We wanted to have a peaceful and orderly march in a part of our capital city. A right which we will always defend. A right that we always ... (cheers).[3]

Having come this close to invoking rights, Tyndall immediately turned away from such language to his preferred topic, the malice of his opponents:

> The fact that there has not been peace and order this afternoon, the fact that people have had to board up their windows and shut themselves in their homes, the fact that businessmen have had to close down their shops and lose money, these are all things which we enormously regret but this fact is entirely due to the red terrorists.[4]

The answer to anti-fascist attacks, Tyndall insisted, was the arrest of his opponents:

> The police did a splendid job. They could have done an even better job had they been allowed to go in with tear gas, with rubber bullets (Cheers) and the whole of the works of crowd control. And let me make this promise to the police ... we will give the police all the necessary equipment, we'll give them the money they deserve, we'll give them the backing they deserve, and we'll give them the authority to sort the Red mob out. (Cheers) (Get the Reds. If they're Red, shoot them dead).[5]

Today, the descendants of the Front complain that left-wing attacks are an infringement of their freedom of expression. But the Front largely disdained that approach, only rarely invoking the right to free speech. It refused to admit the reality of its own physical defeat. After Lewisham, that night's evening news featured a frightened old woman sitting with her feet on the pavement, dazed and distraught. The decontextualised image failed to name her as a member of the National Front, Esther Sizer. Today's far right would have sent 72-year-old Mrs

Sizer on a tour of the TV studios, presenting her as an innocent victim of leftist violence. The NF published her photograph on the back of one of its pamphlets and left her story otherwise untold.[6]

Martin Webster's justification of the Front's decision to march through Lewisham, published in the Front's members' magazine *Spearhead*, made the case for silencing anti-fascists: "I cannot discuss these matters as Court cases are pending," Webster wrote, "But it is obvious that the Police were used by the Political Authorities of the State to suppress the right of National Front members to counter-demonstrate, a right which they always grant to the NF's opponents." He threatened violence to defeat the Front's opponents, saying that "the National Front will refuse to accept that its members may be prevented by the Police from partaking in rights which are enjoyed by citizens of other political associations."[7]

In a letter to the Labour Prime Minister James Callaghan, John Tyndall warned against any ban on Front marches. "The violence at Lewisham," Tyndall insisted, "was organised, not by the National Front itself but by its extreme opponents." This sounds like the contemporary right with its photographs of gagged leaders, its invocation of free speech, and its claims of victimhood. But Tyndall moved quickly beyond such arguments. The Labour government, Tyndall argued, should proscribe the socialists who were responsible for Lewisham. The state needed to ban the SWP, the IMG, and other Marxist groups. After that, the government should also ban the Noting Hill Carnival.[8] Far from defending free expression even for himself, Tyndall's unremitting focus was on the curtailment of free speech for those who disagreed with him.

The right breaks through

In France, in the early 1980s, a different approach towards free speech was to prove fruitful to one of Tyndall's contemporaries in the far right, Jean-Marie Le Pen. Like John Tyndall, the French fascist was the leader of a party which combined both fascist and populist wings. Le Pen had fought in the Algerian War, and, on his return to France, he became one of the main spokesmen of the settlers' campaign against Algerian independence, a campaign which insisted on its loyalty to France while supporting terrorist tactics in Algeria and France, in which 2,000 people were killed. These activities made him a man of the far right, and not necessarily a fascist. Yet the Front was established in 1972, following motions passed at the congress of an avowedly neo-Nazi party, Ordre Nouveau. ON's chief strategist François Duprat persuaded ON to set up the Front National in 1972, after which he was, in effect, the FN's deputy leader until Duprat's death in 1978. Le Pen, with his complex political trajectory, was intended to act as a shield, disguising the fascist character of the FN's membership and structure, and enabling the party to present itself (just as its British counterpart was trying to do) as populist and electoral rather than fascist. Early recruits to the Front included Victor Barthélémy, who became the Front National's Administrative Secretary and had been a General Secretary of Jacques Doriot's war-time fascist Parti

Populaire Français. Barthélémy had recruited a French unit of the Wehrmacht and worked for the PPF in Mussolini's Salò Republic. Within the FN, Duprat published Holocaust denial literature including British fascist Richard Verrall's *Did Six Million Really Die?*[9]

The moment at which Le Pen was transformed from an embarrassment in French politics to one of its main players began in May 1982, with correspondence between Le Pen and the Socialist President, François Mitterrand. In recent elections, the FN had won a mere 0.2 percent of the vote. Le Pen complained that he was being unfairly deprived of an audience:

> Monsieur le President, our movement [i.e. the FN] has just held its sixth congress in Paris. If your only means of information was state television, you would not have known anything about it. In effect, this makes the situation of political formations which are not represented in the National Assembly, which was already very unjust before you, and this is further aggravated in that.[10]

Mitterrand promised Le Pen his support. "It is regrettable that the congress of a political party is ignored by Radio-Television ... the incident that you referred to will not be repeated."[11] Over the following months the FN leader made numerous television appearances, and his party won a first breakthrough in spring 1983, when its candidate Jean-Pierre Stirbois secured 16.7 percent of the vote in local elections at Dreux, a small town outside Paris. The Gaullist right in the RPR supported a joint RPR-FN list, enabling the FN to have three deputies elected to the local council.

According to Le Pen himself, the escape from the margins came about from a single friendly TV interview, on the programme *l'Heure de verité* in February 1984. This was, Le Pen claimed, the turning-point: "An hour is nothing, but it was enough for me to get rid of the monstrous and carnival-like mask that all my opponents have so generously applied to me."[12]

Le Pen's appearance on *l'Heure de verité* was controversial. The Communist Party leader George Marchais complained that the FN leader was scheduled to speak on 6 February 1984, 50 years to the day since a previous generation of French fascists had attempted to storm the French parliament. The broadcaster agreed to put the programme back, but only by a week. Several newspapers reported the issue of Le Pen's appearance in sensationalist terms, insisting that the Front National leader had been "deprogrammed" and "suppressed."[13]

Le Pen used his appearance on *l'Heure de verité* to present an image of the Front as an outsider party being wrongly denied the publicity to which it was entitled. In effect, Le Pen's party was saying to the electorate that you did not need to believe in the FN to vote for it, you only needed to accept it had been treated unfairly.

After the interview with Le Pen was aired, polls showed the Front's support doubling from 3.5 to 7 percent of the vote. The party received hundreds of enquiries for membership and was able to recruit a generation of candidates for office. That year, the Front won 11 percent in European elections. It has been a force in French politics ever since.

Le Pen's imitators

Saying that the Front broke through by manipulating an argument that it was being unfairly silenced explains how it achieved that result, not why it was capable of success. Plainly, there was a part of the electorate open to vote for a far-right party. The Front stood at a forgiving distance from the Second World War, near enough to benefit from the support of an aged and aggrieved generation of Vichy support-ers who believed that they had been wrongly forced out of politics, but not so close as to be defeated simply by rhetorical calls to the memory of the Resistance. All over Europe and beyond, a kind of political system was breaking down, in which the left and the right had been fixed in a competition which went back to the role played by the major combatants in 1945. The left in particular was about to suffer a collapse of self-belief, shaped by role played by the Soviet Union in bolstering "Communism." The rulers of the Eastern bloc were bitterly unpopular with their own people – the realisation of their lack of support preceded the collapse of the Soviet Union in 1989–1991, which was then treated as a global referendum on the left. The French Socialist Party turned towards a support for neo-liberal econom-ics, antagonising millions of working-class voters who had previously supported it.

After 1984, there were any number of figures on the international far right who sought to imitate the Front National's breakthrough, and in particular to copy its complaint of being ignored by the media. In Britain, in 1996 the writer David Irving initiated libel proceedings against a historian Deborah Lipstadt, who had accused him of denying the truth of the Holocaust. Initially, his libel action received favourable press coverage. The *Times Higher Education Supplement* suggested that in criticising Irving other historians were subjecting him to "per-sonal attack" and "stifl[ing] free-ranging debate." The *Times* bemoaned the decline of the liberal tradition which would previously have "uph[e]ld his right to express any view no matter how odious." One historian Donald Cameron Watt described Lipstadt's publishers as "certainly out for blood,"[14] and agreed to testify for him. Yet it was Irving who had initiated these proceedings, not Lipstadt; he was the one demanding that she be silenced. But so strong was the ideological fear that the far right might be refused a platform, or the left respon-sible for its isolation, that many writers simply could not see what was in front of them. The proceedings were drawn out and took four years to determine. In the end, Mr Justice Gray found that:

> David Irving is content to mix with neo-fascists and appears to share many of their racist and antisemitic prejudices … [he is] a right-wing and pro-Nazi polemicist … [this agenda causes him] to manipulate the historical record in order to make it conform with his political beliefs.[15]

It was only after the conclusion of the case and once the judge had given his judgment that most journalists seemed to grasp what was at stake – not Irving's right to lie about the Holocaust, but Lipstadt's free speech right to criticise him for those lies.

The 1980s and 1990s were a period of realignment on the British far right after the spectacular collapse of the National Front in the 1979 general election. In the 1980s, the main carrier of the physical force tradition was the group Red Action, led by former members of the Socialist Workers Party, who had been forced out of that party in 1981, and sought to continue 1970s–style anti-fascism. From 1985, Red Action mainly worked in Anti-Fascist Action, an alliance with other groups including the Newham Monitoring Project, *Searchlight*, and Workers Power. Red Action/AFA speakers would sometimes use the phrase "no platform" to describe their activities. So a major street confrontation in 1992 (the "Battle of Waterloo"), when hundreds of supporters of the far-right music scene were attacked by a crowd of more than a thousand anti-fascists and prevented from attending a Skrewdriver concert,[16] was described afterwards as an example of no platform.[17] The phrase was explained as "a metaphor for a basic denial of free speech to fascists, or those that might wish to debate with them. It is not a liberal concept."[18] Or, in the words of Mark Hayes, a historian of Red Action:

> The first people thrown into the concentration camps under fascism would be communists, socialists, anarchists, and trade unionists – this fact alone, it was felt, bestowed upon Red Action the moral right, indeed the obligation, to resist. It also recognised that a key part of fascist strategy was to 'control the streets' in order to 'march and grow' as the Nazis did in Germany prior to 1933. Red Action (and AFA) aimed to make that claim look ridiculous and thereby completely discredit them in the eyes of working-class communities.[19]

For the 43 Group, the characteristic form of political action was knocking over speakers' platforms midway through a fascist speech. For AFA, it was a group of anti-fascists taking the ground on which a fascist paper sale was due to happen and holding it against attack.[20]

By 1994, Tony Lecomber, the architect of the BNP's "rights for whites" electoral strategy was telling the group's members, "The days of street warfare [are] over … no more marches, meetings, punch-ups."[21] Such language became pervasive within the BNP at the end of the 1990s, with the choice of a new leader, Nick Griffin, who was elected on a platform of modernising his party. This meant closing down the public events which the likes of AFA had disrupted in favour of a focus on elections, where opportunities for anti-fascist disruption would be limited.

On taking over the leadership in autumn 1999, Griffin re-modelled his party along the line of the Front National, copying its language, and establishing a party magazine *Identity* in imitation of the Front's magazine *Identité*. As with Le

Pen 15 years earlier, Griffin had the immense good fortune of being in office while events outside his party bestowed a legitimacy on it. As with the leader of the Front National, his success was not down simply to external factors; rather, Griffin showed a tactical flexibility and was rewarded for it.

In January 2001, the *Oldham Chronicle* ran an article, "Huge rise in race attacks on white men." This story was based on a claim by Chief Superintendent Eric Hewitt of the Oldham police that, in 12 months, the police had investigated 572 racial incidents, and that 60 percent of those to suffer had been white. The figures were extraordinary, and you might have expected journalists to question them. Only 14 percent of the town's population was Asian, so where had all these anti-white attacks come from?[22] The regional press, however, treated them as gospel truth.

The situation escalated when 76-year-old war veteran Walter Chamberlain was shown on national television, his face beaten. One detective told the *Manchester Evening News* that an Asian gang had attacked the white pensioner. The rumour was that, before approaching Chamberlain, his attackers had shouted, "Get out of our area," and these words made the paper's headline. Yet when the police interviewed Walter, he denied that he had been attacked for being white. His son told the press, "[W]e don't think it was a race issue at all."[23]

The police and the *Oldham Chronicle* succeeded in creating an impression of constant racial tension. The white population of the city was told it was the victim of an Asian race mafia, and that hostile authorities were preventing the widespread discussion of a real scandal.

On 31 March 2001, the National Front attempted to march through Oldham. Anti-racists organised a protest which was supported by 1,000 people. The next month, attempted marches by the Front sparked further demonstrations in Oldham and Bradford. Again, the *Oldham Chronicle* ran pieces favourable to the BNP, criticising Asian youth, and reporting without comments the BNP's claims that its St George's flags were being taken down by the council. Members of the BNP and the NF organised further marches on 5 and 27 May. Following the third demonstration, the far-right gangs refused to disperse, but congregated in Oldham's pubs, waiting for trouble. When white crowds took to the street, the police allowed them to march, taking them through Asian areas. When Asian crowds gathered to protect themselves from attack, the police attacked them. In response to repeated arrests and harassment, young Asian men hurled petrol bombs, torched cars, and shattered windows. A survey of 45,000 residents in neighbouring Burnley found that 58 percent of the local population blamed the riots on "racism by Asian people."[24]

Following the riots, Nick Griffin was able to win a vote of 16 percent in Oldham. It was the BNP's best result on election night, and the highest vote secured by a far-right party in a British parliamentary election up to that point.

That night, the Returning Officer refused to allow Griffin to make a speech, fearing that it would stoke racial tension. Griffin was filmed at the count, alongside BNP organiser Mick Treacy, wearing a face mask to show that he had been gagged. This was, undoubtedly, a clever piece of propaganda, connecting the relatively small and transient fact of Griffin being denied a single opportunity to give a speech to the much larger feeling, widespread in small-town North West England, that white people were the victims of racism and were being prevented from complaining. The image of a gagged Nick Griffin contributed to the party's genuine breakthrough a year later, when the BNP stood in 66 wards across Britain, securing votes of between more than 10 percent in 27 of them, and the election of 3 councillors in Burnley.[25]

The success of the stunt required not just the invocation of free speech, but a large group of people who believed their speech rights were being infringed, and who saw a connection between their own situation and Griffin's.

Without that believed link, the appeal to free speech could fall flat, as happened to the same party a decade later, when the BBC invited the party's leader onto its Question Time programme. After numerous protests, and with hundreds of anti-fascists milling outside BBC Television Centre, the programme's organisers chose to change their format. In this episode only, the panellists were each allowed to repeatedly ask questions of their own, as well as take questions from the floor, and the repeated focus on Nick Griffin tired and debilitated him, causing him to look dishonest. One exchange went as follows:

Young audience member, in skullcap: Sir Winston Churchill put everything on the line so that my ancestors wouldn't get slaughtered in the concentration camps. But here sits a man who says that that's a myth, just like a flat world was a myth. How could you say that? How could you?

Nick Griffin: I cannot explain why I used to say these things, I can't tell you, no … (boos from audience) any more than I can tell you why I've changed my mind, I can't tell you the extent to which I've changed my mind, because European law prevents me.[26]

Under intense pressure, and aware that the audience was turning against him, Griffin reverted to what he had previously found was his strongest argument – that some mysterious authority was unfairly silencing him. Yet because he did so in an implausible and untruthful way, he undermined what had until then been an effective plan for the far right to win over wavering voters.

By the late 1990s, there were an increasing number of far-right groups which showed no obvious link to the fascist past. They presented themselves as anti-political rather than right-wing. The new groups' commitment to multi-party politics was seemingly sincere. Several figures in the non-fascist far right were able to go much further than Le Pen or Griffin in presenting themselves as provocateurs, the champions of a free-wheeling and iconoclastic commitment to free speech.

One innovator of this approach was the Dutch filmmaker, politician, and businessman Pim Fortuyn, a former social democrat who had once applied unsuccessfully to join the Communist Party. Fortuyn started moving to the right from the early 1990s. Fortuyn claimed that the liberal and tolerant character of Dutch society, its acceptance of women's rights and of gay male sexuality, was under attack from Islam. He presented himself as someone who spoke in a graphic and shocking language with echoes of leftist discourse. He described his sexual encounters with other gay men in Rotterdam basements. As Fortuyn luxuriated in the public eye, he became increasingly narcissistic and ever-more dependent on social structures which supported right-wing thought. He argued that Holland was deteriorating because of a lack of patriarchal authority figures. He came out as Catholic. He insisted that Islam was not merely an evil religion, it was also an ethnicity: a person of Moroccan heritage born in Holland, he insisted, was Muslim and not Dutch. He complained that the media was a "left-wing church."[27] Fortuyn was killed in 2002 by a left-wing environmentalist, Volkert van der Graaf, after which Fortuyn's party came second in the Dutch national elections. He bequeathed to the Dutch far right a style of politics which for years afterwards shaped such successor parties as Geert Wilders' PVV.

Post-9/11 politics provided many opportunities for similarly Islamophobic politicians to represent themselves as the victims of a great global conspiracy which prevented them from telling the majority how evil Islam was. These included the decade-long controversy which began in 2005 when the Danish newspaper *Jyllands-Posten* posted a dozen cartoons depicting the Islamic prophet Muhammad, including one in which his black turban had been drawn as a ticking bomb. The images were accompanied by text observing that "some Muslims" demanded "special consideration of their own religious feelings. This is incompatible with secular democracy where one has to be prepared to put up with scorn, mockery and ridicule."[28]

Gavan Titley's *Is Free Speech Racist?* addresses the way in which the *Jyllands-Posten* debate saw European politicians lecture their Muslim minorities. Centrist politicians have employed what he terms a "pedagogy of offence," in which Muslims were expected to be grateful for the tough love their betters showed in mocking them. The key misunderstanding, he argues, was a "neglect of power."[29] The newspapers refused to acknowledge their greater status than the minority they baited, or their own connections to the state and its repressive apparatus.

Then came the 2006 controversy in France when Robert Redeker was criticised for publishing a piece in *Le Figaro* arguing that Islam was a uniquely immoral belief-system, being a religion which glorified in death and suffering and was in every case opposed to "generosity, open-mindedness, tolerance, gentleness, freedom of women and morals."[30] Redeker's few critics were overwhelmed by a hostile media which invoked an old slogan of secularism (*laïcité*) previously employed against a vastly powerful enemy, the Catholic Church of the early 1900s, and now used to justify the humiliation of an impoverished non-white minority.

In France, attacks on Muslims continued over the next decade, with the hostility of far-right politicians echoed by Conservative and Socialist presidents and even members of France's shrinking far left. Hemmed in, and subject to abuse, a small number of Muslims responded with acts of grotesque violence, including the 2015 attacks on the *Charlie Hebdo* building, the siege of the Hypercacher kosher supermarket, and further terrorist attacks in November of the same year. The killings were interpreted as a war against freedom of expression and an attack on the liberal state. For President Hollande, "The Republic equals freedom of expression." For Prime Minister Manuel Valls, "France carries freedom of speech everywhere." Just to show how serious France was about the rights of everyone to speak freely, 3,500 raids were carried out on the homes of Muslims, just 6 of whom were subsequently accused of support for terrorism.[31]

By autumn 2020, this idea had become so powerful that when the *Financial Times* and *Politico* responded to a terrorist attack (the murder of history teacher Samuel Paty) by both denouncing it and siting it within a history of French attacks on Muslims, they came under intense pressure to take down their articles and did agree to remove them from their websites. Laws enabling the funding of higher education were rewritten to require fidelity to the Republic. Any critique of the state or of its treatment of Muslims was denounced as tantamount to murder.[32]

All across Europe, the idea of free speech had taken on a different meaning. No one (either on the left or the right) was saying any longer that the free speech rights of the public needed to be protected from the state. Rather, the predominant use of free speech was as an ideological totem. If you were on the right, you called your actions speech and denounced your opponents for criticising them. The most sophisticated of left-wing approaches combined a defence of free speech with an objection to its mystification in the services of empire. But this was an unusual position. More common was either a resurgent universalism that was coy about the consequences of the French state's racism, or an empiricist anti-racist position that protested individual instances of state violence while refusing to draw any connections between them.

It was in this context that the far right was able to achieve repeated political breakthroughs from 2016 onwards, by posing as the muscular defenders of free speech, and by insisting that their opponents sought to prevent a much-needed debate.

The strategy brings rewards

Between 2016 and 2018, the far right achieved breakthroughs almost everywhere, in some countries through increased success for parties of fascist origin (France, Austria), elsewhere through the rise of parties which had taken up anti-migrant and Islamophobic politics late and were now rewarded for them (Italy), or in some cases through the adoption by previously centre-right parties of new kinds of candidates, who drew on the violence and racism of social media and made alliances with those further to their right (as in the United States).

A recurring feature of right-wing politics since 2016 has been the insistence that the right is being unfairly treated. This tactic has been shared by the centre- and far-right. In Spain, during the Coronavirus pandemic, the far-right VOX party complained that it was subject to a "media dictatorship," with its main Twitter account banned by the platform for spreading hate speech during the pandemic, and its messages routinely censored by verification agencies set up to stop the spread of fake news at a time of a health emergency.[33] The claim that leaders are being persecuted because they tell unwelcome truths has been part of the appeal of such figures as Donald Trump, Jair Bolsonaro, and Benjamin Netanyahu. Even in circumstances where the right has held political power and dominated public discourse for many years it has still found a way to complain that it is being unfairly prevented from speaking.

The centre of the campaign for the free expression of far-right speech is the United States where, at some point in the mid-to late-1980s, the dominant approach of right-wing politics flipped over from the idea that free speech was a bad idea and that it led to the toleration of ideas which should be denied a platform, to the realisation that free speech might prove a useful political weapon which could be turned against the left.

George Bush and the attack on political correctness

The emergence of the new politics of free speech can be traced back to 1991, and a speech given by President George H. W. Bush, who told students at the University of Michigan that free speech was "under assault throughout the United States, including on some college campuses," and blamed "political correctness," an ideology which "declares certain topics off-limits, certain expressions off-limits."[34] His remarks were widely reported in the US and elsewhere.

Up until 1991, when students were criticised by the American right it was not because they were *against* free speech, but because they spoke too much. In 1987, University of Chicago Professor Allan Bloom published his best-selling book *The Closing of the American Mind*, whose success was the inspiration for Bush's speech. Bloom criticised the student left for rejecting the closed syllabi of their past, with their fixed ideas of the Western literary tradition, and for insisting that other books be read as well – books written by women and black authors. In contrast to today's culture warriors, Bloom was an avowed and unapologetic elitist. The greatest democratic danger, he warned, was enslavement to majoritarian public opinion. He assumed that civil society could only be hostile to the ideas that interested him, a self-identified member of the elite. He saw students as an arrogant and hostile mob. But even Bloom did not pretend that the despised young were inhibiting the free speech of their enlightened elders. Their mistake was to rebel against a closed curriculum and to require the addition of female and non-white authors to the Western canon. They were reading too widely and speaking out of turn.[35]

In George H. W. Bush's "political correctness" speech, traces of that older politics could be found: the President still complained (in similar terms to Bloom) of left-wing students "abusing the privilege of free speech,"[36] suggesting that the answer was less speech and not more. It was only over the successive years that the logic of his attack was fully internalised by conservatives, giving rise to today's ideological capture of free speech by the right.

To grasp the novelty of this move we need to recall that, in the 1970s, prominent conservatives opposed the rights of fascists to march, with commentators such as Irving Louis Horowitz and Victoria Curtis Bramson insisting that symbols of genocide were intended to invoke the Third Reich and could not deserve the protection of the US constitution.[37] By the 1990s, the point had been grasped that left-wing students deserved much greater condemnation than the Republican outliers on their right. The task of right-wing pundits was not to oppose right-wing militia, but to flatter them. The successors to Frank Collin had to be re-imagined as eager Republicans, people taking honourable positions just a little too far.

Following the election of Donald Trump to the presidency in 2016, a series of right-wing provocateurs sought to impose themselves on university campuses, insisting that their constitutional right to free speech required universities to provide them with platforms. A key figure was the expatriate British journalist Milo Yiannopoulos, who had risen to prominence during the gamergate controversy. This was a campaign of online harassment against women which began when blogger Eron Gjoni published a 10,000-word online screed blaming his former girlfriend, the game designer Zoë Quinn, for the breakdown of their relationship and insinuating her career had been boasted by a cabal of left-wing journalists who had traded positive reviews of Quinn's games for sex. Yiannopoulos, the tech editor at *Breitbart*, denounced Quinn. In so doing, he built the mass audience for that website. He established the national profile which Breitbart's Chief Executive Steve Bannon traded for a position as Trump's Chief Strategist.[38]

Milo Yiannopoulos and the invocation of free speech

By winter 2016–2017, Yiannopoulos had settled on a new strategy to keep himself in the public eye, by organising a series of speaking events in universities ("the Dangerous Faggot" tour), which was intended to culminate in an intentionally provocative mass rally at the famously liberal U.C. Berkeley campus. In February 2017. Yiannopoulos's typical speech saw him boasting about partying, making crude jokes, and interspersing his material with conventional far-right talking points, emphasising the stupidity of women, of trans people, and of social justice warriors.[39] His events were surrounded by violence. At a talk given by him at the University of Washington, an anti-fascist protester was shot by a supporter of Yiannopoulos.[40] His appearance at the University of California, Davis, had to be cancelled after protests.[41]

The far-right news site *Breitbart* published an article a day before the Berkeley talk, saying Yiannopoulos would use it to claim American universities have become "sanctuary campuses that shelter illegal immigrants from being deported." This message protesters interpreted as a threat that he would name undocumented students, putting them at risk of harassment or deportation.

In response, protesters shut down the U. C. Berkeley talk, starting fires, setting off fireworks, and breaking windows until the event had to be cancelled.[42] A comment piece in Berkeley's student paper *The Daily Californian* justified the action:

> If you condemn the actions that shut down Yiannopoulos' literal hate speech, you condone his presence, his actions, and his ideas; you care more about broken windows than broken bodies.[43]

Berkeley College Republicans filed a lawsuit against the University for failing to protect Yiannopoulos's speech. To the near unanimous approval of mainstream opinion, President Trump called for funding to Berkeley to be slashed unless the University could guarantee a respectful audience to his allies.[44] Delighted by what he saw as a moral victory, Yiannopoulos told his followers, "Free speech belongs to everyone, not just the spoilt brats of the academy."[45]

The Berkeley protest involved different groups of people with little central organisation, some applying tactics of mass mobilisation, and others less concerned with how their actions were seen. Protesters shouted, "Nazi scum your time has come" and "when fascists come to town what do we do? We shut shit down."[46] But Milo's followers were not a solid army of fascists with a history of violence against their enemies. Rather, they were a ragtag group of individuals at every point on the right-wing spectrum, from conservatives to supporters of the alt-right. The left played into the hands of Milo's argument that the left were violent troublemakers and censors, uninterested in political principle but determined to prevent anyone else from speaking.[47]

Yiannopoulos proposed to return to the Berkeley campus in September 2017, threatening to hold a Free Speech Week. This second round foundered due to the disorganisation of the event organisers, Berkeley Patriots, who billed such high-profile speakers as Ann Coulter and Steve Bannon without taking such baby steps as contacting the speakers and seeing if they were free.[48]

Between 2016 and 2018, complaints about over-sensitive students were a constant story in the American press. In two years, the *New York Times* alone published 21 opinion pieces about the threat posed to free speech by campus activism.[49]

If the right's campaign to take back Berkeley has since faded from public memory, this is due to the protest which took place at Charlottesville in August 2017. This, too, was billed as a free speech rally. However, for most people watching, it was clear that the right was not genuinely interested in asserting its own right to speak so much as demanding that its opponents be silenced. Take, for example, the distinctive sights and sounds of Charlottesville – a crowd bearing Nazi-style burning torches and chanting "Jews will not replace us."[50] Within the frame of far-right politics, this is a claim of victimhood. It asserts that there exists a well-funded conspiracy of Jews, who plan the genocide of white people, which is to be achieved by allowing black and Muslim immigration. If you do not believe that there is a hidden government of Jews secretly plotting the downfall of the white race, then it is impossible to hear that slogan "Jews will not replace us" as a statement of collective defence. It becomes, instead, what the slogan is very plainly intended to be: a declaration that the marchers intend to harm Jews and the protesters' other racial enemies.

Tommy Robinson

Although the Charlottesville right was unable to deal with the problem of anti-fascist opposition, a model of how to organise using free speech had been established, and others were able to take it up with greater success. On 6 May 2018, the various parts of the British far right came together to hold a free speech demonstration in Whitehall. Billed as a Day for Freedom, the purpose of the event was to protest against Twitter's decision to close down an account held by Stephen Yaxley-Lennon ("Tommy Robinson"). The decision to close Robinson's account was made in the aftermath of the prosecution of Darren Osborne, who in June 2017 had driven a van into Finsbury Park Mosque, killing a worshipper, Makram Ali. At Osborne's trial, it was revealed that he had received direct Twitter messages from Robinson.[51] The thought which upset Twitter executives, in other words, was that there might be a link between their platform and murder.

Robinson's support for free speech was partial and at odds with his previous campaigns. The moment at which he emerged as a leader on the British right came in 2009, in response to a homecoming march by the 2nd Battalion of the Royal Anglian Regiment which had been picketed by a small number of provocateurs from Anjem Choudary's organisation, Islam4UK. So angered was Robinson by the idea that Islamists were entitled to express themselves freely that he joined the first protests of what became the English Defence League. As he explains in his memoir:

> They had placards calling our troops, 'Butchers of Basra' and saying, 'Anglian soldiers go to hell.' And the police had simply guided them to a vantage position where they could hurl insults, while guarding them from people who were understandably pissed off by it all.[52]

In these few sentences it is possible to trace almost the entirety of Robinson's subsequent career: the anger of white people at Muslim outsiders who have forced their way into the country; the betrayal of the British people by the police who were supposed to protect them; the untrustworthiness of Britain's liberal establishment which permits Muslims to insult even the worthiest of people, serving soldiers. Most outrageous of all, in Robinson's account, is the idea that Muslims in Britain are entitled to abuse and to offend, i.e. to speak.

Numerous right-wing figures declared their support for Robinson in 2018, including Raheem Kassam of Breitbart London, and Anne-Marie Waters of For Britain. By far the most important was Gerard Batten, the leader of the UK Independence Party, an organisation which had recently enjoyed the support of millions of British voters. Robinson and Batten both agreed to be photographed with their mouths covered in masking tape.

On 25 May 2018, Robinson was arrested. He had stood outside Leeds Crown Court, filming the proceedings of an ongoing criminal trial, in which Asian men were accused of sexual offences. In June and July of that year, while Robinson was in prison, marches were held in his support, with the June protest involving some 15,000 people. This was the largest public mobilisation in the history of the British far right, comfortably exceeding the 800 supporters of the National Front who were at Lewisham, or the 2,000 British Fascists who were at Cable Street.

No doubt part of the reason why Robinson was able to draw this crowd was that hundreds of thousands had already started to see him as a martyr for free speech, even before his imprisonment. More than half a million people signed a petition demanding Robinson's release, and it was retweeted by many figures on the global right, including Katie Hopkins in the UK, Alex Jones of Infowars in the US, and Donald Trump Jr. The latter's father even allowed Sam Brownback, the US Ambassador for International Religious Freedom, to lobby the British ambassador in Washington, demanding Robinson's release.[53]

By early 2019 Robinson had built a huge platform on social media: with around 1,000,000 friends on Facebook he had a larger platform than Britain's (admittedly unpopular) Prime Minister Theresa May, and nearly as many as Jeremy Corbyn, the leader of Britain's Labour opposition party. All sorts of fundraising campaigns were also carried out for Robinson during his imprisonment. Robinson has never been elected to political office. The one time he has even stood, as an Independent in the European elections in May 2019, he received a mere 2 percent of the vote. In his late-30s Robinson, whose history of employment amounted to 5 years as an apprentice and then a qualified engineer,[54] followed by a few years as a self-employed decorator, lived in a £950,000 home in Bedfordshire.[55] False claims that he had suffered for his opinions combined with the gullibility of Robinson's supporters to make him rich.[56]

For many years, the far right in Britain (as elsewhere) had been adept at concealing the radicalism of its answers beneath the cloak of liberal values. Attacking Muslims was presented as the work of defending Western heritage, or women's or LGBT equality. Free speech was the latest, and the most successful of these attempts at liberal co-option.

Robinson's success should act as a warning to anti-fascists, that even if the idea of free speech is subject to widespread ideological abuse, its content is popular. Its tactical claiming by the far-right has provided the latter with a route out of isolation.

Notes

1 S. Beauman, 'What Lies Behind the Front,' *Sunday Telegraph*, 2 October 1977.
2 M. Walker, *The National Front* (London: Fontana, 1977), pp. 1–2.
3 'Address by John Tyndall, Chairman of the National Front, to His Supporters,' *Lewisham: What Are You Taking Pictures For?* (London: Half Moon Photography Workshop, 1977), p. 6.
4 'Address by John Tyndall,' p. 6.
5 'Address by John Tyndall,' p. 6.
6 M. Webster, *Lifting the Lid Off the "Anti-Nazi League"* (London: NFN Press, 1978) reproduces a photograph of the 72-year-old Ms Sizer, who is said to have marched only because she was "fearful that she [would] be a mugger's victim." The same source also acknowledges that she had been a member of the NF for five years.
7 M. Webster, 'The Lewisham Outrage,' *Spearhead*, July 1977, p. 17.
8 J. Tyndall to Rt. Hon. J. Callaghan, 18 August 1977, National Archives, HO 418/26.
9 D. Gordon, *Immigrants and Intellectuals: May '68 and the Rise of Anti-Racism in France* (London: Merlin Press, 2012), p. 144; S. E. Atkins, *Holocaust Denial as an International Movement* (Toronto: Praeger, 2009), p. 91.
10 E. Faux, T. Legrand, and G. Perez, *La main droite de Dieu* (Paris: Éditions du Seuil, 1994), pp. 12–20.
11 Faux, Legrand and Perez, *La main droite*, p. 22.
12 J. Rydgren, *The Oxford Handbook of the Radical Right* (Oxford: Oxford University Press, 2018), p. 274.
13 P. Davies, *The Extreme Right in France: The Extreme Right in France, 1789 to the Present: From de Maistre to Le Pen* (London: Routledge, 2002), pp. 146–147.
14 R. Evans, *Telling Lies about Hitler: The Holocaust, History, and the David Irving Trial* (London: Verso, 2002), pp. 28–30.
15 *Irving v Penguin Books Limited, Deborah E. Lipstadt* [2000] EWHC QB 115, para 13–162.
16 D. Hann, *Physical Resistance: A Hundred Years of Anti-fascism* (London: Zero Books, 2013), pp. 351–352.
17 "If the anti-fascist movement in Europe had implemented a policy of No Platform for fascists with the same commitment that we showed at Waterloo, then Rostock would still be just a small town in Germany." AFA's Eamon Kent, quoted in 'The Battle of Waterloo,' *Fighting Talk Glasgow*, winter 1992.
18 Debate between Huddersfield and London Anti-Fascist Action, discussed in A. Shaw, 'Know Your Enemy Part 2,' *Red Action*, 3/4, December/January 1998/99.
19 M. Hayes, 'Red Action – Left-Wing Political Pariah: Some Observations Regarding Ideological Apostasy and the Discourse of Proletarian Resistance,' in E. Smith and M. Worley (eds), *Against the Grain: The British Far Left from 1956* (Manchester: Manchester University Press, 2014), pp. 229–246, 239.
20 The battles to prevent the British National Party from selling their papers at Brick Lane are described in S. Birchall, *Beating the Fascists: The Untold Story of Anti-Fascist Action* (London: Freedom Press, 2010), pp. 207–216.
21 Birchall, *Beating the Fascists*, p. 355.
22 D. Renton, 'A Day to Make History'? The 2004 Elections and the British National Party,' *Patterns of Prejudice* 39/1 (2005), pp. 25–45.
23 'War Veteran in "Racist" Attack,' *BBC News*, 24 April 2001.
24 Renton, 'A Day to Make History.'
25 G. Macklin, *Failed Führers: A History of Britain's Extreme Right* (London: Routledge, 2020), p. 490.
26 'BNP Nick Griffin on BBC Question Time,' *YouTube*, 23 October 2009. Accessed 15 December 2019.
27 P. Mair, 'What's Going on in the Netherlands?' *London Review of Books*, 14 December 2006; I. Buruma, *Murder in Amsterdam: The Death of Theo van Gogh and the Limits of Tolerance* (London: Penguin, 2006), pp. 50–57.

28 F. Rose, 'Muhammeds Ansigt [The Face of Mohammed],' *Jyllands-Posten*, 30 September 2005.
29 G. Titley, *Is Free Speech Racist?* (Cambridge: Polity, 2020), p. 101.
30 R. Redeker, 'Face aux intimidations islamistes, que doit faire le monde libre?' *Le Figaro*, 19 September 2006; S. Sands, *The End of the French Intellectual: From Zola to Houuellebecq* (London: Verso, 2018), pp. 245–247.
31 Titley, *Is Free Speech*, p. 64.
32 N. Fadil, 'Radical Free Speech,' *Contending Modernities*, 2 December 2020.
33 '"The media censorship," free speech and the radical right: The case of Spain's VOX party,' *Centre for the Analysis of the Radical Right*, 7 July 2020.
34 'Excerpts from President's Speech to University of Michigan Graduates,' *New York Times*, 5 May 1991.
35 New York: Simon and Schuster, 1987. Also D. D'Souza, *Illiberal Education: The Politics of Race and Sex on Campus* (New York: Macmillan, 2009).
36 'Excerpts from President's Speech'.
37 I. L. Horowitz and V. C. Bramson, 'Skokie, the ACLU and the Endurance of Democratic Theory', Law and Contemporary Problems 43 (1979), pp. 328–349.
38 D. Renton, *The New Authoritarians: Convergence on the Right* (London: Pluto, 2019), pp. 116–117, 129–131; Z. Quinn, *Crash Override: How Gamergate (Nearly) Destroyed My Life* (New York: Hachette, 2017).
39 J. Butler, 'Milo's Stumble,' *London Review of Books*, 22 February 2017.
40 'Couple Charged in Shooting of Protester at Milo Yiannopoulos Event in Seattle,' *Guardian*, 25 April 2017.
41 B. Poston, 'UC Davis Republicans cancel speech by Breitbart's Milo Yiannopoulos Following Protests,' *Los Angeles Times*, 14 January 2017.
42 J. C. Wong, 'UC Berkeley Cancels "alt-right" Speaker Milo Yiannopoulos as Thousands Protest,' *Guardian*, 2 February 2017.
43 G. Lukianoff and J. Haidt, *The Coddling of the American Mind: How Good Intentions and Bad Ideas Are Setting up a Generation for Failure* (London: Allen Lane, 2018), p. 84.
44 L. Dearden, 'Donald Trump Threatens to Withdraw Federal Funds from Berkeley University after Breitbart Editor Talk Cancelled,' *Independent*, 2 February 2017.
45 K. Steinmetz, 'Fighting Words: A Battle in Berkeley Over Free Speech,' *Time*, 1 June 2017.
46 D. Murray, 'Some "Anti-Fascists" Need to Look in the Mirror,' *Spectator*, 4 February 2017; R. Soave, *Panic Attack: Young Radicals in the Age of Trump* (New York: All Points Books, 2019), pp. 79–82.
47 M. Oppenheim, 'UC Berkeley Protests: Milo Yiannopoulos Planned to "Publicly Name Undocumented Students" in Cancelled Talk,' *Independent*, 3 February 2017.
48 E. Helmore, 'Far-Right "Free Speech Week" at Berkeley Collapses in Recrimination and Discord,' *Guardian*, 24 September 2017.
49 P. E. Moskowitz, *The Case Against Free Speech: The First Amendment, Fascism, and the Future of Dissent* (New York: Bold Times, 2019), p. 114.
50 Hunton and Williams LLP, *Final Report: Independent Review of the Events in Charlottesville, Virginia* (Richmond: Hunton and Williams, 2017).
51 A. Gilligan, 'Tommy Robinson Winds Up Bigots and the Cash Floods In,' *Times*, 5 August 2018; L. Dearden, 'Darren Osborne: How Finsbury Park Terror Attacker Became "Obsessed" with Muslims in Less Than a Month,' *Independent*, 1 February 2018; 'Former EDL Leader Tommy Robinson Suspended from Twitter,' *ITV News*, 28 March 2018.
52 T. Robinson *Enemy of the State* (London: The Press News Ltd, 2015), p. 134.
53 D. Smith, 'Trump Diplomat Lobbied UK over Tommy Robinson,' *Guardian*, 14 July 2018.
54 M. R. Hill, 'Who Is the Real Tommy Robinson?', *Telegraph*, 18 October 2013.
55 M. Hyde, 'There's No Such Thing as a Free Lunch?' *Guardian*, 25 October 2018; A. Gilligan, 'Tommy Robinson Is Best-Funded Politician in UK,' *Times*, 10 March

2019; A. Martin and M. Ledwith, 'Syrian Refugee, 16, Who Was Filmed Being "Waterboarded" by School Bullies Is Suing Facebook "For Not Stopping Tommy Robinson Posting Accusations He Violently Attacked Three English Girls,"' *Daily Mail,* 20 January 2019.

56 D. Renton, 'Tommy Robinson's Memoir: The Landlords' Road to Socialism,' *Lives; Running,* 6 February 2019.

PART II

Law

7

THE WRONGS OF HATE SPEECH

In the second section of this book, attention shifts from history to law. The most important response to US-style free speech protections to have been published in the last decade is Jeremy Waldron's *The Harm in Hate Speech*.[1] Waldron's book is repeatedly invoked by free speech theorists as the most coherent expression of the views they disagree with. In the next three chapters I, like them, treat Waldron as an exemplary statement of a wider argument. But I do so from the perspective of an anti-fascist, i.e. not to assert a universal right to expression, but to assist people seriously considering the revocation of a fascist's invitation to speak.

For Waldron, the typical form of hate speech is a sign: a poster telling Muslims they are not welcome in the United States, a swastika, or a burning cross. Such hate speech, he argues, has the purpose of telling the people who see it that they should expect to be shunned, excluded, or beaten. It draws its malign power from the reality that those targeted have suffered violence previously. Hate speech reminds its targets of that terror and exults in it.

Waldron is a New Zealand-born scholar who has lived recently in the United States and taught at the New York University School of Law. Born in 1953, he travelled to England in 1978 and studied in Oxford. He was in Britain, in other words, during the 1979 election where the National Front collapsed, and at the time of the Southall protest where another anti-racist from New Zealand, Blair Peach, was killed. Waldron was much the same age as the generation who formulated no platform. Its ideas were all around him.

In *The Harm in Hate Speech*, Jeremy Waldron makes several points against the idea of free speech which has become hegemonic since the late 1970s. Waldron argues that the long battle against censorship ended the way it did because a majority of people stopped believing that the state required protection from its critics. In ordinary free speech discourse, Waldron suggests, people make the same assumption about racial groups as they do about the state: that mere words cannot harm them. In liberal theory, the state needs to be kept away from speech. By interfering with free expression and limiting who can be heard, it risks undermining the idea of democracy. The state is "thick-skinned enough" Waldron argues, "to be able to shrug off public denunciations," indeed to seek to impose its opinions on political dissidents, but given the recent history of "racial segregation, second-class citizenship, racist terrorism,"[2] it is wrong to treat minorities as if they were similarly immune to humiliation.

Waldron asks: who is the object of the hate speech in free speech discourse? If we think of the key moment as something like the decision of the courts to allow marches through Skokie in 1977–1978, the decision-maker was a judge. Liberal free speech discourse is almost always directed at the same decision-maker: without any defining characteristics of their own, i.e. middle-aged, middle-class, and white. The judge who can say that they despise racist speech, while defending the right of the speaker to persist, is admirable within their own mental universe: they have defended the rights of the ignorant racist. But what, Waldron asks, "about the direct targets of the abuse. Can their lives be led, can their children be brought up, can their hopes be maintained, and their worst fears dispelled, in a social environment polluted by these materials?"[3]

Waldron also takes issue with the formulation of hate speech as mere speech. This suggests something casual and impermanent, whereas much hate speech is printed or posted online and remains on display, sometimes in perpetuity.

Drawing on old decisions of the US Supreme Court, including *Beauharnais v Illinois*, which asserts the rights of states to punish libels which are directed at groups as well as those aimed at individuals,[4] Waldron explores the concept of group libel. This can occur, he writes, when seemingly factual statements are made which have the purpose of demeaning an entire group of people as, for example, in the statement "All Muslims are terrorists."[5]

Waldron's focus on the group is intrinsic to any serious plan to restrict hate speech. All societies in the last two hundred years have had laws to restrict the use of language that promotes violence. The doctrine of hate speech however is aimed at something different from this. It posits that what makes language demeaning is its relationship to structures of social oppression which are not principally or only located in language. Speech is hateful not merely because of its unpleasant content but also because of the history of violence suffered by Jews in Europe or by Muslims in America, their experience of detention and murder.

Waldron asks: what place does hate speech have in a just society? For liberal constitutionalists, free speech is necessary: by giving people the chance to hear and reject hateful language, you increase the chances that they will understand the world better, even if that comes about through the rejection of the views they encounter. To which Waldron responds that more is at stake than whether our collective understanding of the world will be advanced.

When a society is defaced by burning crosses, Waldron writes, then black people's feelings of self-worth will be diminished. Racist appearances, he argues, tend to confirm to racist realities: a sign outside a home saying the home is for sale only to Christians implies a community in which Muslims and Jews are unwelcome. A fair society, he maintains, has an interest in affirming the dignity of its members. He speaks of "environmental" goods, atmospheres of mutual respect:

> When a society is defaced with antisemitic signage, burning crosses, or defamatory racial leaflets, that sort of assurance evaporates. A vigilant police force and Justice Department may still keep people from being attacked or excluded, but people no longer have the benefit of a general public assurance to this effect, provided and enjoyed as a public good, furnished to all by all.[6]

Waldron writes of "assurance," a public good, in which all citizens are entitled to share certain minimum standards. This virtuous state, he argues, is "diffuse" but also "general, sustained, and reliable."[7] The beneficiaries of laws prohibiting hate speech are, in other words, being assured by the law that they are members of society in good standing with it. By having laws against hate speech on its statute book, society tells members of a minority group that they are entitled to live full and equal lives, just like everyone else.

In standard liberal free speech discourse, the participants in speech are disembodied. "Speech" itself, is portrayed as a good, irrespective of what is said to who. Waldron surpasses this approach by giving the audience a body – by making it black or Jewish or Muslim.[8] In setting out who is the target of hate speech, Waldron focusses on its ethnic minority casualties. In setting out why hate is wrong, however, Waldron's attention turns away from their damaged lives towards the needs of society. He envisages an unspoken contract in which members of a racial minority ask society to treat them as equals. Then, if that dignity is afforded to them, they reciprocate by treating their neighbours with kindness and sympathy.

There have been other writers, for example Richard Delgado and Jean Stefancic, who give an even more vivid account than Waldron of the capacity for hate speech to do harm:

> Minorities may come to believe frequent accusations that they are lazy, ignorant, dirty, and superstitious … Racial tags discourage interracial behaviour and even that with members of one's own group. The consequences of racism may also include mental illness and psychosomatic disease, including alcoholism, high blood pressure, and drug addiction. The rate of depression is considerably higher in minority communities than in society as a whole. Women who had fallen prey to internet stalking, trolling and "revenge porn" report similar distress, nightmares, and inability to function or work.[9]

Achille Mbembe expresses the same basic idea with greater economy: "'Race' is the name for the rage of those who, constrained by subjection, suffer injuries, all manner of violence and humiliations, and bear countless wounds."[10]

Such approaches focus not on the liberated children of the oppressed in whose name Waldron is writing, but their suffering parents living in our own time. They complement Waldron's approach, sharpening his demands for justice. They remind us of the basic truth that hate speech includes not merely seemingly moderate and temperate words which derive their pain from the context of discrimination. Hate speech also comprises the most bitter and painful of insults.

Part of the importance of Waldron's book is that it engages with some of the most common liberal arguments for free speech. He sets out the argument (which can be traced back to the Victorian philosopher John Stuart Mill's pamphlet *On Liberty*)[11] that free speech is necessary because it is indefensible for anyone to maintain that another person's speech is wrong.

Waldron's answer to Mill's argument is to concede the possibility that falsehoods might contribute to the discovery of the truth but to insist that possibility applies only for a limited time.

On the broad approach taken by Waldron, and applying his insights to fascism, he is surely right. Debates do end; no one suggests that 16-year-old geography students should be required to learn that the world is flat; or aspiring physicists made to endure lectures on the enduring wisdom of geocentric astrology. If fascism taught the world anything, that lesson was learned in 1945 with the triumph of anti-fascist politics all over Europe and with the determined effort that was made after the war's end to create human rights instruments which would protect the rights of refugees, eliminate racial discrimination, etc.

Similar reasoning can equally be applied to another of Mill's arguments, that it is arrogant for anyone to say that they speak the truth. The problem with this idea of political speech (or, in Mill's term for it, "opinion") is that it assumes all political speech is addressed to the future, when a very great deal of it exists to explain the past. Here, again, Waldron's idea that the passage of time can serve to prove the falsity or otherwise of any truth claim is surely right. Anyone living in Europe in 1918 who said that Hitler and Mussolini would bring prisons and genocide to Europe was making a falsifiable prediction about the future, and there was a chance that their prediction might have been wrong. Looking back on the past from a century later, that element of prediction no longer applies. It is not arrogant, nor conceited, nor over-simplistic, to say that the fascist regimes brought untold suffering to Europe; this is exactly what they did.

Waldron rejects the idea that racism and religious bigotry need to be kept alive to prevent the emergence of a banal consensus in which everyone is an anti-racist and therefore the potential harm of racism is no longer understood. He concludes his book by arguing that hate speech is a fundamental assault on the ordinary dignity of members of racial and religious communities, their self-regard, and their sense as people of good standing in society.

I find many of Jeremy Waldron's arguments persuasive. They begin, as this book does, with a sense of the difficulty of any serious commitment to free speech and the potential harm of any attempt to argue that speech exists or should exist in a unique zone of toleration where everything is permitted. Waldron's arguments are ones which anti-racists have argued repeatedly in relation to pro-posed meetings of hateful groups. They are, moreover, arguments which are deeply embedded in the law. Member States of the European Union, and the United Kingdom, proscribe harassment, defined by the EU Equal Treatment Directive as "where unwanted conduct related to the sex of a person occurs with the purpose or effect of violating the dignity of a person, and of creating an intimidating, hostile, degrading, humiliating or offensive environment."[12]

In Waldron's concept of hate speech, the harm of such language is that it is a form of discrimination which derives its force from the subaltern status of those on which it preys. The Equality Act 2010 is based on a similar understanding. So, if someone directs hateful language at a black person, or a woman, this is harass-ment related to race or sex. Indeed, the Act goes further than Waldron, whose prohibition is limited to race and religion, in outlawing harassment in relation to age, belief, disability, gender reassignment, sex, or sexual orientation, etc.

For Waldron, the evil of such language is "environmental," and the same lan-guage appears in both European and UK law. He objects to hate speech because it violates the "dignity" of its targets, by which he means their ability to feel that they are equal members of society. Again, the same word appears in the Directive.

The best way to understand Jeremy Waldron's book is that it was not simply a statement of social ethics, directed at an American audience; it was also a clarifi-cation of principles which are already embedded in European and UK law.

Content exceptions

The virtues of Waldron's book can be seen in the way in which he deals with the question of whether it is legitimate to prohibit certain forms of speech only. Again, this is a distinction which is grounded much more obviously in EU and UK rather than US law. The distinction between these two approaches can be seen by comparing the language of the First Amendment to that of Article 10 of the European Convention on Human Rights. The former, on its face, appears to prohibit any restriction on free speech at all:

> Congress shall make no law respecting an establishment of religion or pro-hibiting the free exercise thereof; or abridging the freedom of speech, or of the press; or the right of the people peaceably to assemble, and to petition the Government for a redress of grievances.

The latter, by contrast, makes free speech an explicitly qualified right, emphasis-ing not just the rights of a speaker but their duties and responsibilities:

1. Everyone has the right to freedom of expression. This right shall include freedom to hold opinions and to receive and impart information and ideas without interference by public authority and regardless of frontiers.

2. The exercise of these freedoms, since it carries with it duties and responsibilities, may be subject to such formalities, conditions, restrictions or penal-
   ties as are prescribed by law and are necessary in a democratic society, in the
   interests of national security, territorial disorder or crime, for the protection
   of health or morals, for the protection of the reputation or rights of others,
   for preventing the disclosure of information received in confidence, or for
   maintaining the authority and impartiality of the judiciary.

This idea of legitimate "restrictions" on free speech provides the content to the
law of free speech as practiced in the UK. The purpose of Article 10 to protect
democracy. In the words of Lord Bingham, then Lord Chief Justice of England
and Wales, Article 10 is

> an essential condition of an intellectually healthy society … The free com-
> munication of information, opinions and argument about the laws which a
> state should enact and the policies its government at all levels should pursue
> is an essential condition of truly democratic government.

It plays a "central role in the Convention," protecting "free speech in general and
free political speech in particular."[13]

The UK courts have held that "freedom of expression constitutes one of the
essential foundations of a democratic society." It applies not only to opinions
"that are favourably received or regarded as inoffensive or as a matter of indiffer-
ence, but also to those that offend, shock or disturb." Freedom of expression "is
subject to a number or exceptions which, however, must be narrowly interpreted
and the necessity for any restrictions must be convincingly established."[14]

The following examples are some of the cases which have been heard by
the European Court of Human Rights. In 1985, the journalist Jens Olaf Jersild
released a radio interview with a group of activists, the Greenjackets, who made
abusive remarks about immigrants and ethnic minorities in Denmark. Jersild was
convicted of aiding and abetting the youths in making racist comments (including by plying them with beer, presumably with the intention that they would
make offensive remarks). On application to the ECHR, the Court found that
Jersild had been informing the public about a social issue and his speech should
have been protected.[15]

In 2003, Pavel Ivanov was convicted in the Russian courts of incitement
to racial hatred following a series of anti-semitic articles on the subject of the
"Ziono-Fascist leadership of the Jewry." The European Court of Human Rights
held that any infringement of his right to free speech was necessary in a democratic society and proportionate.[16]

In 2007, Károly Fáber, a supporter of the far-right Hungarian party Jobbik,
was convicted after having displayed a striped flag 100 metres away from a demonstration by anti-racists. The flag was associated with the country's war-time
pro-Nazi regime and it was accepted that its use would cause unease among those

who suffered in the war. Nevertheless, his behaviour was limited to showing the flag and had not been violent. The ECHR upheld Fáber's complaint that his right to free expression had been unlawfully infringed.[17]

In 2009, an Austrian national, E. S., spoke at two seminars in which she accused the Muslim prophet Muhammad of being a paedophile, for which she was convicted of disparaging religious doctrines and fined €480. The ECHR held that the principle of free speech should take priority in all cases except where speech was likely to incite religious intolerance. Balancing the need to protect free speech, the fact that E. S. had made numerous incriminating statements, and the fact that her punishment had been limited to a fine, the Court rejected her complaint.[18]

Outside the narrow context of speech calculated to give rise to an immediate and imminent threat of lawless action, there is no direct equivalent in US Constitutional law of the requirement in EU human rights law of expression to be subject to limits prescribed by law. Nor is there any consensus that certain forms of speech are particularly amenable to restriction.

In the last half century, the US Supreme Court has repeatedly opposed "content-based restrictions." So, in 1972, the US Supreme Court considered the case of *Chicago Police Dept. v Mosley*, concerning a city ordinance which made it unlawful for protesters to picket within 150 feet of a school except during a labour dispute. During school hours, the black postal worker Earl Mosley walked the public sidewalk adjoining the school, carrying a sign that read: "Jones High School practices black discrimination. Jones High School has a black quota." The Supreme Court held that: "the First Amendment means that government has no power to restrict expression because of its message, its ideas, its subject matter, or its content."[19] This phrase has been used out of its original context repeatedly, and is said to provide an irrefutable argument against those who would prevent fascists from speaking.

Waldron challenges the idea that content restrictions are always unjustifiable. Drawing on the work of other legal theorists and the decisions of the Supreme Court, he concludes that this doctrine originates in a certain understanding of government and the idea that citizens can in all circumstances be trusted. In the American constitutional tradition, it is assumed that isolated racists or fascists can never secure a majority for their ideas. Indeed, it is said to be patronising to members of oppressed communities to assume that the law should protect them. Rather, the "marketplace of ideas" will always weigh pernicious political speech and ensure it is rejected.

Waldron hosts, as it were, a dialogue between supporters of the First Amendment and those who warn of the dangers of hate speech:

> Why can't government presume that people's sense of the place of minorities in social life is resilient, even in the face of a proliferation of hateful material proclaiming the opposite? But the question answers itself, particularly in the context of a society that has a history of racism or intercommunal

conflict. Nobody knows when that heritage of hate and conflict is really over. Old fears die hard; old nightmares are never entirely put to rest.[20]

Waldron would portray himself as a realist: racism is not finished, nor does it show any signs of dying away. Therefore, if a prohibition on hate speech has the effect of creating both a slightly stronger state and less racism, he is content with that bargain.

In so far as Waldron argues that hate speech remains pervasive, he has the better of the argument. For whatever points we might make that the people are usually wiser than their governors, and no matter how keenly we might insist that society is capable of becoming more equal than it is now, the reality remains that ideas of the far right are still capable of winning an audience. They rise in scarcity and crisis, and our world has known plenty of both in recent years.

The ECHR tradition and fascism

So far, this chapter has spoken only of Article 10 ECHR, which provides protection for free speech. Also relevant is Article 17 of the European Convention which provides that:

> Nothing in this Convention may be interpreted as implying for any State, group or person any right to engage in any activity or perform any act aimed at the destruction of any of the rights and freedoms set forth herein or at their limitation to a greater extent than is provided for in the Convention.

Among the cases which the Court of Human Rights has considered under Article 17 are the following. In 1984, an Association for the Defence of the Memory of Marshal Pétain placed an advertisement in the *Le Monde* newspaper celebrating the legacy of the France war-time collaborationist Vichy Regime. The authors were convicted of making a public defence of the crimes of collaboration. The judges of the Court of Human Rights found the criminal conviction disproportionate. The debate that the authors wanted was as to the general social measure of the Vichy Regime, a matter about which historians disagree. The outcome would have been different, the Court held, if the authors had sought to deny genocide. "As such, [their project] does not belong to the category of clearly established historical facts – such as the Holocaust – whose negation or revision would be removed from the protection of Article 10 by Article 17."[21]

In *Norwood v United Kingdom*, a supporter of the British National Party was convicted in 2002 of displaying insulting images, after affixing in his window a large BNP poster representing the Twin Towers in flames and carrying the words "Islam out of Britain – Protect the British People." The Court held that Article 17 applied. "The Court, and previously, the European Commission of Human Rights, has found in particular that the freedom of expression guaranteed under Article 10 of the Convention may not be invoked in a sense contrary to Article 17." Accordingly, it held that any infringements of his rights had been lawful.[22]

In 2004, Bruno Gollnisch, a university professor and supporter of the Front National, was suspended from teaching and research duties within his college for five years, after saying at a press conference that there had been no gas chambers in the concentration camps and that the Holocaust had been exaggerated. The Court held that his contribution to the spreading of Holocaust denial and disorder within his university was incompatible with his responsibilities as a teacher to his students. Accordingly, it upheld his conviction.[23]

The Court also dismissed a complaint brought by footballer Josip Šimunić, who claimed he had been wrongly fined in 2013, after shouting, at an international football match, "For Home" several times. Each time the spectators replied "Ready." While the origins of the chants preceded the fascist era, they had also been used as an official greeting of the Ustaša movement, which originated from fascism, and symbolised hatred towards people of a different ethnic identity. The applicant was a famous footballer and should have known better. His application failed.[24]

Article 17 was included in the Convention since it could not be ruled out that a person would attempt to rely on the rights enshrined in the Convention to prevent everyone else enjoying those same rights.[25] It creates the intellectual space in which some, but not all, content exceptions will be legal. It is an analogue, in human rights law, of the principle of no platform. It employs a similar reasoning, which can be traced back to Milton, the idea that those who would suppress the rights of everyone else cannot expect their speech to be protected.

Waldron and Holocaust denial

The purpose of this book is to ask whether, and when, it can be appropriate for anti-fascists to seek to disrupt or prevent a fascist meeting from going ahead. That question is narrower than Waldron's and yet the two are linked. The main argument in this book for preventing fascist meetings is that fascism seeks the active suppression of all other ideas – not merely the ideas of the far left, its recurring adversary, but also of the centre-left, and even of the centre-right. But I do not suggest that this one justification exhausts all possible reasons to limit fascist speech.

It could also be said that fascism does not deserve a platform because any fascist speech carries with it an implied argument that Hitler and Mussolini's descendants have earned the right to rule again. The promotion of fascism requires some reckoning with the past. The history of the 1930s was so murderous and so bleak that there is no possibility of fascism's redemption without its supporters lying about what happened.

Any of the contemporary fascist strategies for explaining the past involve a deceit of one sort of another, whether that takes the form of denying the extent of the Holocaust or blaming those deaths on fascism's enemies before calling for a second genocide.

In this model of contemporary fascism, a representative figure might be someone like Andrew Anglin, the editor of the *Daily Stormer* website, which derives its name from a paper published by Julius Streicher, the most obsessive of Hitler's anti-semitic followers. Anglin has attacked numerous journalists and politicians in Britain and the US either for being Jewish or having a relationship with Jews: including fellow right-winger Alex Jones for having a Jewish wife, and far-right website *Breitbart* for opening an office in Israel.

The *Daily Stormer* claims to be "the most censored publication in history."[26] Its style guide calls on its writers to "dehumanize the enemy, to the point where people are ready to laugh at their deaths." Anglin explains to his writers:

> The unindoctrinated should not be able to tell if we are joking or not. There should also be a conscious awareness of mocking stereotypes of hateful racists. I usually think of this as self-deprecating humour ... This is obviously a ploy and I actually do want to gas kikes.[27]

Reflecting on the rise of figures such as Andrew Anglin, Alexander Brown's *Hate Speech Law* suggests a refinement of Waldron's theories.[28] For Waldron, dignity is associated with the living. Brown argues that one way to understand hate speech laws which prohibit Holocaust denial is that they protect both the dignity of the living and the good name of the dead – meaning, the fifty million people who died in the Second World War, the six million Jews who died in the Holocaust, the millions more of Hitler's racial victims, and the hundreds of thousands of others who were killed by him. In this model, neither the few living survivors of the Holocaust nor the much larger numbers of the dead can have civic dignity unless society is willing to accept their innocence and limit the speech of those who exult in their killing or would re-enact it.

There is a famous passage in Walter Benjamin's "Theses on the Philosophy of History," which was written while its author was a refugee on the run from Hitler's armies, in which the philosopher wrote that

> Only that historian will have the gift of fanning the spark of hope in the past who is firmly convinced that even the dead will not be safe from the enemy if he wins. And this enemy has not ceased to be victorious.[29]

Brown's refinement of Waldron's position takes the logic of that argument and converts it from a negative fear into a positive instruction. The task of those who come after is to keep those who were killed safe from an enemy who would desecrate their gravestones, pull down their memorials, and extinguish even the memory of the dead.

Notes

1 J. Waldron, *The Harm in Hate Speech* (Cambridge, MA: Harvard University Press, 2012).
2 Waldron, *The Harm*, p. 31.
3 Waldron, *The Harm*, p. 87.
4 343 US 250 (1952).
5 Waldron, *The Harm*, p. 28.
6 Waldron, *The Harm*, p. 96.
7 Waldron, *The Harm*, p. 163.
8 G, Titley, *Racism and Media* (London: SAGE, 2019), pp. 148, 152.
9 R. Delgado and J. Stefancic, *Must We Defend Nazis: Why the First Amendment Should Not Protect Hate Speech and White Supremacy* (New York: New York University Press, 2018), pp. 8–9.
10 A. Mbembe, *Critique of Black Reason* (Durham: Duke University Press, 2017), p. 10.
11 London: John W. Parker and Son, 1859.
12 Directive 2002/73/EC of the European Parliament and of the Council of 23 September 2002; section 26(1) Equality Act 2010. In the US, Title VII of the Civil Rights Act of 1964 outlaws discrimination and harassment in the workplace on the basis of a protected category (race, colour, religion, sex, or national origin, etc.). Most states have statutory schemes mirroring or expanding Title VII (e.g. by offering a wider set of protected categories). Unlike EU and UK law, Title VII does not expand its protection beyond the workplace.
13 *Animal Defenders International, R (On The Application of) v Secretary of State for Culture, Media, and Sport* [2008] UKHL 15, para 27.
14 *BBC Petitioners (No3)* 2002 J.C. 27, para 13–14.
15 *Jersild v Denmark*, application no. 15890/89.
16 *Ivanov v Russia*, Application no. 35222/04.
17 *Fáber v Hungary*, application no. 40721/08.
18 *E. S. v Austria*, application no. 38450/12.
19 *Police Department of the City of Chicago et al. v Mosley*, 408 US 92 (1972).
20 P. Waldron, *The Harm in Hate Speech* (Cambridge, MA: Harvard University Press, 2012), p. 153.
21 *Lehideux and Isorni v France*, application no. 24662/94.
22 Application no. 23131/03.
23 *Gollnisch v France*, application no. 48135/08.
24 *S. M. v Croatia*, application no. 60561/14. For a broader discussion of the use of Article 17, and its use by the ECHR in relation to Turkey, S. Tyulkina, *Militant Democracy: Undemocratic Political Parties and Beyond* (London: Routledge, 2015), pp. 98–104.
25 *Ždanoka v Latvia*, no. 58278/00, ECHR 2006-IV, para 99.
26 Accessed 24 July 2020.
27 J. Moore, 'The Daily Stormer's Playbook to Turn People into Nazis,' *GQ*, 14 December 2017.
28 A. Brown, *Hate Speech Law: A Philosophical Examination* (London: Routledge, 2015), pp. 96–97, 146.
29 'Theses on the Philosophy of History,' in W. Benjamin (ed), *Illuminations* (London: Fontana, 1992 edn), pp. 245–256; here Thesis VI, p. 249.

8

HATE SPEECH, NO PLATFORM, COMPETING RIGHTS

I do not doubt that in the actual circumstances considered in this book – that is, a proposed fascist speech to which many people object – the instincts of Waldron and of people who share his understanding of hate speech would be similar to those who support no platform. Advocates of each group would agree in demanding that the event be cancelled. But there are differences between the two approaches, both as to why they would refuse a speech to proceed and who would be responsible for ending it.

For Waldron, the wrong of hate speech is the combination of its actual unpleasantness and the group identity of its prey. Those who apply no platform are also concerned with preventing attacks on fascism's ethnic minority (and left-wing) opponents. They combine this rejection of fascist violence with a dislike of fascism's dictatorial and censorious instincts.

Those who object to hate speech envisage two opposed groups of people and a neutral referee (the state) standing over them. In arguments for no platform, the group entitled to limit free expression is an insurgent people, perhaps the members of a trade union or student union, perhaps participants in a mass movement or a street protest.

In this and the next chapter I will set out why advocates of no platform have been cautious in seeing the state as a neutral body capable of being won consistently to an anti-racist or anti-fascist cause; and why appealing to the state – or to any benign authority – changes the politics of those objecting to fascist speech, turning them from insurgents into petitioners.

At the start of his book, Waldron invokes the situation of a hypothetical Muslim family walking through the streets of New Jersey and of their antagonist, a person motivated by hatred, who is carrying signs expressing his contempt for all Muslims. This chapter raises a complexity which is acknowledged in no platform, but barely recognised in hate speech theory. What if the aggrieved observers respond to the intimidation? What if they tear down a hateful sign?

What it the scene reassembles, and a group of anti-fascists joins it? What if they and a crowd of fascists find themselves asserting their speech rights each in conflict with the other?

The purpose of hate speech, whether in Waldron's formulation or in the general approach of contemporary left-wing politics, is to defend groups of people who have suffered oppression. But, in so far as the law sets up a series of binaries, they are different ones, not the oppressed versus the privileged, but two groups of people, either of whom might suffer discrimination. It is integral to our law that discrimination can apply in either direction: that either a man or a woman might suffer at the hands of a policy which indirectly discriminates on grounds of sex, or that an act of direct discrimination on grounds of race might harm either black or white people.

Second, in Waldron's critique of hate speech the injured parties are racial or religious minorities. Waldron appears to believe that it is possible to distinguish with certainty between groups of people who have genuinely suffered harm and to protect them, and others who falsely claim to have suffered. Those with a bogus claim of suffering do not have any say in determining who should be heard. But how do you deal, then, with their allegations? In the law as it stands today in the UK, EU, or US, the correct legal answer is to say that a white person might well be the casualty of harassment on grounds of race and the law might well protect them. But that is not Waldron's answer, nor would it be the answer of most anti-racists or anti-fascists.

Third, even if the problem of bad faith could be dealt with, there is a separate but related problem of the disparate nature of power. For in evaluating whether a speech should be permitted, we must deal with the reality that a speaker might be in some respect powerless. Waldron largely avoids the problem by assuming that hate speech is the act of white racists, anti-semites, and Islamophobes. But, as previous chapters have shown, the dominant style of far-right organising proceeds through allegations of victimhood, through complaints that fascist and far-right speakers are being denied platforms while others are allowed them, that policies of welfare spending benefit the wrong people (i.e. Muslim, Asian, and black people), and that the increasing presence of black and Asian people in Europe and the United States reduces white domination and in that way leads to white suffering, even an imagined genocide.

Civil and criminal law

This chapter focusses on the civil law governing free speech restrictions. The reason for this choice is that, in the scenario with which this book opened, a speech is proposed, and a group of people are discussing whether to seek to have it cancelled. If the scenario were to come to court, the most likely route it would take would be an application to a judge for a civil order (an injunction) prohibiting the speech from taking place, or for an order striking down a ban on fascist speech. This, it seems to me, is the place to which hate speech arguments are always tending, i.e. towards a rerun of Skokie, but in the hope that this time the judges will agree with the anti-fascists.

If the case came to court through the criminal law the situation would be slightly different. The body which prosecutes crimes is not a group of demonstrators but the state. In a criminal trial, what is at stake is behaviour which is so bad that the state is entitled to prohibit it. On that terrain, a part of the state (i.e. the judiciary) does indeed often find that the behaviour of some far-right speaker is criminal and should be punished. But the offence is an offence of a dual character, aimed both against (in Waldron's terms) a minority group and against the state itself.

One way to see these criminal dynamics play out is to look in more detail at the trial and imprisonment of Tommy Robinson in summer 2018 for contempt of court. It began with Robinson outside Leeds Crown Court and livestreaming (i.e. filming himself projecting a speech to tens of thousands of his online followers). In Robinson's version of events, he was simply reporting on the trial, as any other journalist would. The only difference between him and other reporters was that he had chosen a different mechanism for transmitting his commentary to his audience.

While his followers listened to him, Robinson gave his version of what the trial was about, namely that a group of Asian men had committed sexual offences against women and now, at long last, were about to receive their due punishment.

As Robinson spoke, he was seen by members of the Court, taken before a judge, and pleaded guilty to contempt, after which he was imprisoned. The subsequent court proceedings were complicated, with the Court of Appeal finding that the Judge had been wrong to deal with Robinson that day rather than adjourn the case for sentencing. The Court granted Robinson's appeal but ordered a rehearing. The matter then returned to the High Court, where Robinson was convicted and sentenced to several months' imprisonment. Robinson's advocates argued that his rights to free speech were protected by the European Convention on Human Rights, and that he was entitled to use even words which might shock, offend, or disturb. However, the Judges looked at the words used by Robinson and found that they did not merit protection. Robinson had not been simply reporting the trials, he had incited his supporters to violence. He had said:

> You want to harass someone's family? You see that man who was getting aggressive as he walked into court, the man who faces charges of child abduction, rape, prostitution – harass him, find him, go knock on his door, follow him, see where he works, see what he's doing. You want to stick pictures online and call people and slander people, how about you do it about them?[1]

The case concerned an application for an order committing Robinson to prison for contempt of court. Robinson had breached a reporting restriction order which prohibited any reporting of the trial until after the conclusion of that trial.

The content of the material Robinson published gave rise to a substantial risk that the underlying trial would be impeded. By confronting some of the defendants as they arrived at court, doing so aggressively, and filming and broadcasting his material, he had interfered with the administration of justice.

In all these ways, the Court made it clear that Tommy Robinson's wrongdoing was not only his harassment of the defendants. Rather, it was his attempted frustration of existing court proceedings which led to his imprisonment.

In the case of a public campaign to limit the rights of a speaker, those dynamics are rarely available. The harm on which a successful no platform campaign depends is the malice shown by the speaker to other members of the public. No crime has yet been committed – the most that can usually be said is that a fascist and his followers tends to employ violence, they have done so often before, and that this can be part of the reason for refusing them a platform now. That is before we grapple with the central weakness of a civil case: the difficulty in identifying who is the protagonist, i.e. who is principally at fault, when each side is seeking to silence the other.

The fascist as victim

Waldron repeatedly refers to racial and religious minorities. At times[2] he acknowledges that discrimination does also take place on grounds of sex and concedes the need to protect women from language which reduces their social dignity. Such points are, however, incidental to his main argument, which is about racial or religious rather than gendered hate. All Waldron's examples are of groups of people who have suffered violence at some time or another in recent history on account of their race or religion. His account is divided into a series of pairs: the anti-semite who can be silenced, and the Jew who would suffer derision; the Islamophobe and the Muslim; the black person and the white racist. That dichotomy reflects the approach of social justice advocates who are rightly concerned to assert the rights of the oppressed.

The law, however, chooses a different and broader approach. In the US, Title VII of the Civil Rights Act of 1964 protects employees and job applicants from employment discrimination because of their race, colour, religion, sex, etc. The Age Discrimination in Employment Act of 1967 and Americans with Disabilities Act of 1990 prohibit age and disability harassment and discrimination in the workplace, respectively, in similar terms.

In the UK, section 26 of the Equality Act 2010, prohibits discrimination or harassment "related to a relevant protected characteristic." Nine protected characteristics are set out in the act, including age, disability, race, religion, sex and sexual orientation.[3] The term "related to" is akin to the phrase "because of" in Title VII: it requires a limited causal connection, without specifying the race (etc.) of either discriminator or their victim.

Often it is said that the Equality Act is mirrored, that (with the exception of disability discrimination law which cannot be invoked to protect non-disabled people) it equally protects women and men from sex discrimination, black and white people from race discrimination, and so on.[4] Occasionally discrimination claims are brought by people on the privileged side of each binary, arguing that in their case a rule discriminates against them, even though they are a member of the more privileged group. So, although UK anti-discrimination law provides a modest scope for positive action (section 159 Equality Act 2010), this has remained underdeveloped, essentially because any rule which protected only women or black people (etc.) would be direct discrimination against men or white people, and under the Equality Act direct discrimination is (with the exception of age) always unjustifiable and unlawful.

The significant obstacle that the mirrored character of anti-discrimination law places in the way of using the law to prevent hate speech is that there is no starting presumption that an oppressed group (or in Waldron's terms, a minority) is allowed special access to a judge to demand that the Court intervenes while a more privileged group is refused that same access. Imagine, for example, that in Southall in 1979 a local resident of Asian (Punjabi Sikh) heritage had asked a judge to grant an injunction prohibiting the local council from permitting the National Front to hold an election meeting in the vicinity of her home, and that the same law had applied then as applied now. In those circumstances, the National Front might just as easily apply to the Court for a mandatory injunction requiring the meeting to be permitted, saying that the National Front was an all-white organisation, and that a refusal to allow its meeting to go ahead would violate the dignity of its white members. Simply on the terrain of equality law, there is nothing in principle which stops a white racist organisation from making that request.

In practice, whenever anyone applies to the Court for an injunction, whether a prohibitory or a mandatory one, a court will only make the order if it would be just to do so. The best shield in equality law against decisions which would cause injustice is the evidence of the case, and a judge's real but rarely articulated concepts of fairness and equity.

In recent times, it has become common to hear advocates of white privilege insist that they are the only true egalitarians. Slogans such as "White lives matter" or "Rights for whites" require their advocates to believe that, despite all the evidence that black people in Europe and the United States are less likely to be employed than whites, are paid less, are housed in worse conditions, and so on – that somehow black people, Muslims, or Jews are the beneficiaries of social privilege.

We have seen how Waldron uses the term "dignity," to mean an atmosphere in which each individual is respected and capable of achieving their own self-worth. This is, of course, not the only possible meaning of that term. Francis Fukuyama's book *Identity* distinguishes between two different ideas of dignity. In the democratic concept of self-worth (in Greek, "isothymia") all people are essentially equal, and the way to achieve respect is to be a person of equal standing with everyone else: to have the same political and economic rights as them.

In the older, aristocratic idea of dignity ("megalothymia"),[5] a person could achieve full sell-worth only by being superior to others. In this conception, value cannot be shared; rather, fulfilment requires the subordination of others. From that perspective, the future demanded when people speak of "Rights for whites" is not an equality of treatment but an inequality of treatment, the superior living standards to which white people are entitled, indeed a wider differential than this period of late capitalism will allow. Such a way of looking at the world is of course ripe for dissatisfaction and belief of injustice, for no matter how far the democratic revolution of the past century is turned back, it is still the case that workers, women, black people, and other exploited or oppressed people will never be as subordinate as the far-right imagination demands.

The far right has long based its demands to act on false claims of victimhood. In 1930, for example, the Communist Party emerged as the largest party in the German capital city of Berlin, winning 27.3 percent of the city's votes. The Nazis' response was to target the districts where the Communists had the greatest support: Wedding, Friedrichshain, Neukölln, bribing tavern owners to turn their premises into Nazi bases, and then setting off in the evenings in groups of 10–12 so-called roll commandoes to beat or kill their chosen Communist rivals. Forced to testify by a left-wing lawyer Hans Litten, Hitler defended this tactic, insisting that the phrase roll commando, "in and of itself has nothing to do with the elimination of people." Rather, the troops of the SA were being sent out from the taverns defensively, to protect other fascists from attack: "The SA is forbidden to commit violence or provoke it … But if a person really oversteps the boundary of self-defence you can't hold a person responsible for that."[6]

As the decade wore on, the fascist states invoked self-defence repeatedly: insisting that Communists needed to be jailed because otherwise they would destroy Italy and Germany, that Italian military expansion was necessary because Italy had no colonial possessions of her own and was a "proletarian" nation among the colonial states, or that war was needed to protect the oppressed German minorities of Eastern Europe (the German-speaking Poles, in whose name the invasion of that country was justified). As early as December 1939, the mass murder of Polish citizens was being justified as acts of "reprisal." The same language was used repeatedly in Italy to justify the collective punishment of towns accused of harbouring partisans.[7] In 1944, V1 and V2 rockets fired at London were called *Vergeltungswaffen* or "reprisal weapons."

Hitler and his admirers persuaded themselves that the Jewish populations of Europe and America were such a powerful adversary – with a control over culture, politics, and the news – that they had dragged the rulers of Britain and the US into war with Germany in 1914–1918 and again in 1939 and 1941. They managed to justify even genocide as self-defence.

This chapter will now proceed to give examples of recent cases where judges have had to address the issues of victimhood and work out for themselves whether someone deserves to be silenced. They are cited not to say that the law gets these sorts of disputes generally wrong or right (in many of the cases I will cite, the decisions reached were ones which many social activists will applaud). I am making the different point that choosing who is the casualty of hate speech and who is its protagonist is a harder task than Waldron suggests, and that the common-sense position adopted by many courts is unlikely to favour anti-fascists in particular.

Two oppressed groups

One difficult issue which the law has had to confront is what happens when the source of hate speech is someone who themselves has a protected characteristic. In 2012 and 2013, the Employment Tribunal in Britain heard a case brought by Ronnie Fraser of Academic Friends of Israel against the lecturers' University and College Union complaining of harassment. The claim was a claim of harassment on grounds of race. Mr Fraser complained that his union had passed motions which criticised the actions of the Israeli government and supported the boycott of Israeli universities, and had invited Mr Bongani Masuku, International Relations Secretary of COSATU, to speak at its events, a trade unionist who had written on his own blog of the need to make "every Zionist … drink the bitter medicine they are feeding our brothers and sisters in Palestine."[8]

The panel were unimpressed by Mr Fraser's insistence that other campaigners had wrongly disagreed with him. Most of the allegations, the Tribunal found, were not complaints of harassment. Mr Fraser was not saying that he had been distressed by the behaviour of members of his union, or of its leadership's failure to restrict them. Rather, what he objected to was that he had lost a series of arguments. With regard to one of the controversial motions, the Tribunal found:

> It was open to Congress to consider that motion. Its legality was not in question. The vote was valid, and the outcome was the product of the union's democratic processes. The "unwanted" conduct was that of the members who proposed and supported the motion and Congress as a whole which passed it. As we have already explained, no claim lies against the Respondents in respect of these actions. Nor was the Respondents' conduct "related to" the Claimant's protected characteristics. Nor did their conduct produce the prescribed effect upon him. Nor would it have been reasonable for it to do so. And even if the Claimant could base his complaint on the decision of Congress to pass the motion and even if that decision produced the prescribed effect on him, it would not be reasonable for it to have done so.[9]

If we recast this decision in terms of hate speech, what the Tribunal was saying was that the speech complained of was not aimed at Mr Fraser, but instead was for a political purpose (i.e. to criticise Israeli state actions). It was not bad enough to be harassment.

The panel held that those who participate in politics had a lesser entitlement to complain against hateful opinions. By entering the terrain of contested political debate, they had placed themselves in a context where other people were likely to antagonise them:

> The Claimant is a campaigner. He chooses to engage in the politics of the union in support of Israel and in opposition to activists for the Palestinian cause. When a rugby player takes the field, he must accept his fair share of minor injuries ... Similarly, a political activist accepts the risk of being offended or hurt on occasions by things said or done by his opponents (who themselves take on a corresponding risk). These activities are not for everyone. Given his election to engage in, and persist with, a political debate which by its nature is bound to excite strong emotions, it would, we think, require special circumstances to justify a finding that such involvement had resulted in harassment.[10]

From the perspective of hate speech – with its assumption of a one-sided battle between an aggressive majority and a silent and righteous minority – this approach seems harsh. Why should a member of a subaltern group protesting injustice be expected to have a thick skin?

But from the point of view no platform, with its assumption of a struggle between two vocal groups of people, separated principally by the righteousness of their respective causes, this idea of two competing sides seems much more familiar. Most anti-fascists are used to the idea that the arguments in which they take part will be heated and contested and things will be said and done at the edges. There is a struggle between violent fascists who would introduce general censorship, and anti-fascists who insist on the rights of everyone to speak. No one involved in anti-fascist politics would maintain that anti-fascists are always on the receiving end of insults or attacks. Rather, we celebrate moments such as Cable Street or Lewisham when an anti-fascist crowd chose to confront the fascists, resisted them with force, and prevented them from marching.

The interest of Mr Fraser's case is that it was an instance of a campaigner insisting on his subaltern status and seeking to use it to restrict the speech of people who disagreed with him. Essential to Mr Fraser's case was the idea that he was a member of a disadvantaged group (Jews), that all, or effectively all, Jews supported the existence of the state of Israel, and that by allowing the members of the union to pass policies which criticised the state of Israel his trade union had infringed his dignity and failed to treat him as an equal member of the union.

Mr Fraser accused his union of enabling hate speech and insisted that he, as its target, was better placed than anyone else to understand its hurt. His parents had fled Nazi Germany in 1939 and members of his family had died in the Holocaust. While parts of Fraser's legal case were poorly conceived, as a piece of politics they captured the moment we are in, and a way of doing politics which can be found at every point of the political spectrum.

Witnesses for Mr Fraser included the Chief Rabbi, the President of the Board of Deputies of British Jews, and Mr Whine of the Community Security Trust, the organisation which provides security and intelligence on security issues to the Board of Deputies. Denis McShane MP and John Mann MP (more recently an advisor to the Government on anti-semitism) also gave evidence on his behalf. Mr Fraser's solicitor was Anthony Julius, Chair of the *Jewish Chronicle*, and the veteran of the defence of the historian Deborah Lipstadt in which his client had been sued for libel by the Holocaust denier David Irving and won. At the start of the case, it must have seemed to the Tribunal that Mr Fraser's arguments contained an almost unique moral authority. Here was a member of an oppressed group, receiving the support of the official bodies who were entitled to speak for almost every other member of that minority community.

Yet one of the problems faced by Mr Fraser in bringing his claim was that a large proportion of the people he complained about were other (anti-Zionist) Jews. The people who had proposed motions to the union's Congress criticising Israel, or who had denounced him in emails were themselves in many cases Jewish. In ignoring his complaints, Mr Fraser accused the union of applying a racist distinction between "good Jews," who were allowed platforms and "bad Jews" who were not. But what, the Judge asked, about the anti-Zionist Jews who had criticised Fraser and proposed the motions he disliked – where did they fit in? Mr Fraser's answer was to say that their opinions did not count, since they were merely a fringe within Jewish opinion. Employment Judge Snelson suggested that Mr Fraser was falling into the same dualities he deplored in others.[11]

For Mr Fraser, all of this was beside the point. His case was not an argument between two groups of oppressed people. His case was brought against the union. He was a member of a minority, and a person who was entitled to protection. As he saw it, an individual and a community were asserting their need for dignity. Applying the logic of hate speech and nothing else, you might have thought that Fraser deserved to win. This is worth remembering, not to praise Fraser, nor to adopt (or refute) his arguments, but rather to say that the hate speech approach can be used by a wider set of people than most activists have realised. It is already being employed, and widely, by people from the centre-ground of politics hoping to silence those further to their left.

Groups in bitter and protracted conflict

At the heart of Waldron's theory of hate speech is the idea that members of subaltern groups should be protected from hateful speech. Those who object to unwanted speech on the grounds that it is hate speech assert that there is a plausible distinction to be drawn between benign and hateful speech. For something to be bad enough to constitute hate speech, such language must be worse than unpleasant; it must also draw some of its negative effect from the subordinate status of the people at which it is aimed. Yet a difficulty with this approach comes when you try to develop the idea that groups of people are oppressed and require protection. As this chapter has indicated, that is not the approach of the law, which refuses to distinguish between groups of people who are capable of suffering harassment and those who are immune to it.

Moreover, the set of characteristics through which social power and powerlessness are understood has expanded, and now includes race, sex, disability, sexual orientation, age and religion or belief, as well as class. This is the benign consequence of social movements rightly demanding recognition of the powerless and winning well-earned victories. Yet, this expansion of our ideas of the oppressed means that there are increased opportunities for fascists and the far right to pose as disadvantaged in relation to the members of another subordinate group. Previous chapters have given the examples of Theo van Gogh and Milo Yiannopoulos presenting themselves as the gay victims of Islam. And that stance has not gone without reward.

When judges are faced with free speech arguments pitting against each other two groups of people, each claiming to stand in defence of their legitimate rights, they often fill that void with quite simple common-sense ideas, principally the notion that whoever is taking the initiative in any conflict and offending another group of people is automatically wrong.

You can see this unacknowledged reasoning in the case of *Forstater v CGD Europe*, which concerned a tax specialist who had worked for several years as a consultant but found that her contract was not renewed, and blamed her employer, arguing that it had refused her employment because for several months she had been speaking out on social media against proposed measures which would have made it easier for people to have a gender other than the one reported on their birth certificate recognised by law.

In so far as UK and European law prohibits discrimination on grounds of religion or belief, it does so by restricting protection to beliefs which are compatible with human dignity and the fundamental rights of others. The question for the Court was, accordingly, whether Ms Forstater's beliefs were entitled to legal protection. For Employment Judge Tayler, the key to the case was the "absolutist" character of Forstater's beliefs.[12]

As far as Ms Forstater was concerned, the question of a person's sex was for her and no one else to decide. She considered that if a trans woman said she was a woman, that statement was untrue, even if that person had a Gender Recognition Certificate. She believed there were two sexes, male and female, there was no spectrum in sex, and there were no circumstances whatsoever under which a person could change from one sex to another, or to be of neither sex. She said she would generally seek to be polite to trans persons and would usually seek to respect their choice of pronoun but would not feel bound to; if a trans person who was not assigned female at birth was in a space that was intended to be for women only, then Ms Forstater would object to her presence. In Ms Forstater's opinion, the words man and woman described a person's sex at birth and were immutable. A person was either one or the other, there was nothing else in between, and it was impossible to change from one sex to the other.[13]

From Ms Forstater's view that sex is biological and unchanging, there is logically no debate between trans and non-trans (or even trans-exclusionary) opinion. The discussion was between some women and the men who sought to oppress them.

> Yes, I think feminists and non-gender conforming and trans people are natural allies ... But I think there are also a group of misogynist people, and others who want to undermine protections for women and children that have become entryists to the Trans Rights Activists movement that are not natural allies to women: gamergaters, incels, narcissists, extreme porn advocates.[14]

Trans people were blamed for ills to which they had not contributed. By "gamergaters," Ms Forstater meant such ardent misogynists as Milo Yiannopoulos, whose contempt for trans rights was indistinguishable from her own. What was being expressed in this passage was really the degree of Ms Forstater's contempt for people she disagreed with. The result of her mind-set was a conflict where trans people were seen as irredeemably wrong, and two groups of people (women and trans people) were pitted together in a moral war which could end only with one group voluntarily agreeing to be silent, to cease campaigning for its rights, and quit society and politics for ever. One group of bad people – gamergaters – had to be fitted alongside the other bad people (those who believed in gender reassignment) even if in fact they were mortal enemies. That is what the Tribunal meant in characterising Forstater's views as absolutist.

The Court found that such opinions required Ms Forstater to cause distress to other people. So, while Ms Forstater considered herself a polite person willing to accede to other people's requests, the reality was that she sought out trans women and made a point of referring to them as men. In Ms Forstater's words, "While I may choose to use alternative pronouns as a courtesy, no one has the right to compel others to make statements they do not believe."[15]

Employment Judge Tayler treated Ms Forstater as the active party in any debate, and the one responsible for causing undue distress to others.

> The Claimant could generally avoid the huge offense caused by calling a trans woman a man without having to refer to her as a woman, as it is often not necessary to refer to a person sex at all ... I do not accept that there is a failure to engage with the importance of the Claimant's qualified right to freedom of expression, as it is legitimate to exclude a belief that necessarily harms the rights of others ... The human rights balancing exercise goes against the Claimant because of the absolutist approach she adopts.[16]

Most commentators decided that this was a good or a bad decision according to how they evaluated the underlying merits of either trans- or trans-exclusionary politics. The supporters of the former welcomed the decision, the latter opposed it with equal force. What is of more interest for this book however is that the judgment depends on an unspoken idea of who is right or wrong in a debate according to who is making life difficult for others. While many theorists of hate speech would welcome this approach, and see it as operating in line with their understanding of free speech debates, advocates of no platform are more likely to find it troubling.

Anti-fascists are more likely to grasp that there is a sustained conflict between fascists and anti-fascists, which is incapable of being finally determined at any one demonstration. Given that the conflict is enduring it is possible to take a snapshot of any particular given moment, isolate it from its context, and (without needing to misrepresent what happened) portray anti-fascists in that moment as the source of the conflict and the party seeking to restrict the rights of others. If we focus on who is the active party in a debate and who is challenging the free speech rights of others, then it is likely that there will be many occasions when anti-fascists are the dynamic force. If so, then the law is likely to reject our demands repeatedly and support people we disagree with.

When the person demanding free speech is a fascist

Between 2004 and 2012, the civil courts in Europe and the European Court of Human Rights had to grapple with a case which turned on the same issues as this book: i.e. should the supporter of a fascist party be permitted to speak? The claimant in that case was the member of a party led by fascists and asserted his right to speak – in this case, by standing for his party in elections. The protagonists in this situation, his left-wing critics, insisted that the risks caused by his employment meant he could not legitimately remain there and should be dismissed from his post.

An election candidate for the British National Party Mr Redfearn found employment as a bus driver. The trade union Unison wrote to his employer Serco complaining about Redfearn's employment and raising its members' fears of racial hatred. Unfortunately, Unison's objection to Mr Redfearn was based solely on the fact that he had stood for the BNP during elections. There was no suggestion that he had organised in his workplace or said or done anything untoward there. Given the message of this book that no platform works best as a tactic when most of those watching accept that the person being targeted is a fascist, this was a significant error from the outset.

Serco dismissed Mr Redfearn in June 2004, ostensibly on grounds of health and safety. Redfearn then brought a claim against Serco for unlawful direct discrimination. He had been employed continuously for just six months and was not eligible to bring a claim of ordinary unfair dismissal. He was also limited in a second respect: the UK was due to introduce in 2006 laws prohibiting discrimination on grounds of religion or belief. However, they had not been introduced yet, and the only protection which Mr Redfearn could invoke was the prohibition against discrimination on grounds of race. At the Employment

Tribunal, Redfearn argued his dismissal had been indirectly discriminatory on grounds of race, reasoning that membership of the BNP was limited to whites,[17] and that by imposing a requirement that members of the British National Party could not work for Serco, the company was imposing on its staff a requirement which every black employee could satisfy but a proportion of its white staff could not. It was discriminating indirectly, in other words, against whites and the discrimination could not be justified. Serco's General Manager James Binnington gave evidence that

> members of the public [were] strongly opposed to BNP's policies might wrongly associate Serco with the BNP, which might in turn lead to attacks on Serco's minibuses which would jeopardise the health and safety of Serco's staff and its vulnerable passengers.[18]

Very few judges, after this initial hearing, were persuaded that the fears raised by Binnington of these possible attacks were at all credible.

The Employment Tribunal rejected Mr Redfearn's claim in forthright terms. He appealed, and the Employment Appeal Tribunal ruled in Redfearn's favour, insisting that he had been the victim of discrimination. In the EAT's view, the phrase "on racial grounds" encompassed any detriment suffered by a worker where race was in any way a factor at all, irrespective of the motives of the employer. At the Court of Appeal, the decision of the EAT was heavily criticised. Lord Justice Mummery, one of Britain's most experienced employment judges, found that its approach had been wrong in principle and inconsistent with the purposes of equality law.

> Taken to its logical conclusion [Mr Redfearn's counsel's] interpretation of the 1976 Act would mean that it could be an act of direct race discrimination for an employer, who was trying to improve race relations in the workplace, to dismiss an employee, whom he discovered had committed an act of race discrimination, such as racist abuse, against a fellow employee or against a customer of the employer. I am confident that that is not the kind of case for which the anti-discrimination legislation was designed.[19]

On the face of it, the above account seems to be a ringing endorsement of the policy of anti-discrimination legislation, going back to the Race Relations Act 1976, and a finding that the law must not be used to protect the free speech rights of racists. But Mr Redfearn then applied to the European Court of Human Rights and, in 2012, the Court ruled in Mr Redfearn's favour.

The Human Rights Court was much more focussed than its British counterparts on Article 10 ECHR which protects free speech. (These were lesser consideration for the UK courts because, as noted above, the prohibition on discrimination on grounds of belief had not come into UK law at the time of Mr Redfearn's dismissal.) The Judges reminded themselves that,

What the Court is called upon to do in this case is not to pass judgment on the policies or aims, obnoxious or otherwise, of the BNP at the relevant time (the BNP is, in any case, not a party to these proceedings), but solely to determine whether the applicant's rights under Article 11 were breached in the particular circumstances of the instant case.[20]

The Court's view was that, on the facts, Mr Redfearn was the victim of an injustice. There had been no objections made to his presence in the workplace other than a general complaint about his membership of the BNP. No consideration had been given to transferring him to a non-customer-facing role. The Court held that, although the Race Relations Act was "not primarily intended to cover a situation such as the present one," the Courts should have given the Act "a liberal interpretation" to protect Mr Redfearn.[21]

The issue in the case was not the superiority of either the British or European courts: there have been very many cases where the latter has been far ahead of the former. The question is rather whether race equality law can be used to protect the free speech rights of people who promote fascism. In two of the four courts which heard Mr Redfearn's case, including the most senior and last of them, it was found that the law could and should have been used in this way.

The Court's reasoning appears to have been that, in a conflict between two groups of people as to who should speak, the priority should be given to whichever party does the least damage to the free speech rights of the other. This, of course, was also the reasoning in *Forstater*. On this judicial logic, whoever is the active party is wrong and their demands should be rejected, whether they are calling for their own right to speak or for the restriction of someone else's speech. Such politics, the next chapter will argue, are a recurring position, not merely of judges but of other parts of the state which intervene in defence of fascist speech.

Notes

1 *HM Attorney General v Yaxley-Lennon (Rev 2)* [2019] EWHC 1791, para 69.
2 P. Waldron, *The Harm in Hate Speech* (Cambridge, MA: Harvard University Press, 2012), pp. 89–97.
3 Equality Act 2010, section 4.
4 Only disability discrimination is not mirrored (i.e. there can be no discrimination against a person on the grounds that they are not disabled): Equality Act 2020, section 6.
5 F. Fukuyama, *Identity* (London: Profile, 2019), pp. 21–22.
6 B. C. Hett, *Crossing Hitler: The Man Who Put the Nazis on the Witness Stand* (Oxford: Oxford University Press, 2008), p. 89.
7 C. Pavone, *A Civil War: A History of the Italian Resistance* (London: Verso, 2013), p. 540.
8 I. Chernick, 'High Profile Hate Speech Case Heard in South Africa's Constitutional Court,' *Jerusalem Post*, 28 August 2019.
9 *Fraser v University & Colleges Union*, ET Case No: 2203290/2011, para 166.
10 *Fraser v UCU*, para 146.
11 *Fraser v UCU*, para 53.

12 *Forstater v CGD Europe and others*, ET Case No: 2200909/2019, para 83.
13 *Forstater v CGD*, para 77.
14 *Forstater v CGD*, para 27.
15 *Forstater v CGD*, para 35.
16 *Forstater v CGD*, para 91.
17 *Serco Ltd v Redfearn* [2006] ICR 1367, CA, para 16.
18 *Serco v Redfearn*, para 25.
19 *Serco v Redfearn*, paras 43–44.
20 *Redfearn v the United Kingdom* [2012] ECHR 1878, para 47.
21 *Redfearn v the United Kingdom* [2012] ECHR 1878, para 51.

9

HATE SPEECH AND THE STATE

About a third of the way through Waldron's *The Harm in Hate Speech*, the author recalls being in Leamington Spa in 1978 when an unnamed "racist agitator" was sentenced to a short prison term for covering the streets of the West Midlands town with posters depicting British people of African ancestry as apes. The figure at the centre of Waldron's story was not the agitator, or indeed the black families of the town, but the judge:

> After [the racist's] conviction by the jury, he was sentenced by a crusty old English judge, who (one might have imagined) would have little sympathy with this new-fangled hate speech legislation. But the judge gave the defendant a stern lecture to the effect that we cannot run a multiracial society under modern conditions if people are free to denigrate their fellow citizens in bestial terms. There was some shouting from the gallery as the defendant was taken away. The case made a deep impression on me.[1]

This incident is one that Waldron has referred to elsewhere, been criticised for invoking, and addressed again.[2] It is easy to understand why Waldron felt so protective of this memory; for the judge's focus on running "a multiracial society under modern conditions" is exactly Waldron's own focus, on the necessity of building a rational and well-ordered society.

Indeed, knowing more of the trial, what becomes ever clearer is how much of Waldron's analysis turns on this one incident. For on 29 January 1979, a Leamington Spa resident Robert Relf was indeed convicted and sentenced to 15 months in prison for conduct likely to cause racial hatred: that is, posting leaflets (one called "Jungle News")[3] in shop windows, portraying black people as apes, stating they were all violet criminals, and using various racist epithets to describe them. This trial raised the issues which were at the heart of Waldron's idea of hate speech.

Hate speech arguments assume a judge, either literal or figurative: a kindly neutral figure fully appraised of the facts who can choose wisely between competing accounts, and on whose ultimate fairness all well-meaning people can depend.

In this way, hate speech can be included within a wider set of arguments whose outcomes have been the juridification (i.e. legalisation) of so much of life. For it is one of the ways in which the neo-liberal transformation of British life has been experienced since 1979 that all sorts of disputes which were previously determined without reference to the law are now decided in judicial or quasi-judicial hearings. The best-known example is the shift from the resolution of industrial disputes through often-unruly unofficial strikes and their relocation to the sterile environment of the Employment Tribunal.[4] But, in fact, the process is much more widespread. Over the past 25 years, criminal offences have been created at a dizzying rate, including more than 3,000 between 1997 and 2006 alone,[5] as well as a proliferation of offences prohibiting hate speech.[6] Very much of what we consider politics now takes place through the law. In 2003, when Britain went to war in Iraq, protesters demanded the prosecution of Tony Blair for his breaches of international law. In 2016, when Jeremy Corbyn's opponents in the Labour Party came within a whisker of deposing him, the forum they chose was an application to the High Court. In 2018 and 2019, when opponents of Brexit sought to pre-empt a no-deal departure, they did so by issuing Judicial Reviews which were won by them (twice) in the Supreme Court.[7]

Robert Relf's 1979 trial was in fact the second set of proceedings involving him. In the first, Relf had made his Leamington Spa home available for sale to "positively no coloureds."[8] He was prosecuted under the Race Relations Act, ordered to take the sign down, and jailed when he refused. Relf went on hunger strike against his imprisonment, was widely supported by the tabloid press, and released early. He then took part in speaking tours for various far-right groups, before seeking to begin the same cycle of publicity all over again. In January 1979, that previous history of punishment and release would have been known to everyone in court.

Waldron's "crusty old English judge" was a former barrister by the name of His Honour Judge Mynett QC. Mynett had been a former Squadron leader during the war. As a criminal advocate, he defended rather more often than he prosecuted.[9]

From the press accounts of the trial we can piece together a little of what Mynett said. A court reporter for the *Coventry Evening Telegraph* heard Judge Mynett telling the convicted Robert Relf, "In these days, one cannot take other than a very serious view of this,"[10] which sounds rather more like generic judge-speak (a very serious offence …) than a genuine commitment to the multicultural England that Waldron recalls.

Waldron's account ends in the Crown Court, but to have a sense of the total-ity of the case, it is worth setting out what happened next. Relf appealed to the Court of Appeal. There the presiding judge was a different figure, Lord Justice Lawton. Forty years before, Lawton had been not a judge but a student politi-cian, a founding member of Cambridge University's Fascist Association. Then, as a junior barrister, he had represented Oswald Mosley in libel proceedings. He was also employed by the fascist leader to negotiate the acquisition of land on Sark, to build a fascist radio station capable of broadcasting into Britain during the coming world war. In late 1937, Lawton was in Belgium again negotiating on behalf of Mosley. In November 1938, the future Lord Justice Lawton negotiated the agreement by which the German Nazi regime supplied the funds for Mosley's station, a victory he celebrated with a trip to a Paris brothel.[11] Lawton had been, in other words, for many years one of Britain's leading fascists – but this history was no obstacle to his subsequent promotion to one of the highest judicial offices in the land.

At the end of the Court of Appeal proceedings, Lord Justice Lawton, like Mynett before him, gave a speech celebrating the necessity of laws prohibiting hate speech and justifying them. "It is sometimes forgotten," Lawton intoned,

> that the common law of England for centuries has taken the view that it is an offence for anyone to stir up hostility against any section of the Sovereign's subjects. Most of the immigrants are now British Citizens, and those who are not are living under the protection of the Crown, and they too are entitled to be protected from those who wish to stir up hostility against them.[12]

It was another stern lecture, but in so far as Lawton was willing to acknowl-edge the equality of his fellow black citizens it was only at second hand, in so far as they were the subjects of the sovereign, the protected children of the Crown. Patronisingly, he acknowledged that many immigrants were now British Citizens (for more than a decade, no immigrant had been allowed to settle in Britain without a white grandparent or a British passport). Then, being as leni-ent as any judge could without inviting inquiries into his own past and ongoing politics, Lawton reduced Relf's sentence from 15 to 9 months.

The point of revisiting this story is not that the former fascist Freddie Lawton was the true face of the judiciary, or that his presence somehow negates that of the more liberal Judge Mynett. The point, rather, is that both are representative of the judiciary. There are judges who are natural liberals and others who are more authoritarian. One strategy for defending property does not take prec-edence over the other. Both have an equal chance to constitute the law.

The state is an assembly of people broad enough to encompass many strains of political opinion, stretching from the former fascist to the conservative and reaching even to the liberal. The state encompasses all these views. Where the state will not go, however, is so far as to allow fascism's unruly opponents on the streets to challenge the police. It will not sanction any challenge to the authorities, or the creation of any rival force which desires a fully egalitarian society and sees the defeat of fascism as merely a step towards that more equal future.

A two-, or a three-sided, conflict?

A previous chapter of this book quoted Jeremy Waldron's warning that, should hate speech be allowed, then even a "vigilant police force"[13] would be insufficient to restore the faith of members of minority groups that they were truly considered equal. For many members of ethnic minorities, whether in Britain, Europe, or the United States, the idea of a police force acting with vigilance to crush all instances of racism is not the usual experience.

The state is not a single body. Rather, it is an assemblage of competing parts, different ones of which can play different functions at different times. The contemporary state compromises not just coercive aspects such as the police, prisons, and the criminal courts but also fire services and institutions for maintaining social health and education. State actors have multiple responsibilities: to balance the interests of both the repressive elements of the state and its more benign components, and to measure the interest of each against the needs of the people (even if, for many politicians, the latter seems to mean only the interests of their voters and the rich). It is wrong to treat this complex whole as a monolith, and this chapter does not.

Those complexities acknowledged, it is a discernible fact that, since 1945, in the United States and in almost every country in Europe, police forces have responded to clashes between fascists and anti-fascists by siding with the former rather than the latter, most recently (and very visibly) in clashes in Portland in the wake of George Floyd's murder at the hands of Minnesota police. As one author Talia Levin wrote in late 2020, drawing on the experience of anti-fascists since 2016:

> Anti-fascists and the police have a particularly antagonistic relationship … police forces throughout the country have disproportionately focussed their attention on leftists. Excessive police violence, lopsided arrest counts, and the punitive posting of mug shots associated with leftist activists have added to the hostility that already exists between leftist organisers and the police.[14]

If, in liberal theory, the courts and the police are ideally placed to put an end to hate speech (including speech of fascist origin), why has that not happened more often? Empirical studies of the 1940s have shown that the Metropolitan Police intervened more often on the side of fascists, and against the interests of anti-fascists.[15] The police arrested the latter at roughly three times the rate of fascists, in a context where both groups used violence, and although the fascists were organising in the aftermath of the war so that you would expect them to find considerable public disfavour. Police intervention also took other forms: for example, policemen would appear in court and insist that a particular speech had been orderly and respectful, while from the police notes which are now in the archives it is clear that the speech had dripped with open racist abuse.[16]

For one historian of British fascism, Graham Macklin, the decisions made by the Metropolitan Police in the 1940s are best understood if that force is seen as not pro-fascist or as anti-fascist but simply pro-police. In the force's eyes, they were the mere guardians of free speech and were, by definition, above the fray. The problem was that they were not neutral or inactive. Rather, they were imposing themselves on local communities, several of which (especially in Jewish areas of north and east London) did not want insulting and provocative marches routed through their area. Moreover, the longer that clashes between fascists and anti-fascists went on, the more force the police were required to use in order to remain the masters of the situation.[17]

Why, ultimately, were the police more likely to arrest ant-fascist rather than fascist meetings? Macklin's explanation begins with the police's conception of themselves as the sole body legitimately tasked with protecting the public from violence:

> The salient fact driving police hostility to fascist or anti-fascist demon-
> strators was their desire to protect their position as the guardians of pub-
> lic order … [T]he Commissioner of the Metropolitan police was fiercely
> opposed to direct action anti-fascism on the ideological grounds that it was
> not for "Communists" to dictate who should and should not be allowed to
> hold meetings.[18]

What Macklin conveys is that the police's ideas of themselves as simply holding the ring while two groups of undesirables fought each other, led them to inter-vene repeatedly. As the police saw it, the anti-fascists were the dynamic force in the conflict. The left was taking the initiative, forcing confrontations with the far right. Therefore, mere ordinary policing required them to arrest the left rather than fascists. Anti-semitism and anti-Communism also played their part, but the essential problem was something else. It was that the police saw anti-fascists as instigators and as challengers to their monopoly use of force. This was the institutional pressure requiring them to intervene on one side. It was the same logic that we encountered in the previous chapter, the same idea of the state as a neutral force which has, in reality, caused it to side with the far right.

Anti-fascists as troublemakers

A recurring point of controversy between anti-fascist and anti-racist approaches to political organising is that the latter is rooted in the self-emancipation of black people and others targeted by racism. The danger of anti-fascism, as the historian of the black Atlantic Paul Gilroy has warned, is that it portrays "neo-fascism as the most dangerous embodiment of contemporary racism," taking race "away from the centre of political culture" and "relocate[ing] it on the margins where these groups are doomed to remain."[19] The alternative to this danger, he argued, is to take black people's lives, their experiences and their struggles against the state, and to make these central to the strategies of the left in Britain and beyond. In his words:

> What anti-racism must do it if expects to be taken seriously by the black settlers in whose name it claims to act is to transcend this sociologism and move towards the longer-term aims of demonstrating the historical dimensions of "race" and bringing black fully into historicity, as actors capable of making complex choices in the furtherance of their own liberation.[20]

In contrast to this model of political change, anti-fascism is by contrast more footloose. It stands on the side of the anti-racists in their conflict with institutional racism but chooses to give greater priority to a single enemy (fascism) and confronts it on whatever ideological terrain it finds, whether racism, sexism, homophobia, the harassment of disabled people, or anyone else. A consistent anti-fascist might agree with Gilroy that fascism is on the margins now, and that as a matter of priorities it would be a waste of energy to harry it beyond a certain point. One place where they must disagree with him is in his assumption that history stands like an angel behind us, guaranteeing that fascism can never emerge from the margins to which it is forever doomed.

In the 1970s, a key task facing anti-fascists was to win the support of prominent black campaigners in the struggle against white racism. There is a long-standing controversy as to whether, how well, or how long they achieved this. Gilroy's arguments fitted within this context: he wanted to see more campaigns like Rock Against Racism, and ones that went further than RAR in creating a space for black self-liberation. In this context, he saw the Anti-Nazi League and the shift from anti-racist to anti-fascist politics which accompanied its launch as a step backwards.

The poet and songwriter Linton Kwesi Johnson wrote for the magazine *Race Today* and was one of the Race Today Collective's highest-profile members alongside Darcus Howe and Leila Hassan. In summer 1976 (i.e. at the time that Rock Against Racism was launched) Johnson was sceptical of the new initiative, fearing that it would be absorbed by the alphabet soup of existing, white-led socialist groups. He believed that "Sections of the white left in this country were trying to exploit the conditions that blacks found themselves in and trying to win us over to their various ideological positions. They saw us as victims."[21] After 1977, and the success of the Battle of Lewisham, when black and white anti-fascists working together defeated a march by the National Front, Johnson reconsidered. "What persuaded me to discard my cynicism about their motives was the Lewisham riot in 1977; that made me sit up and pay attention to what they were doing." For several years afterwards, Johnson participated in RAR as a performer and campaigner. With the benefit of hindsight, Johnson is proud to have been part of the movement: "Rock Against Racism was a great initiative. It isolated the fascists and helped to bring a significant number of black and white youth together with a shared vision of change."[22]

What is it about that protest that changed Johnson's opinion of anti-fascists? In the collective memory of 1977, Lewisham is often characterised as a moment of black and white unity in struggle. The Front sought to march through South East London and were repulsed. The crowd which fought them was a multiracial crowd, both black and white, and many other things besides. This is how it is portrayed, for example, in David Widgery's memoir, *Beating Time:*

> As the day became more brutal and frightening and the police, furious at their failure, turned to take revenge on the counter demonstrators, there was one big flash of recognition on the faces in the groups: between dread and socialist, between lesbian separatist and black parent, between *NME* speed freak and ASTMS branch secretary. We were together.[23]

It is easy to see in this image of a united crowd echoes of other, older protests; the Catholic dockers and the Jewish garment workers who clasped hands at Cable Street.

But Lewisham did not end with the dispersal of the Front, the bitter speech given by their Chairman John Tyndall, and his demands that the police "sort the Red mob out." Rather, protests continued well into the evening, when a younger, blacker, crowd took the fight from the National Front (who had fled the scene) to the Metropolitan Police, who were regarded locally with no less contempt than the fascists. One of those who remained on the scene through both moments of the struggle was a young Irish student Einde O'Callaghan:

> At that time, the pavements along Lewisham High Street were being newly paved with conveniently sized bricks. These were used to pelt the police. It was quite terrifying at first. We were occupying the street facing a line of police. Behind us were large numbers of young blacks who were lobbing half-bricks over our heads into the middle of the police – miraculously none of us seemed to be hit. The police would charge us, our line would part, and the young blacks would simply melt away into the side streets. Then the whole thing was repeated facing in the other direction. At some stage, the police brought out the riot shields, the first time they had been used on the "mainland."[24]

There is no way of knowing which Lewisham is the one that sparked Linton Kwesi Johnson's interest but it is worth taking seriously the possibility that it was the second of these protests – the one against the police, the vision of left political action creating a space for black urban insurgency – which gave him the greatest hope.

Johnson has a counterpart, in the US, in James Baldwin, whose 1965 speech to the Cambridge Union had this to say about the forces of the American police:

> Sheriff Clark in Selma, Ala., cannot be dismissed as a total monster; I am sure he loves his wife and children and likes to get drunk. One has to assume that he is a man like me. But he does not know what drives him to use the club, to menace with the gun and to use the cattle prod. Something awful must have happened to a human being to be able to put a cattle prod against a woman's breasts.[25]

To speak of Jim Clark was to speak of white America writ large. Racism, Baldwin argued, took a toll on its protagonists as well as on those it targeted. "It is a terrible thing for an entire people to surrender to the notion that one-ninth of its population is beneath them." Racism, he continued, had to be rejected. He invited his (predominantly white) audience to grasp that Americans were both black and white, and that Baldwin himself had ancestors who had been each. "I am not an object of missionary charity," said Baldwin, "I am one of the people who built the country." He raised the hope of a "new identity," to be forged in the fight for a different, equal, America.[26] And this could not happen, Baldwin's example shows, without weakening the power of the police.

From this perspective, the message of anti-fascism might be rather different than from how it is often understood. Seen through the prism of anti-racism (or any analogous project of resisting social inequality), the circuits of narrative meaning might go something like this. There are two ways in which such a struggle can end well:

One model of successful political organising

- Black people encounter racism (i.e. both popular and state racism).
- Black people are – perhaps – joined by white people. If not, then so be it.
- Black people are changed in conflict with racism, and learn to acquire a sense of their enemies as well as their own power: in the struggle, they become both the subjects and the objects of their own lives.

Another model of successful political organising

- Black people encounter racism (i.e. both popular and state racism).
- White people also encounter racism and are also repelled by it.
- White people agree to participate in a joint struggle against racism.
- Black people are changed in conflict with racism, and learn to acquire a sense of their enemies as well as their own power: in the struggle, they become both the subjects and the objects of their own lives.

- White people too are changed in the same struggle – they work as genuine equals of black political campaigners, not subordinating black people to white demands nor treating black people as objects of charity.
- Both black and white people become both the subjects and objects of their own lives.

In either route, and without needing to assume that only one of them is preferable, consistent anti-racist or indeed anti-fascist politics requires an idea that the oppressed are capable of resistance. The conflict of anti-racists with racists and with the state becomes the central moment by which people can take back control of their lives.

In Achille Mbembe's *Critique of Black Reason*, the transformation from struggle to liberation is characterised in the following terms:

> It served as a call to a people who were caught in the grip of their freedom, to take charge, to name themselves, to spring to life, and if they refused, they had at least to admit their bad faith in not doing so. They had to make a choice, risk their lives, exposed themselves and "draw on their most hidden resources." Such was the precondition for achieving liberty.[27]

One thing we may notice in this account, a sign of the similarity between anti-racist and anti-fascist accounts of their movements is the emphasis on individual and collective choice. The Italian anti-fascist Domenico Adriano recalls the collapse of the Italian state in 1943. "I suddenly became an adult … from that day I made my choice." Vito Salmi, condemned to death at the hand of a fascist firing squad told one friend, "I've done this of my own free will, so you mustn't cry." This sense of people finding themselves in response to oppression informs Sartre's ironic dictum, "Never have we been so free as under German occupation."[28]

The weakness of hate speech approaches is that they stop at the beginning of the narrative I have outlined: the oppressed encounter oppression. There is no role for struggle which becomes instead a task of persuasion. In hate speech analysis, there is no sustained attempt to distinguish between different strategies for stopping unwanted opponents. The overriding task is to stop hostile and demeaning language. If that can be done by protest, then all for the good. If it cannot, then it is appropriate to rely on the goodwill of an intervening authority, the state.

The point is not quite that hate speech approaches assume that the oppressed are incapable of resistance and require a neutral arbitrator (the state). It would be fairer to say that if some referee can be found then opponents of hate speech will deal with them. But the relocation of conflicts from a political to a legal setting has its cost. The oppressed are most likely to succeed there if they are meek and if they approach the state as their superior and change themselves to meet its demands. Continued protest removes their moral sheen – risks the danger that those resisting racism might be wrongly seen as the aggressor – and makes it harder for them to win their case.

The model which I have outlined of no platform does not require any judicial interlocutors, well-meaning or otherwise. The contribution of white anti-racists might (on occasion) be welcome. But, even if they choose not to contribute, a struggle is still needed both to challenge the power of personal and institutional racism, and to produce free people liberated from oppression.

As soon as you assume a conflict with the forces of the state it becomes hard to see the latter as a neutral force. If a successful struggle could take the form of thousands of people throwing bricks at a police station, then why would you expect the same police officers to agree with the anti-fascists, when they say that a fascist group should be banned from speaking? The police, organising as the police, can reasonably be expected to look with greater favour at the people who end their marches by demanding more power for the state. A judiciary, which depends on the police to bring criminals to court, could hardly disagree with them.

This surely is the point at which no platform departs from hate speech. Hate speech, in the words of the anti-fascist historian Devin Zane Shaw, "defers responsibility for community self-defence … to the state."[29] No platform, by contrast, does not seek a fair hearing in any court. Its supporters are trying rather to build their own power, and the power of the workers and oppressed people with whom they are in an unfinished dialogue.

No platform imagines an argumentative and militant people asserting their own rights.[30] No platform displays no excessive animus in relation to the state. It simply refuses to accept the logic that the rights of oppressed people, or indeed the rights of everyone to live free from fascism, require them to present themselves as the polite, deferential petitioners to a benign authority.

Rather, no platform sees the state as an agent in a three-sided conflict, with fascists on one side, anti-fascists on another and the police fighting assiduously in their own interests (with the press, the judiciary, etc., no distance behind). It acknowledges that the risk of co-option do not disappear simply if the authority being petitioned is not a police officer or a judge but an employer, or (as so often these days) a social media platform.

Notes

1 J. Waldron, *The Harm in Hate Speech* (Cambridge, MA: Harvard University Press, 2012), p. 58.
2 J. Waldron, 'Boutique Faith,' *London Review of Books*, July 2006; A. Lewis, *Freedom for the Thought We Hate* (New York: Basic Books, 2007), p. 163; Waldron, *The Harm*, p. 7.
3 *R v Relf and Cole* [1979] 1 Cr App R 111 at 112.
4 D. Renton, *Struck Out: How Employment Tribunals Fail Workers and What Can Be Done?* (London: Pluto, 2012).
5 N. Morris, 'Blair's "Frenzied Law-Making",' *Independent*, 16 August 2006.
6 P. Embery, *Despised: Why the Modern Left Loathes the Working Class* (Cambridge: Polity, 2021), pp. 123–126.

7 *R (Miller) v Secretary of State for Exiting the European Union* [2017] UKSC 5; *Miller, R (on the application of) v The Prime Minister* [2019] UKSC 41.

8 J. Fenton, 'An Evening with Robert Relf', *New Statesman*, 9 July 1976.

9 *Times*, 25 September 1984.

10 'Threat by Jailed Relf,' *Coventry Evening Telegraph*, 31 January 1979.

11 S. Dorrril, *Blackshirt: Sir Oswald Mosley and British Fascism* (London: Viking, 2006), pp. 434, 436, 442.

12 *R v Relf and Cole* [1979] 1 Cr App R 111 at 113.

13 Waldron, *The Harm*, p. 96.

14 T. Lavin, *Culture Warriors: My Journey to the Dark Web of White Supremacy* (London: Monoray, 2020), p. 225.

15 D. Renton, *Fascism, Anti-Fascism and Britain in the 1940s* (Houndmills: Palgrave, 2000), pp. 101–129.

16 Renton, *Fascism, Anti-Fascism*, pp. 111–112.

17 G. Macklin, '"A Plague on Both Their Houses": Fascism, Anti-Fascism and the Police in the 1940s,' in D. Renton and N. Copsey (eds), *British Fascism, the Labour Movement, and the State* (Houndmills: Palgrave, 2005), pp. 46–67.

18 Macklin, '"A Plague on Both Their Houses,"' p. 51.

19 P. Gilroy, *There Ain't No Black in the Union Jack: The Cultural Politics of Race and Nation* (London: Routledge, 1987), p. 148.

20 Gilroy, *There Ain't*, p. 150.

21 A. D'Ambrosio, *Let Fury Have the Hour: Joe Strummer, Punk and the Movement That Shook the World* (London: Nation, 2012), p. 216.

22 D. Rachel, *Walls Come Tumbling Down: The Music and Politics of Rock Against Racism, 2 Tone and Red Wedge* (London: Picador, 2016), p. 104.

23 D. Widgery, *Beating Time: Riot 'n' Race 'n' Rock and Roll* (London: Chatto and Windus, 1986), pp. 45–47.

24 D. Renton, *Never Again: Rock against Racism and the Anti-Nazi League 1976–1982* (London: Routledge, 2018), p. 82.

25 N. Buccola, *The Fire is Upon Us: James Baldwin, William F. Buckley Jr., and the Debate over Race in America* (Princeton: Princeton University Press, 2019), p. 384.

26 Buccola, *The Fire is Upon Us*, pp. 386–387.

27 A. Mbembe, *Critique of Black Reason* (Durham: Duke University Press, 2017), p. 167.

28 C. Pavone, *A Civil War: A History of the Italian Resistance* (London: Verso, 2013), pp. 32, 34, 39.

29 D. Z. Shaw, *Philosophy of Anti-Fascism: Punching Nazis and Fighting White Supremacy* (London: Rowman & Littlefield, 2020), p. 68.

30 A. Malkopoulou and L. Norman, 'Three Models of Democratic Self-Defence: Militant Democracy and Its Alternatives,' *Political Studies* 66/2 (2018), pp. 442–458.

PART III
Politics

10

THE BATTLE AGAINST HATE SPEECH GOES ONLINE

So far, the account in this book has assumed a struggle over speech rights which takes place in some public space: a square, outside a public broadcaster, or at university. But a recurring feature of politics in the last ten years has been that arguments over speech take place to an ever-greater extent online. From this perspective, one of the most important figures in the global far right has been the American far-right celebrity Richard Spencer. Around 2010 Spencer launched a radio station (Vanguard Radio) and a website AlternativeRight.com. On the latter, he interviewed celebrities from various right-wing traditions, both right-wing Republicans (such as Pat Buchanan, former Communications Director to Ronald Reagan) and mimetic fascists (including Matthew Heimbach of the Traditional Workers Party). Spencer was seeking to present himself as the American equivalent of the European New Right, a writer and intellectual. Borrowing the name for his website from the paleo-conservative writer Paul Gottfried, Spencer drew in marginal figures from numerous points at the far edge of US conservatism.

By 2014, a second group of people had been attracted to the alt-right. Many were not either fascists or conservatives, or at least not in the usual senses of those words. They were podcasters and bloggers rather than political organisers. Some called themselves "Men's Rights Advocates," and described the websites and online forums on which their views were welcome as the "manosphere." Others spoke of the "Dark Enlightenment," a philosophy which shared with certain strands of leftist thinking the idea that history was accelerating, except, in the mind of writers such as Curtin Yarvin or Nick Land, the direction of progress was towards elitism leadership, a new aristocracy of the spirit rather than political or social democracy.

Between summer 2016 and summer 2017, the alt-right in the United States was at the sharp edge of right-wing politics worldwide. It, better than anyone else, seemed to have grasped how to build a relationship between online culture and politics. At one event, Richard Spencer announced his admiration for the figure of the internet troll. The troll was the soul of the internet, he insisted, and the alt-right the soul of the troll.[1]

Spencer's notoriety was reinforced by a series of events: an alt-right conference in November 2016 where he declared "Hail Trump!"[2] Trump's inauguration two months later when Spencer was punched in the streets, and through 2017 the various marches that built up to the Unite the Right rally at Charlottesville. Spencer has found it almost impossible to live up to the part of the right-wing prankster. For someone who had built his career publishing dull and predictable books warning in semi-academic racist prose that the white race was on the verge of genocide, it was not an easy task reinventing himself as an Abbie Hoffman or a Jerry Rubin of the right. He was just too conventional, with his fashy haircut and his slate-grey suits. He drank. His former wife went to the courts with credible allegations of domestic violence.

A previous chapter described how, in early 2017, it was an effective strategy for the far right to seek invitations to speak on campus, with the explicit intention of provoking left-wing counter-protests, in response to which the right could present itself as the custodian of free speech. By the end of 2017, the balance of the argument had shifted. After the murder of Heather Heyer at Charlottesville, those watching from the side-lines were noticeably less forgiving of far-right provocations, and recognisably more sympathetic to anti-fascist protesters.[3] Richard Spencer sought to rebuild his popularity with a university speaking tour.[4] However, its centrepiece, a planned "alt-right" conference in Detroit in March 2018, had to be cancelled after protests. Venue after venue refused to host his talks. Events organised by the Traditional Workers Party were stopped by a flash mob of protesters. Spencer complained: "I don't think that it's a good idea for me to host an event that is wide open to the public."[5] Then, in August 2018, a Unite the Right 2 rally in Washington attended by barely 50 people was vastly outnumbered by a crowd of several thousand anti-fascist protesters.[6]

From this moment onwards – with the far right outnumbered in the streets and largely isolated (save for its patron in the White House), the major internet platforms were increasingly disturbed by complaints that they enabled the likes of Spencer.

Shane Burley, the historian and author of *Fascism Today*, has listed some of the examples of deplatforming that took place in 2019 and 2020. They include the *Daily Shoah* podcast, which was removed from iTunes, Twitter, and Facebook. By spring 2020, Andrew Anglin of the *Daily Stormer* was on the run. Spencer's audience too had collapsed. "Deplatforming," Burley wrote, "meaning removing certain figures and groups from the mass platforms that they share with the rest of us, was a death sentence for key players in the Alt Right."[7]

In summer 2020, the British anti-fascist campaign Hope not Hate published a piece agreeing with Burley. The author Joe Mulhall gave the example of Britain First. As of spring 2018, that group had an impressive online presence with two million likes on Facebook, making it the most popular political page in the country after the Royal Family. However, Facebook removed its page (as did Twitter). Two years later, Britain First had receded to much smaller platforms already dominated by the far right: Gab and the messaging app Telegram. Its audience on each (11,000 and 8,000 people) was 1 percent of what it had been.[8]

Former *Breitbart* journalist Milo Yiannopoulos has complained, in similar terms, of being forced onto sites with a marginal, far-right audience: "I can't post without being called a paedo kike infiltrator half a dozen times … I can't make a career out of a handful of people like that. I can't put food on the table this way."[9]

Over the next year, there would be further cases of deplatforming. In June 2020, Unilever, one of the world's purchasers of advertising space, announced that it would cease to advertise on Facebook, Instagram, or Twitter, blaming the prevalence of "divisiveness and hate speech" on these platforms. Within two days, Facebook was promising to tighten its policies, including by restricting content that contained hateful speech against migrants. Over the following weeks, YouTube banned former Klan leader David Duke, Richard Spencer, and so-called "race realist" Stefan Molyneux. Reddit deleted more than 2,000 subreddits including r/The_Donald.[10]

In November 2020, Steve Bannon encouraged violence against FBI director, Christopher Wray, and the infectious disease expert Dr Anthony Fauci, calling for them to be decapitated and their heads posted outside the White House as a "warning." Twitter banned Bannon (Facebook, however permitted Bannon to keep posting).[11]

One of the purposes of this book is to argue for no platform. Although deplatforming sounds like it should be the same idea updated for social media, it actually means lobbying social media companies to shut down far-right pages. Calling it deplatforming does not change the reality that it is significantly unlike no platform. Unlike the latter, this decision to ban far-right websites takes in a very wide set of speech practices directed potentially at any subaltern group. Again, unlike no platform, the agents of change turn out to be the huge platforms, and the businesses (the likes of Starbucks, Unilever, and Verizon) who buy advertising space from them.

If you stop history in summer 2020, then the equation is straightforward: the social media companies were willing to stop hateful voices who brought bad publicity to them. Their social interventions have whittled down the right's potential audience and made it harder for fascists and their allies to organise. The problem is accounting for the period between 2010 and 2018 when the same companies refused to close far-right pages. If deplatforming was such an obvious and all-round good, why did the companies refuse to employ it earlier?

The problem of effectiveness

Part of the answer is that deplatforming was not principally a response to antifascists making demands of the companies. Rather it was an attempt by them to relate to a much broader social movement: the uprising in American cities against racism in summer 2020. By the start of July 2020, there had been some 5,000 Black Lives Matter protests, in which more than 20,000,000 people had participated, and protests had been staged in a wider range of locations (including in small towns) than at any point in recent US history.[12] Such was the breadth of this movement, that the owners of social media had to do "something," in the same way that sports franchises felt no choice but to permit their stars to take the knee, or universities took an anxious look at the names of their historic buildings, or book publishers began to reassess their backlists. This book argues that, in quieter times, it would be a tactical mistake for anti-fascists to focus on deplatforming; but saying that is not in any way to criticise the street protesters who by confronting the state and the police were acting in the very insurgent spirit which is needed for any significant historical change.

On a longer perspective, if we want to understand why deplatforming did not happen sooner, part of the answer might be that discrimination has become hard-wired into our society: part of how we think and act and talk. As I set out earlier, in speaking of 1970s Britain, activists serious about challenging institutional racism could not do so without also challenging a series of institutions which divide along racial lines: our immigration prisons and our citizenship laws, our police, our courts, our newspapers. If we think of sex discrimination and homophobia, they are likewise structured into the nuclear family, our education system, etc. The corporate platforms that have been built up to profit from speech might look anxiously at their own spaces; they are incapable of challenging the police or the courts in the name of anti-racism or anti-sexism.

A 2018 documentary for Channel 4's Dispatches series showed the training Facebook gave to its staff, in which employees were shown images of a toddler being beaten by a man and a girl kicking another young woman unconscious. The show described how Facebook staff were encouraged to see such violent images as the means to drive viewer engagement and increase advertising revenue.[13] The same cynicism informed decisions to tolerate Britain First and Tommy Robinson. As one early investor in Facebook Robert McNamee put it, right-wing extremism was "the crack cocaine of their product – the really extreme, really dangerous form of content that attracts the most highly engaged people on the platform."[14]

Between joining Twitter in 2009 and summer 2017, Donald Trump posted more than 30,000 times, acquiring 36,000,000 followers. Every time he posted, and newspapers or television companies reported his latest outrage, he drove people onto the site to read him. From the perspective of the owners of the platform, he was devoting an incredible amount of time to boosting its profile. One financial analyst, James Cakmak, estimated that if Donald Trump had to leave Twitter the company's value would fall by $2,000,000,000.[15] From that perspective, we can start to see why social media companies were so slow to criticise his tweets – even when they promoted racism, sexism, or violence, and even when they retweeted obscure figures from the neo-Nazi fringe. The businesses gained more from hosting Trump than they could from challenging him.

This calculation was not fixed for all time. The media platforms assumed a thriving economy outside the computer screen, with real-world companies treating Facebook, Twitter, etc., as previous generations might have seen a busy inner-city road, as an opportunity to plaster countless advertising messages. There was always the possibility that if enough advertisers spoke out, the maths could turn against the right.

Indeed, this was what happened in summer 2020. The campaign Stop Hate For Profit brought together the likes of the Anti-Defamation League, the NAACP, Color of Change, Free Press, and Sleeping Giant. It was not just Unilever who, under the influence of the Black Lives Matter protests, threatened to withdraw its advertising from the social media giants. Some 900 companies including Coca-Cola and Ford Motor Company signed up to the campaign, urging the social media platforms to tighten up their rules.

But the victories which were won were only possible in an extremely favourable context: the dying days of the Trump administration, at a time when it felt as if the Republican President, by failing to acknowledge the risk of Coronavirus or fight the disease, had betrayed large parts of his own voting base.[16] This was a time when public support for Black Lives Matter was overwhelming, and businesses wanted to be seen offering campaigns for race justice more than the usual empty platitudes of support. Those had not been the circumstances of the preceding decade during which the social media companies repeatedly gave a platform to the right.

In summer 2020, the campaign for deplatforming seemed to go from success to success. But it was a strategy which bore concealed risks. A previous chapter has described how the impetus to the rise of a Tommy Robinson street movement was provided by the decision of Twitter to close his account in 2018. In Britain, deplatforming increased Robinson's support. There have been other instances of the same unintended consequences: for example, the rise of the far-right media celebrity Laura Loomer who was banned from Twitter in November 2018, after numerous stunts, including denying the citizenship of prominent Muslim politicians, interrupting a performance of Shakespeare's *Julius Caesar* to denounce "violence against the right," and boasting about refusing to take rides from "Islamic immigrant[s]" on Uber. Loomer was backed by Trump, and in August 2020 secured the Republican nomination to stand for Congress in the Palm Beach district of Florida.[17] (Loomer went on to win over 150,000 votes, or 39 percent of the poll, in a traditionally Democrat seat.)[18] So, while banning is rarely in the interest of any of these figures, it provides an opportunity to the right, and where the right takes up that chance it can magnify its audience.

Moreover, it is not unrealistic to think that, over a longer timescale, the right could succeed in building up such platforms as Gab or Parler, until they reach the point where they are mass media providers, capable of competing with the likes of Facebook. There is still a long way for them to go: at the start of August 2019,

Gab was claiming that it enjoyed a million regular visitors, three times as many as at the start of the year but less than 0.1 percent of the audience of Facebook. By November 2020, Parler was claiming 10,000,000 users worldwide.[19] It seemed unlikely that the right-wing platforms would be able to compete seriously with the main social media platforms any time soon. But 20 or 25 years ago, few people would have predicted the growth and takeover of sites such as Reddit, let alone the capture of parts of them by the far right, or the use of sites such as 8chan or later Telegram to promote terrorism.

One way you can tell the story of anti-fascism is as a series of political innovations by each side. So that in 1930–1934, Mosley built the British Union of Fascists as parties for disgruntled Conservatives; after which the left retaliated (i.e. innovated) by forcing its way into fascist meetings and daring to attack the right with violence. This tactic embarrassed the BUF, barely one tenth of whose members at the time of Olympia were still paying their subscriptions 12 months later. In response, the BUF innovated again by relocating geographically and aiming at a milieu of East End anti-semites. The left retaliated with mass protests appealing to parts of the same audience: Cable Street. After which the right, innovated once more, turning towards a generation of middle-class pacifists, a strategy which worked until internment.

The conflict between left and right is a struggle marked by conflict and repeated bursts of political creativity, with each side capable of adapting to hostile circumstances. It follows that no single strategy is guaranteed of success for all time. The best any anti-fascist tactic can achieve is simply a period of relative hegemony. From that perspective, we should anticipate that the right will retaliate to online deplatforming with strategies of its own. As of 2020, deplatforming appears to work; it is unlikely to seem quite as successful in 10, or in 20 years' time.

The traditional free speech warning against attacks on hate speech is that they risk empowering the state (or, in this case, the owners of the largest social media companies). The danger is that Facebook and other platforms already use these powers widely. Journalists Julia Angwin and Hannes Grassegger have accused Facebook of making its decisions arbitrarily. They cited the example of a Republican member of Congress, demanding the murder of his political opponents and those posts staying up untouched, while relatively banal posts by Black Lives Matter supporters were removed.[20]

The left and the right are never simply fascist or anti-fascist but combine multiple other causes. What we achieve in one moment of struggle can have all sorts of unintended consequences elsewhere. So, one of the most censored forms of political speech has been pro-Palestinian activism. West Bank media outlets Quds News Network and Shehab News Agency have had their Facebook accounts closed. The Palestinian Authority's ruling party Fatah had its page blocked by the platform. So ubiquitous was Facebook's determination to close pro-Palestinian speech that campaigners responded with a hashtag, #FBCensorsPalestine.[21]

In September 2020, Facebook temporarily closed accounts of activists who had given support for the campaign of indigenous people in the Wet'suwet'en territory against the construction of a 670-kilometre hydrofracturing ("fracking") gas pipeline through British Columbia in Canada. Two hundred people were told that they had "infringe[d] or violate[d] others' rights or ... violate[d] the law" and prevented from using the social media platform. While Facebook said it had taken this action "mistakenly," and not as a result of corporate lobbying in favour of the gas pipeline, notably only opponents of the pipeline were censored.[22]

In November, another "accidental" censorship took place, after three members of the Egyptian Initiative for Personal Rights were arrested and jailed, penalised after they had met with foreign diplomats and briefed them on the human rights abuses carried out by that country's military regime. Twitter closed down the EIPR account for several hours, before backing down under pressure and switching the account back on.[23]

By late 2020, the social media platforms were conscious of a need to be seen not merely banning right-wing hate speech but also incendiary political comment when it came from the left, if only to insist that they were not favouring one side over another but treating all comment the same once it crossed an invisible line. So, Facebook and Instagram began to refuse links to anti-fascist and anarchist pages, including the American pages It's Going Down, CrimethInc. and the German site Enough is Enough. In a statement, Facebook accepted that these groups were not "dangerous organisations," nor did they "organi[se] violence." However, it claimed that individual supporters of these group had shown "violent behaviour," and on that basis, it was appropriate to "restrict [anti-fascists] ability to organise on our platform."[24]

The lesson seemed to be that a well-connected protest movement might overturn a social media ban; but the further left you were, the harder it was to prevent such censorship.

Leftists sometimes fall into the trap of assuming that hate speech arguments are likely to prove especially fruitful to them, since the people they oppose are often the defenders of racial or sexual privilege. But one of the lessons of the past few years is that, both online and offline, justice campaigns have been defeated by an argument to the effect that their levelling intentions in fact conceal a hateful purpose. In Britain, we have seen that argument employed effectively against both advocates of gender recognition for trans people, and supporters of Palestine. A similar dynamic could be seen in the decision of the UK government in 2016, to adopt the International Holocaust Remembrance Alliance definition of anti-semitism and its associated examples,[25] which have the effect of treating most if not all pro-Palestinian advocacy as racist.

In November 2020, Tony Lerman, previously the Director of the Institute for Jewish Policy Research (JPR) in London, looked back on Labour's crisis. There was clear evidence of Labour members trading in classic anti-semitic tropes relating to Jewish bankers and Holocaust denial, Lerman accepted. Yet, he insisted, it was

> [T]he suppression of open discourse around Israel-Palestine – whether it is
> a Palestinian narrating the simple truth of their own family's experience of
> ethnic cleansing, accusations that Israel is an apartheid state, BDS advocacy
> … and so on – that fans the flames of the antisemitism story.[26]

If the British government, many local councils, and the Labour Party[27] have all
adopted the IHRA's reasoning and prohibited pro-Palestinian speech, it would
be bold to expect Facebook or Twitter to do any better.[28]

The purpose of this book is to put the case for preventing certain kinds of
speech without falling into censorship. There is no clear means to make the
social media businesses accountable for the decisions they take as publishers. In
increasing their power to decide that (this week) Breitbart or the *Daily Stormer* as
an unreliable source, we are also increasing their freedom to reduce access to the
Guardian or *Truthout* in favour of Fox News. In calling on the platforms to act,
the left and protest movements are petitioning businesses with different interests
to our own.

Social media platforms are private spaces

Social media platform are intensely undemocratic spaces. The previous chapters
have criticised hate speech doctrine (of which deplatforming is only the most
recent variant) for its dependence on some assumed neutral authority to carry out
the request to prevent unwanted speech. But, in comparison to the usual focus
of hate speech approaches, i.e. the state, private companies are a bastion of power
almost always unresponsive to popular demands.

There are no elections to decide the composition of Facebook's Board of
Directors or of its Governance or Oversights committees. Its members hold their
positions for as long as they retain the support of the group's founder. The reason
Mark Zuckerberg is so powerful is not just his status as Facebook's founder, but
in particular the corporate structure he established, creating two categories of
share: 2,400,000,000 Class A shares, which are open to purchase by ordinary
investors through the stock market, and 398,000,000 Class B shares, which are
his exclusively for life. In contested votes, under Facebook's rules, each Class B
share is given a voting weight equivalent to ten times the value of each Class A
share. Even if every single individual shareowner agreed, and there was a complete unanimity of all opinion save for Zuckerberg's, he would still out-vote all
the other investors every time.[29]

Deplatforming assumes that some privileged actor can be used to guarantee
the online speech rights of oppressed people, whether through the intervention of sympathetic businesses or the law. But the way in which free speech law
has been used in the United States in controversies such as campaign funding
has been to prioritise the rights of the rich and the corporate entities behind
which they shield, at the expense of everyone else. So, in *Citizens United v Federal
Election Commission*, the Supreme Court ruled that the "prohibition on corporate

independent campaign expenditures is an 'outright ban' on speech in violation of the First Amendment."[30] The consequence has been to reinforce a political system in which it is considered normal, even essential, that billionaires fund candidates, who spend roughly a hundred times as much in each election as their counterparts for office in Europe. It has massively entrenched what was already a system of government by and for the rich.

Or, to take another example, in 2018, when employers sought to destroy the limited remaining power of America's public sector trade unions, the mechanism they chose was to attack arrangements under which employees had union fees automatically deducted from the employer at source. The Supreme Court ruled that such an arrangement violated the First Amendment rights of workers who did not want to join trade unions, with Justice Alito writing for the Court that, "fundamental free speech rights are at stake."[31]

The point is not just that, in general, free speech is used to protect the rights of companies in relation to the rights of ordinary citizens, so that free speech is like a set of scales which are loaded not on the side of unhindered expression but of oligarchy. In US law, private space is considered an empty zone, in which the First Amendment's free speech protections simply cease to apply given the absence of a governmental actor. With very limited exceptions (such as where a private space, like a shopping mall, becomes a well-established public gathering place), the parallel free speech protections incorporated in most state constitutions have been held not to protect protests or other speech on privately owned property. State courts have held that free speech rights cease to apply as soon as the speaker crosses the gate of a private property.[32]

Even in Britain and Europe, our notions of free speech assume a public space. The leading case under Articles 10, 11, and 13 of the European Convention of Human Rights is *Appleby v UK*, which concerned the rights or otherwise of people in Tyne and Wear who were protesting against the granting of planning permission to a local college to build on the town's only available playing field. The one place which could provide them an opportunity to petition publicly was itself a privately owned supermarket. It refused permission, and that decision was supported by the European Court of Human Rights, the ECHR holding that human rights law protects the rights of the individual to speak on private property (against the refusal of the owner to permit freedom of expression), only if there was no other way in which speech could be expressed, and the refusal would "destroy" altogether the petitioner's chance to speak.[33]

Some readers will recall a time when online discussion was minimal, when it was something which took place in universities and through an electronic infrastructure which excluded the vast majority of people, and when other means of international communication (e.g. by telephone) was prohibitively expensive. If you had said to anyone 30 years ago that we were on the verge of a transformation in people's ability to speak, opening up interpersonal communication to billions of people, the prospect would have filled every one of us with delight.

While the theme of this chapter is the opportunity provided by the growth of networked capitalism to the far right; this is not to say that social media is only a negative phenomenon. Billions of people devote their creativity and ingenuity to the effort to make that experience as pleasant as possible. A shared experience on this scale could not simply be unpleasant, any more than all "food" or all "water" could be bad. Yet the fact that this speech is mediated – i.e. communication controlled by huge businesses – has replaced the prospect of liberation with something less positive. In his book *The Twittering Machine*, Richard Seymour writes that,

> To inhabit social media is to be in a state of constant distractedness, a junkie fixation on keeping in touch with it, knowing where it is and how to get it … whether or not we think we are addicted, the machine treats us as addicts.[34]

In *Antisocial*, his account of the alt-right and of social media, the left-liberal journalist Andrew Marantz focusses on the rise of clickbait – meaning both the practice of abbreviating content, and the companies which specialise in this kind of media production. The viral internet promotes content which inspires "activating" emotions, i.e. awe, anxiety, anger. It ignores "deactivating" emotions (sadness) and responses (contemplation, analysis). The latter, he argues, are just as essential to us as the former; online capitalism treats them as market inefficiencies.[35]

Seymour focusses on the architecture of social media and the "like" button which was introduced on most platforms between 2011 and 2012. Superficially, the purpose of this function was to make discussions more pleasant. In reality, it has discouraged long, free-ranging, playful interactions between different people in favour of pithy and wry statements – the one-line take-down. The reward for being liked, Seymour observes, is a small hit of dopamine. The process is a dissatisfying one, as with any addiction, for with each repetition of the pleasure-chemical, its positive effect is a little less gratifying. It is not a coincidence that a global fascination with being liked has encouraged a generation of dislikeable politicians: Trump, Salvini, and Modi. [36]

Social media platforms and culture wars

Five or ten years ago, you would often find on the left a critique of the tech giants for their social policies and, above all, for the way in which they had opted themselves out of the tax system. In so doing, these big businesses ensured that most people had worse access to healthcare, education, and so on. Moreover, they contributed to the circumstances which drove the right-wing backlash in 2016–2019. It was precisely because states were weak, impoverished and refused to offer their people any real prospect of serious reform, that centre-right voters found themselves open to the argument that radical outsiders were needed to (in Donald's Trump's phrase) "drain the swamp."

By mid-2020, the wealth of Facebook's Mark Zuckerberg was $80,000,000,000 almost all of it contained in the share price of his company. He was the world's fourth-richest person. And by the time you read this his wealth will almost certainly have grown further: since the company went public in 2012, Facebook's share price has been growing at the rate of roughly $50,000,000,000 a year, earning Zuckerberg a personal wealth bonus (i.e. an effective income) of about $8,000,000,000 a year. Part of the reason his wealth has been able to increase at this rate is that his company has opted out of the tax system. First, it only declares a small proportion of its annual earnings as profits. Second, of the money it chooses to declare as profits, almost all is then routed through offshore tax havens, principally Bermuda, Ireland, Luxembourg, and the Netherlands.[37]

If somehow his wealth could be frozen tomorrow, and Zuckerberg simply never earned another cent in his entire life, his wealth of $80,000,000,000 would be as much as the average American worker could reasonably expect to earn in the next 2,000,000 years or so – that is, for about as long as there have been human beings on this planet.

For 40 years American schools and hospitals and libraries have been steadily defunded, and that even spending on the sorts of infrastructure you need to keep an economy functional (e.g. roads, water, electricity) has been cut substantially. The wealth of the major companies has been achieved, in other words, at public expense. People are poorer, their lives diminished, and they are in greater debt because of a series of behaviours ("neoliberalism") at the heart of which is the diminishing willingness of the rich to pay tax, and for which there could be no better poster boys than the owners of the social media platforms. Why then would anyone give Mark Zuckerberg more power than he already has?

Alternatives to painting social media better than it is

The point of this chapter is not to deprecate the decisions taken by social media platforms to close down far-right activists, but to caution against celebrating these decisions, and to warn against spending time and resources lobbying the social media platforms. There have in fact been numerous anti-fascist strategies which have been used to counter the far right, without relying on deplatforming, but while building the protest capacity of popular movements.

In his sociology of anti-fascist protest movements, *American Antifa*, Stanislav Vysotsky shows that for most of the recent history of American anti-fascist campaigns (i.e. Rose City Antifa, the One People's Project, and similar groups) by far the most common activities have been information- and intelligence-gathering about proposed fascist activities, followed by publicly shaming the men and women who take part in them. Almost all the instances that Vysotsky gives of either task previously took place offline; for example, searching in county courthouse records to track the names of fascists who had been convicted of criminal offences, looking through telephone directories, collecting paper archives of fascist activities and publicising the results of such research through face-to-face meetings, leafletting in the neighbourhood of prominent fascists, or printing magazines containing the identities of fascists.[38] In the last decade, almost all of these activities have gone online. Even as they have done so, they have kept their primary focus on the capacity of the right (and the left) to control the streets.

Such projects imply the existence of a locally based anti-fascist campaign which can then go over from tactics such as intelligence-gathering to street demos and other public protests as the situation demands. They assume collective organising and increase the capacity of anti-fascist groups to protest, rather than leaving everything to the whims of remote tech businesses.

Moreover, there are many things you can do online rather than simply campaign for people you disagree with to be banned. So, in autumn 2020, the anti-fascist coalition Merseyside Anti-Fascist Network was faced with a problem that long-time supporters of far-right groups, as well as advocates of anti-semitic conspiracy theories, were sheltering in popular Facebook groups such as The People's Republic of Liverpool, a page where messages in support of ousted Labour leader Jeremy Corbyn could be read beside claims that the threat of COVID was exaggerated, or that the government had unfairly targeted Merseyside, subjecting the region to Tier 3 lockdowns before anywhere else. Members of MAFN settled on different tactics: criticising their ideas, challenging right-wing speakers, and pointing out their history of involvement in fascist organisations. Where anti-lockdown groups sprang up, MAFN tried to use their existing connections with people who had a history of protesting or left-wing organising to isolate far-right cadres. I give this example not to say that this was a unique piece of campaigning by that group, but rather as an instance of the sort of patient organising that occurs to activists naturally.

A number of left-wing speakers in recent years have built their appeal in part by the way they fascinate the right and live in the heads of the right's own militants: Alexandria Ocasio-Cortez in relation to Fox News, Ash Sarkar in Britain. Between spring 2018 and spring 2019, Ocasio-Cortez's Twitter following grew from 50,000 to 3,500,000 people. An early profile in *Time* magazine described Ocasio-Cortez as the "preferred punching bag of Fox News pundits."[39] It helped her rise that Fox News attacked her; onlookers supported her against them. Between 25 February and 7 April 2019, Ocasio-Cortez was mentioned on Fox News Channel or Fox Business Network 3,181 times, or 76 times per day.[40] Much of this obsession was down to the skilful way in which she was using social media, appealing as often to the non-political views and habits of her supporters as she was to the ideology. Think, for example, of her response to one attempted right-wing take-down on social media: when a Republican supporter unearthed an old college film in which Ocasio-Cortez and student friends had filmed themselves dancing together in the style of the dance scene from the 1985 teen comedy *The Breakfast Club*. Ocasio-Cortez's response was to put out a new film of her dancing to Edwin Starr's "War? What is it good for?" as she walked smiling through the door of her office in Congress.

Ocasio-Cortez was insisting on the rights of women to be elected to Congress, and of the young to be represented. The clip was cultural, it appealed to the tens or hundreds of millions of people who had watched that film or heard that song. It did not respond to the right by insisting on Ocasio-Cortez's weakness, but her power: her joy in her election, and in the simple act of dancing. Think how much weaker it would have been if Ocasio-Cortez had complained of a breach of her privacy or demanded that the video of her dancing with her classmates be taken down from the websites of the private companies on which it was embodied.

Plainly, Ocasio-Cortez's response was made possible by the character of the attack on her, as well as the position she held. It is easy to imagine different kinds of right-wing attack, to which a deplatforming-campaign might be the only available response.

However, the success of these and similar tactics shows that in many circumstances it is possible to confront the right and build up anti-racist or anti-fascist causes, without appealing to the goodwill of the super-rich.

Notes

1 S. Burley, 'The Autumn of the Alt-Right,' *Commune*, 21 February 2020.
2 D. Lombroso and Y. Applebaum, '"Hail Trump!" White Nationalists Salute the President-Elect,' *The Atlantic,* 21 November 2016.
3 J. Wilson, 'How the World Has Fought Back against the Violent Far-Right and Started Winning,' *Guardian*, 19 December 2018.
4 S. Burley, 'The "Alt-Right" Is Building a White Nationalist Mass Movement with "Operation Homeland"' *Truthout*, 18 February 2020.
5 S. Burley, 'The Fall of the "Alt-Right" Came from Anti-Fascism,' *Salon*, 16 April 2018.
6 D. Andone, M. Simon, and S. Sidner, 'White Nationalists Dwarfed by Crowds of Counterprotesters in Washington,' *CNN*, 12 August 2018.
7 Burley, 'The Autumn of the Alt-Right.'
8 J. Mulhall, 'Deplatforming Works: Let's Get on with It,' *Hope not Hate*, 4 October 2019.
9 Mulhall, 'Deplatforming Works.'
10 A. Hern, 'YouTube Bans David Duke and other US Far-Right Users,' *Guardian*, 30 June 2020.
11 Guardian Staff, 'Mark Zuckerberg Defends Not Suspending Steve Bannon from Facebook,' *Guardian*, 13 November 2020.
12 T. Waite, 'Black Lives Matter Is the Biggest Movement in US History, Data Suggests,' *Dazed*, 5 July 2020.
13 A. Hern, 'Facebook Protects Far-Right Activists even after Rule Breaches,' *Guardian*, 17 July 2018.
14 S. Dent, 'Facebook Accused of Shielding Far-Right Activists Who Broke Its Rules,' *Engadget*, 17 July 2018.
15 J. Wittenstein, 'What Is Trump Worth to Twitter? One Analyst Estimates $2 Billion,' *Bloomberg*, 17 August 2018.
16 D. Renton, 'Trump Downplayed COVID at His Town Hall. No Wonder He's Losing Older Voters,' *Truthout*, 16 October 2020.
17 A. Naughtie, 'Laura Loomer: Far-Right "Proud Islamophobe" Wins Republican Primary in Florida,' *Independent*, 19 August 2020.
18 'Florida 21st Congressional District Results,' *New York Times*, 3 November 2020.

19 S. Manavis, 'Can the Right Thrive on Parler?' *New Statesman*, 17 November 2020.
20 J. Anglin and H. Grassegger, 'Facebook's Secret Censorship Rules Protect White Men from Hate Speech but Not Black Children,' *ProPublica*, 28 June 2017.
21 Anglin and Grassegger, 'Facebook's Secret Censorship.'
22 G. Woody, 'How Facebook Tried to Censor Indigenous Struggle,' *RS21*, 7 October 2020.
23 @EIPR, Twitter, 26 November 2020.
24 'This Page Isn't Allowed,' *Freedom*, 21 August 2020.
25 J. Neuberger, *Antisemitism. What It Is. What It Isn't. Why It Matters* (London: Weidenfeld & Nicolson, 2019), p. 38.
26 A. Lerman, 'Fighting Labour Antisemitism Must Not Come at the Cost of Palestinian Rights,' *972 Magazine*, 26 November 2020.
27 D. Renton, 'The EHRC Report: A Missed Chance,' *Labour Hub*, 29 October 2020.
28 L. Harpin, 'UK Anti-Racist Groups Sign Letter to Facebook Alongside Tommy Robinson-Supporting Organisation,' *Jewish Chronicle*, 18 August 2020.
29 M. Hiltzik, 'Facebook Shareholders Are Getting Fed up with Zuckerberg but Can't Do Anything about Him,' *Los Angeles Times*, 17 April 2019.
30 *Citizens United v Federal Election Commission*, 130 S. Ct. 876, 897 (2010).
31 *Janus v AFSCME*, Council 31 – 138 S. Ct. 2448, 2460 (2018).
32 *Prune Yard Shopping Center v. Robins*, 447 US 74 (1980); N. J. Newman, 'A Bloody Problem: Free Speech and Private Property Rights Collide in California,' *American Bar Association*, 14 April 2020.
33 (2003) 37 EHRR 38.
34 R. Seymour, *The Twittering Machine* (London: Indigo Press, 2019), p. 31.
35 A. Marantz, *Antisocial: How Online Extremists Broke America* (London: Picador, 2020 edn), pp. 81–82.
36 Seymour, *The Twittering Machine*, pp. 48–52; O. Laing, *Crudo* (London: Picador, 2018), pp. 43, 86–87.
37 M. Sweeney, 'Facebook Paid Just £28m Tax after Record £1.6bn Revenues in UK,' *Guardian*, 11 October 2019.
38 S. Vysotsky, *American Antifa: The Tactics, Culture and Practice of Militant Anti-fascism* (London: Routledge, 2021), pp. 83–85.
39 C. Alter, '"Change Is Closer Than We Think", Inside Alexandria Ocasio-Cortez's Unlikely Rise,' *Time*, 21 March 2019.
40 D. Bauder, 'Study: Fox News Is Obsessed with Alexandria Ocasio-Cortez,' *AP News*, 13 April 2019.

11

ON BEING SILENCED, MASCULINITY, VICTIMHOOD

This book has noted the complaint of the far right that it is being silenced. This chapter examines that grievance by asking three linked questions, how do the supporters of the far right feel when the chance to speak is taken away from them? Who do they think they are speaking for? And how does this act of speaking for others change them?

The main sources for this chapter are 60 interviews with the supporters of the English Defence League carried out between February 2011 and May 2012 by the sociologist Joel Busher. The first thing he noticed about his interviewees was they spent *a lot* of time online: they argued with their families, they would go on social media and argue for hours there with strangers ("lefties," "trolls," "muz-zies") and would attend EDL demonstrations tired and worn out by all the argu-ing.[1] Activists created a narrative to justify the hours they sacrificed to politics, and central to it was the idea that, although they were expressing themselves in public, and speaking much more than the people around them, they needed to do so – the alternative was to be unfairly silenced.

Repeatedly, Busher was told a variant of the same story. An EDL supporter owned their own house, on the side of which they had fixed a large St George's flag. A stranger (a Muslim, perhaps, or a left-winger) asked them to take the flag down. At first, the stranger was polite – saying the flag made a noise at night-time and disturbed them. But when the EDL homeowner stood their ground, the stranger would reveal the politics beneath their request. Here, for example, is one version of this right-wing folktale, as told to Busher by "Susan" (a pseudonym)"

> I went, "My flag, my St. George's Cross flag offends you?" He went, "Yeah!" So, I went, "Do yourself a favour." I went, "What's coming out of your mouth is offending me." I said, "All it smells of is bullshit, like that." I said, "I live in England, I was born in England." I said, "So do yourself

a favour, put your Reeboks on and do one because I'm not taking it lying down."[2]

Busher heard the same story too often with too many different people casting themselves in the part of the offended homeowner, for it to be true. Or, you could say, that its truths were never intended to be purely literal. The story explained a moment when right-wing opinions were corroborated: it is a story of conversion to activism. It reflected the belief of his interviewees that they were a put-upon and unfairly criticised minority.

Another recurring feature of these stories was that other white people were repeatedly no help at all. They were supposed to show solidarity to the EDL narrator, but instead they had confused themselves with the false idea that black people or Muslims might be capable of suffering racism. When black people or Muslims were criticised, "they" were alright, because "they" could draw on a huge quantity of supportive organisations, Amnesty, Liberty, the unions, etc. But when patriots were reprimanded, there was no one speaking up for them. Another interviewee, "Eddie," explained these double standards, telling Busher about an occasion when Eddie had, on his own account, "confronted" a group of his Asian work colleagues, or, as he called them, "Islamists":

> I just remember the total hand-wringing reaction of this little ginger bas-
> tard … He said [adopting a whining tone of voice], "You were so rude to
> him, you were so rude to poor Usman." I said, "I wasn't rude to the guy at
> all." I said, "Challenge extremism wherever you find it." I said, "If I was
> making pro-Nazi statements or something like that, you wouldn't hesitate
> to be in my face about it, but with them, you just sit there and smile!"[3]

Again, in November 2011 nearly 200 EDL supporters were arrested after a brief march followed by a long drinking session allowing Whitehall to celebrate the fact that an Islamist group "Muslims Against Crusaders" had been banned. They fought with the police officers, and many were arrested. One of the EDL sup-porters, "Rob," complained to Busher about the double standards of civil liber-ties groups who refused to help deserving patriots:

> Where were all – you know, where are Liberty and Amnesty International
> rushing out screaming, "What about these people's human rights?" You
> know? If we were students, rioters, or black youths, whatever they'd be
> bending over backwards.[4]

In the ideology of the far right, it is good that a group such as Muslims Against Crusaders should be harassed by the state and its members jailed. On the same logic, it is reasonable to make racist or pro-Nazi statements at work or to con-front your Asian colleagues – injustice occurs only when a work colleague hears your speech and replies by disagreeing with it.

Being silenced *hurts*

Any study of right-wing activism is likely to note the contrast between the relatively short period in which its members respond to criticism by taking to the streets (their own, private, "St George's flag" moment), and the long period in which they bemoan the large majority of people who are insufficiently patriotic, who are not rallying to the cause, and who betray those who do. Busher's book, for example, ends with a lengthy post from one of his interviewees, "Graham," who wanted the world to know that he had "had the doom well and truly earlier and it's still lingering." He mourned the closed pubs, the hostile faces of new migrants ("the dregs of the third world"), and the absence of butchers save for Halal ones. It was clear where Graham was heading, into longer periods of silence and despair.[5]

There is also a similar sense of misery in the second half of Billy Blake's memoir, *Coming Down the Road.* The book's 260-page account of the EDL's greatest moments opens optimistically enough, with claims that patriotic English people were fed up with being prevented from speaking ("England was in the grip of a political correctness obsession, the cultures of minority groups were being lauded, the host culture ridiculed or ignored").[6]

Halfway through the book, however, "top lads" were leaving the movement, while Tommy Robinson had fallen in with the wrong crowd. Blake blamed the decay of the EDL on outside "dark forces." By early 2011, the EDL was desperately closing its own internet forum, objecting that members were using neo-Nazi slurs and talking points. "Football hooligans and other ordinary activists … were suddenly surplus to requirements."[7] Tommy Robinson began taking to the stage at protests and denouncing disloyal supporters, who would then be beaten up in front of him.

At the end of Blake's account,

> The EDL is in disarray, too many people want a slice of the action and control in some way. Of course, this is only a reflection of the narcissistic society we have allowed to develop, in which people are not happy being a small anonymous cog in a big wheel, the Jeremy Kyle generation crave attention.[8]

The imagination of the far right, in other words, begins and ends with shame. Both at the start and end of the narrative, there is collective decline and individual despair.[9] In author and far-right researcher Talia Lavin's account of white nationalism in the US, the voice which captures this best is a prospective suitor who tells her:

> The world will not forgive us for this, it will not forget. It seeks to destroy this beauty, our beauty. It wishes that we would vanish, that our progeny would never come to pass. It hates and loathes us. This is a heavy burden we must bear, and with it we must arm ourselves against the world.[10]

The supporter of the far right begins as a victim and ends no better.

Even the leaders of the far right express a similar anomie. This was what it was like, for example, to be sitting in court in July 2018, at the time of former EDL leader Tommy Robinson's appeal against his conviction for contempt of court. Robinson was able to follow the proceedings only remotely, relying on a video link from Woodhill Prison. "Can you see your barrister?" the usher asked. "Yeah." "Can you see the judges?" "Yeah. Are they supposed to be that small?" Bored, ignored by the lawyers in court, Robinson was all "please" and "thank you" and trying hard to look serious. "I'm not nervous before a court case," he said, "not usually." Soon enough the sound was switched off, leaving Robinson picking distractedly at his shirt.[11]

When they spoke, his lawyers made every effort to present Robinson as a champion of good relations between different communities. Yes, they accepted, Tommy Robinson's livestreaming from outside Leeds Crown Court breached an order made earlier year, which banned any person from publishing any report of those proceedings. And yes, Robinson was already subject to a suspended sentence from a similar contempt. But Robinson, his barrister Jeremy Dein QC explained, had been learning how to be a journalist. He had been trying to better himself for the purpose of challenging extremism. A reputable solicitor's firm, Kingsley Napley,[12] had apparently trained Robinson and warned him where the line was between legitimate and illegitimate behaviour. Tommy Robinson was a delicate man, Dein continued, the victim of self-doubt. When in prison, he suffered anxiety, butterflies to the stomach. It was grotesque and unfair, Robinson's lawyers said, that he had been kept in prison in solitary conditions.[13]

The women are victims; men must speak out

In his memoir, *Enemy of the State*, Robinson attempted to retell the story of his political career, insisting that this need to defend white women was there from the start. He described his cousin Jeanette, a woman of about his own age. As a teenager, Robinson said, Jeanette was "groomed" by a gang of Pakistani men, persuaded by them to acquire a heroin addiction, after which she was "gang-raped by half a dozen Muslim men."[14] Jeanette apparently returned home, only to escape again. At the end of his story, Jeanette had converted to Islam and married a Muslim. She now had six children. The family could not see her, Robinson complained, even if she remained in Luton. Even if they were on the same street as her, she would be unrecognisable beneath a burka.

There are many reasons to be sceptical about this account. The story is too convenient, it involves too many people doing what Robinson's ideology tells him ought to have happened: a female target, Muslim criminals, and the state shielding them.

The story fits too neatly into older patterns of far-right storytelling. The historian who captures this best is Klaus Theweleit, who for his book *Male Fantasies*, studied the diaries and memoirs of previous supporters of the far right, members of the 1918-era German Freikorps, the immediate predecessor to Hitler's Nazis. In their accounts, Theweleit observed, there were only two sorts of women: "white" (mothers, nurses, or nuns, i.e. carers) and "red." The latter were sexually promiscuous and politically pro-Communist. Supporters of the German right were required to murder or rape them, and if the men failed, they risked being killed themselves.[15]

In Tommy Robinson's story, his cousin Jeanette is a latter-day red woman. She is a race traitor: someone who suffers at the hands of a foreign religion and then compounds the harm by converting willingly to Islam and living among Muslims. She betrays her family. She is sexually active and indifferent to human suffering, even if the suffering is done to her own body. She expresses, in other words, a recurring far-right fantasy in which an entire class of women, even though they are British and ought to be virtuous, are barely human. They are not capable of choice; someone else has to make all important decisions for them. They can become full people (or the nearest female equivalent to it, permitted by far-right ideology) only by setting aside their selfish desires and agreeing to put their lives into the hands of their betters: i.e. patriotic white men.

Children are victims too

By summer 2020, Tommy Robinson's supporters in the North East were promoting themselves as supporters of a new campaign, "Freedom for the Children UK." Where had this slogan come from? In the United States, during the Trump Presidency, a new conspiracy theory emerged that the world was being secretly controlled a small group of Satan-worshiping paedophiles (principally Hillary Clinton, Barack Obama, and George Soros, but also Hollywood celebrities and religious leaders) who operated a global child sex-trafficking ring. As with the British right, this theory revelled in the figure of the male saviour. The theory can be traced back to autumn 2017, and a post on the 4chan message board, by a figure "Q," who claimed to be a high-ranking intelligence officer with access to classified information. His story was that American generals were about to wage a war against the paedophiles, assisted by President Trump, who had recently been photographed alongside several soldiers in uniform and made a typically banal joke: "You guys know what this represents? Maybe it's the calm before the storm." The resulting myth took its name from the original poster: Q Anonymous. In QAnon mythology, Trump's meeting with the generals was a gathering of millenarian significance, the start of the resistance.[16]

While QAnon sounds like the script for a third-rate political thriller, by summer 2020 it had found a presence in US politics and online life and was entering the mainstream. Nearly two dozen candidates for elected office in that year's Congressional elections had declared themselves supporters of the theory. Facebook accounts dedicated to circulating the myth had 3,000,000 followers. Donald Trump's son Eric posted QAnon images and slogans, while Michael Flynn, Trump's former national security adviser, filmed a video of him taking the QAnon loyalty pledge, an edited version of the US oath of office. On a single day in July 2020, the President himself retweeted more than a dozen of the leading QAnon Twitter accounts, and when Republican law-makers criticised the existence of the conspiracy theory, the White House communications team sided with the QAnon supporters against its own members of Congress.[17] QAnon conspiracy theorists were, Trump insisted, people who "love our country." One journalist tried to explain to him what QAnon stood against, an imaginary conspiracy of paedophiles and cannibals, to be defeated only by Trump himself. He answered:

> Is that supposed to be a bad thing? If I can help save the world from problems, I'm willing to do it, I'm willing to put myself out there. And we are actually, we're saving the world from radical left philosophy that will destroy this country.[18]

Through summer 2020, QAnon supporters sought to win recruits by posting images of liberal politicians, such as Joe Biden or Barack Obama, alongside photographs of children, sometimes juxtaposed with images of child trafficking victims, and the hashtag, "#SavetheChildren," which they swamped with pro-Trump messages. In other words, what the movement was based on was a publicly declared self-righteousness, in which its adherents would flaunt their support for vulnerable people,[19] while preventing charities who had worked in the field for decades from getting publicity for their own work or helping vulnerable children.

Neither children nor women can control their own destiny

The right believes it is protecting white women and children from Muslim rapists. This is not a dynamic of giving women or children a platform, but of permitting white men to speak for them. As socialist feminist Kate Bradley observes, "Placing women on a pedestal soon turns to violence and aggression if they prove insubordinate or unhappy with their passive position." From the Proud Boys, with their ideal of the "Veneration of the Housewife," it is a short step to attacks on women, such as Lauren Southern, who was abused for not sleeping with white racist men,[20] or Richard Spencer's wife Nina Kouprianova. A fellow white nationalist, at one point Spencer brought her into his interviews. Weeks later, he was shouting at her that she should kill herself.[21]

The far right's protection of white women sits alongside a misogynistic language of hatred for the weak ("cucks") and the left ("snowflakes"). In both its protective and its denunciatory faces, the most basic belief of the far right in relation to women is that they are not full human beings and require representation by someone else.

Kate Bradley also gives examples of paedophilia within a movement pledged to punishing it. "Richard Price of the EDL and John Broomfield of Britain First were both found in possession of child pornography, whilst Kristopher Allan of the Scottish Defence League was convicted of sexual contact with a 13-year-old child."[22] Jack Renshaw of the British National Party and National Action also railed against Muslim paedophilia before being sentenced to 16 months in prison for sexually grooming 2 children aged 13 and 14.[23] More than 40 supporters of the British far right have been jailed for sexual offences against children since 1999.[24]

Other prominent neo-Nazis have been prone to the same vice: Frank Collin's career as leader of the National Socialist Party of America, and tormentor of Skokie, ended in 1980 when he was convicted of 8 counts of taking indecent liberties with children aged between 10 and 15, and he was sentenced to 7 years in prison.[25]

In speaking for others, the right claims an authorisation to act

When someone outside a social group says, "I believe in its cause and I want it to win," that, in itself, is a normal reaction. It suggests a politics of solidarity. But when the outsider expresses their support so keenly that they lose sight of their distance from the experience on which they draw, the result is rarely healthy. They claim the moral protection of a situation they misunderstand. They can start wielding the standing of their imagined position and use it capriciously. A much wider set of people even than the far right have lied to themselves about who they are and used that self-deceit to justify insulting or bullying behaviour.[26]

Tommy Robinson is an example of this phenomenon. How could anyone criticise him, his supporters argue, when he has pledged himself so publicly to the support of vulnerable white women? But "I've always been comfortable," Tommy Robinson writes in his memoir, "in a bloke-oriented environment," and it is a feature of his memoir that very few women are mentioned: his mother, his wife (good), his probation officer (bad). He is the sort of writer who can describe himself, without finding this in any way unusual or requiring a justification, as "having a bit of a domestic" when describing walking outside his home with his wife.[27]

Participants in far-right politics tell themselves that they are the champion of "women and children";[28] but there is no real-life category of women and children. Rather, the difference between women and children is that women are adults and entitled to speak for themselves, while children are less than adults and still obliged to depend on others to speak for them. To speak of the rights of women and children as a single group is to assume that women have no entitlement to speak and can be heard only if men speak for them.

The invocation of the rights of children in the face of imagined liberal conspiracy serves the purpose of persuading the supporters of the far right that they are simultaneously the victims of history, and the only people capable of avenging an enormous historical wrong.

Supporters of Q and its connected theories were arrested after attacking restaurants wrongly rumoured to have held captive children,[29] assembling bomb-making materials,[30] attacking Roman Catholic churches, derailing trains, stalking politicians, and attacking the buildings where they live.[31] If a child has been punished (and a child is the most powerless person imaginable) then there is in principle no action which goes too far in the task of recusing them. Someone who attacks a child can be beaten; they can be killed, and their killers will have a moral justification. For in order to prevent cruelty to children, any act is legitimate.

To invoke the suffering of non-existent children is to legitimise violence without limit against those who reject the right's conspiracy theories.

Notes

1 J. Busher, *The Making of Anti-Muslim Protest: Grassroots Activism in the English Defence League* (London: Routledge, 2016), pp. 75–83.
2 Busher, *The Making*, p. 82.
3 Busher, *The Making*, p. 102.
4 Busher, *The Making*, p. 77.
5 Busher, *The Making*, pp. 111–112.
6 B. Blake, *EDL: Coming Down the Road* (Birmingham: VHC Publishing, 2011), p. 4.
7 Blake, *EDL*, pp. 124–130.
8 Blake, *EDL*, p. 258.
9 A. Ramsay, '"Queer Eye," Jordan Peterson and the Battle for Depressed Men,' *Open Democracy*, 29 August 2020.
10 T. Lavin, *Culture Warriors: My Journey to the Dark Web of White Supremacy* (London: Monoray, 2020), p. 87.
11 Author's own notes.
12 J. Rozenberg, 'The Contempt of Stephen Yaxley-Lennon,' *Law Society Gazette*, 5 November 2018.
13 Author's own notes; *Re Yaxley-Lennon (aka Tommy Robinson)* [2018] EWCA Crim 1856.
14 T. Robinson, *Enemy of the State* (Luton: The Press News, 2017), pp. 59, 62.
15 K. Theweleit, *Male Fantasies Volume 1: Women, Floods, Bodies, History* (Minneapolis: University of Minneapolis Press, 1987).
16 K. Roose, 'What Is QAnon, the Viral Pro-Trump Conspiracy Theory?', *New York Times*, 19 August 2020.
17 A. Marcotte, 'Is QAnon the New Christian Right? With Evangelicals Fading, a New Insanity Rises,' *Salon*, 13 August 2020.
18 C. Subramanian, 'Trump Says QAnon Conspiracy Theorists "Like Me Very Much" and "Love Our Country,"' *USA Today*, 19 August 2020.
19 A. Breland, 'Why Are Right-Wing Conspiracies so Obsessed with Pedophilia?', *Mother Jones*, July–August 2019.
20 D. Lombroso, 'Why the Alt-Right's Most Famous Woman Disappeared,' *The Atlantic*, 16 October 2020.
21 K. Bradley, 'Always Anti-Fascist, Always Anti-Sexist,' *RS21*, 7 August 2018.
22 Bradley, 'Always Anti-Fascist'.
23 L. Dearden, 'Jack Renshaw: Neo-Nazi Paedophile Who Plotted to Kill Labour MP Jailed for Life,' *Independent*, 17 May 2019.
24 *Far-Right Criminals* (https://far-rightcriminals.com/far-right-sexual-offences/), accessed 2 August 2020.

25 P. Strum, *When the Nazis Came to Skokie: Freedom for Speech We Hate* (Lawrence, KS: University Press of Kansas, 1999), p. 144.
26 H. Freeman, 'God Save us from the Philosemitism of Burchill, Amis and Mensch,' *Guardian*, 7 November 2014.; M. G. Zimeta, 'Did it Have to Be the Hair?' *London Review of Books*, 15 June 2015.
27 Robinson, *Enemy of the State*, pp. 11, 55, 83.
28 As in the Sunderland Campaign, Supported by the EDL, 'Justice for Women and Children.' K. Razzall and Y. Khan, 'Far-Right and Far-Left Extremists Use Abuse for Own Agenda – Sarah Champion,' *BBC*, 20 December 2018.
29 '"Pizzagate" Gunman Sentenced to Four Years,' *BBC News*, 22 June 2017.
30 J. Winter, 'Exclusive: FBI Document Warns Conspiracy Theories Are a New Domestic Terrorism Threat,' *Yahoo News*, 1 August 2019.
31 L. Beckett, 'QAnon: A Timeline of Violence Linked to the Conspiracy Theory,' *Guardian*, 16 October 2020.

12

THE IDEOLOGICAL CAPTURE OF FREE SPEECH

In summer 2020, one of the most sustained attempts to silence a prominent political voice was directed not at a speaker from the far right, but at a prominent intellectual associated with the left. The Cambridge academic and historian of the British Empire and its critics, Priyamvada Gopal, was accused of having employed hate speech and, after hundreds of complaints, her Twitter account was briefly suspended. The story began on 23 June 2020, when Gopal posted on Twitter the following message: "I'll say it again. White Lives Don't Matter. As white lives."[1] The day before, supporters of Burnley Football Club had paid for an aircraft to fly a banner above their ground as their team played: "White Lives Matter Burnley." (The club distanced itself from the stunt and banned its organiser from the club for life.)

Both American and British politics had been polarised since the death of George Floyd, with advocates of racial equality complaining that the police were repeatedly killing young black men and women, while their opponents insisted that it was in principle wrong – and on occasion hateful – to demand that the state treat black people no worse than they treated whites.

Gopal's tweet was intended to summarise in just a few words a point she has made repeatedly elsewhere, including in a comment piece for the *Guardian*. White lives, she has argued, already mattered more than others. When people proclaimed that whites lives mattered, this added excess value to them, tilting society towards white supremacy. Of course white people experienced hardship, but not because they were white. In her words:

> Black lives remain undervalued and in order for us to get to the desirable point where all lives (really do) matter, they must first achieve parity by mattering. It's not really that hard to understand unless you choose not to.[2]

Some 15,000 people responded to Gopal's message on Twitter; most of them with hostile comments of their own.[3] Her employer and the police were inundated with demands for her sacking and arrest. Since Gopal's original post had been by no means unpleasant, it was rapidly supplanted by further fake tweets, purporting to have been written by her, including one that her readers should "carry out a resolute offensive against the whites, break their resistance, eliminate them."[4]

Many of the messages directed against Gopal were ultimately taken down by Twitter. After that, Gopal's harassers took to emailing her directly at her university address. Gopal herself therefore took the unusual step of posting more than 90 of those emails online, including repeated threats to rape or murder her:

> You will be the first to perish …
> Go and neck yourself before someone else does …
> We know where you live, we know your way to work …

And there were dozens and dozens more messages of this sort.[5]

Right-wing journalist and some-time enthusiast for free speech Douglas Murray attacked Gopal. He attacked her for complaining about having received death threats ("a renowned cry-bully move"). Murray called Gopal a "racist" and a bigot. And, while not directly calling for her dismissal from the university, he made it clear that such an act would be wholly appropriate: "Surely nobody who acts in such a deranged and deliberately provocative manner could possibly have any role at an institution of higher learning?"[6]

The *Daily Mail* agreed, with its journalist Amanda Platell claiming that Gopal "supports and endorses the subjugation and persecution of white people" and that she was "incit[ing] an aggressive and potentially violent race war." Under the threat of libel proceedings, the *Mail* apologised, and paid Gopal £25,000 compensation.[7]

The treatment of Gopal was unusual only in that her university supported her, helped her to face down the critics, and in that way, she was able to remain in her job. We might compare her to the American political scientist George Ciccariello-Maher, who, annoyed by the claim that the mere presence of black people in that country amounted to an actual or imminent "white genocide," decided to expose the conspiracy theory by pretending to take it at face value, and tweeted in December 2016, "All I want for Christmas is white genocide." On this occasion, Drexel University sided with the critics, calling the professor "utterly reprehensible" and "deeply disturbing," and placing him on administrative leave. After multiple death threats and threats to attack his family, Ciccariello-Maher resigned his university post.[8]

Why the reciprocal promise of free speech does not apply

There were two distinct ways in which Gopal and Ciccariello-Maher might have defended themselves. In the first, they might have argued that the accusations against them of racism were false. They were speaking *against* hate speech, and the accusations against them of bigotry were manifestly bogus. The difficulty with this approach is that it requires an adjudicator motivated by good faith and with a minimal political intelligence so that they are capable of distinguishing racism from anti-racism. As the case of these two universities makes clear, that is a considerable assumption to make. Moreover, as previous chapters sought to explain, in citing such cases as *Fraser v UCU* and *Redfearn v UK*, even experienced adjudicators of discrimination conflicts have real difficulty in determining who is the victim in a free speech case.

In the second approach, Gopal and Ciccariello-Maher might have argued that there is such a thing as free speech, and that this is a demand which should (in theory) protect the left as well as it protects the right, and that it ought to protect left-wing teachers against hostile outside critics demanding their removal from their posts. Yet neither used "free speech" in that way and it is worth thinking through why not. The simplest reason is that all participants in contemporary political debate have become used to a highly ideological conception of free speech, so that when genuine free speech crises occur outside that context, almost no one in politics (on either the left or the right) is capable of recognising them as such.

A previous chapter described the moment at which the career of British agitator Tommy Robinson was born, in 2009, when a homecoming march by British soldiers was disrupted by a group of political Muslims in Luton seeking, in their own way, to highlight the cruelty of the Iraq war. Waving placards and denouncing soldiers, they antagonised Luton residents to such an extent that a movement of far-right protesters, the English Defence League, was born.

How would Tommy Robinson have responded if one of his supporters had approached and said that the principle free expression protects all speech, even a (rhetorical) attack on British soldiers? That speech cannot be free unless anything is tolerated, no matter how shocking?

The argument would have been rejected with derision. Free speech is not for *Muslims*. And, in this part of his politics, Robinson was no extremist. Rather, he was in line with a policy consensus that stretches from the far right to the large majority of British liberals and to our state, which, in programmes such as Prevent, subjects Muslim speech to policing and curtailment, and threatens those who exceeds the boundaries of what can be said with imprisonment.

The example of Islamist speech illustrates what is in fact a general phenomenon. In contemporary discourse, we have all taught ourselves to understand that free speech applies to certain situations but not to others. It applies to people seeking a platform to speak within a university, i.e. coming from outside. It does not apply to anyone (whether a student or a lecturer) who is already there. It applies to the leaders of right-wing parties who want to employ social media to advance their positions without having to deal with the problem of anyone arguing back against them. It applies to monologues but not to dialogues. It applies to the instigators of political arguments, and not to those who disagree with them, who criticise, or who heckle.

Thus, in the context of Gopal and Ciccariello-Maher, no one would challenge the idea that a person taking to social media to advance the thesis that black people or Jews were causing a genocide of European and American whites was a speech act. That recognition would be a step towards the conclusion either that such speech should be prohibited (as hate speech) or that it should be allowed (as free speech).

There is seemingly no space within our free speech debate to recognise that the people criticising hate speech are themselves speaking, or that any serious application of a right to free expression must protect them too. "Free speech" applies only to the white racist and never to their anti-racist critic. And, because we have all drifted into this shared assumption that only one person's speech rights in any debate can be protected, critics of racism or other forms of bigotry unsurprisingly tend to see "free speech" as a politics which is incapable of shielding them.

Part of this is down to precisely the thing that "free speech" is intended to exclude, in other words, politics. Previous chapters have described how centre-right discourse around free speech changed, in Britain and America, around 1970. After many years of seeing free speech as of limited and partial value, the right began to use free speech discourse. It accepted the principle of free speech, an idea which had always belonged to the left. Then, from 1989–1990 onwards, the right began to treat free speech as an indicator of which side you belonged to: George Bush supported free speech, while "politically correct" students were accused of abandoning constitutional principles. If the students demanded the right to express an opinion, then by definition their demands were not really "free speech" claims, but something else and unworthy of protection.

Since 2016, there has been a further shift in our shared understanding of free speech, so that it has become a value around which conservative and those further to their right can co-operate. Our ordinary "free speech" debate assumes something like the scenario with which this book opened. The body issuing the invitation is a part of the mainstream right: a group of college Republicans inviting Milo or someone further to their right – even a fascist. Everyone has become so familiar to that scenario that we forget that free speech might be employed in other contexts: in defence of a worker's employment, or by the left as well as the right. The centre-right and the far right co-operate, and their alliance is shielded by liberal principle.

The left has been tacit in this process when we should have insisted on our own right to speak. As North American socialists David Camfield and Kate Doyle Griffiths have argued, "free speech isn't a cause the left can afford to leave to liberals or the right."[9]

Online culture

The far right has grown because of a much broader process of politics relocating online. The right is not the only group to have been changed by the encounter with social media. Plenty of people without strong views were also spending too many hours a day online, trying to win an audience and being knocked back. At the time that the English Defence League was growing, so were the giant tech companies. Between spring 2009 when the events in Luton began and summer 2012 when Busher's interviews with EDL members ended, the number of people engaging with Facebook increased from 200,000,000 million to 1,000,000,000 people worldwide. If the far right was growing faster online than other politics, it was still a minority. The right's obsessive use of the internet to build an audience and its passive-aggressive insistence on its own victimhood are not unique to it but are features of this period common to many forms of politics.

This point is developed in Jeff Sparrow's book *Trigger Warnings*. Written from the perspective of wanting the left to defeat the likes of Donald Trump and his emulators in Australia (where Sparrow is based) and Britain, he maintains that its rise has been poorly resisted by a left which has become both more moderate and more didactic since the 1970s. Sparrow makes a contrast between the "direct" politics of the 1960s and 1970s, which could envisage workers and the poor taking charge of society and running it for themselves, with the subsequent rise of "delegated" politics, i.e. the idea that the best the left could do is speak on behalf of the dispossessed in relation to a state whose ascendancy was imagined into the indefinite future.[10] This emphasis on delegation chimes with the themes of the present book, that the shift from no platform to hate speech anti-fascism shifts the subject of history from workers and the dispossessed to the state and business elites, with which the left is supposedly in dialogue.

The change from direct to delegated leftism has been followed more recently, Sparrow argues, by a turn to "smug politics"; that is, the belief of left-wing people that they are better than those they disagree with. A key moment in Sparrow's account is 9/11 (i.e. prior to the rise of social media) when the decline of left-wing infrastructure (unions, parties) meant that left-wing politics increasingly took the form of rooting for left-wing celebrities and cheering as they cut some Fox News presenter or similar down to size. Progressive defences of, say, scientific authority in relation to climate denialism opened the way to a top-down emphasis on political authority. "If progressives couldn't influence society that was the fault of society – or, more exactly, the people who were too stupid and too venal to appreciate the objective correctness of progressive ideas."[11]

Sparrow's purpose is not to suggest that these trends are final or irreversible, but only to warn against a certain direction of travel. If he is correct to any extent, then the left it follows has not been immune to the negative effects of culture wars or of a kind of online politics which risks infantilising everyone. On occasion, we too have claimed the mantle of suffering and demanded a right to be heard on behalf of other people. If we find this behaviour offensive when we see it in the far right, then consistency demands that we object when we see it in our own ranks.

The stakes of no platform have been raised. An earlier chapter described how, 20 years ago, Nick Griffin was able to win the support of voters in Lancashire, by being filmed on election night with his face in a gag. The appeal of that measure was limited to the voters of Oldham and nearby Burnley. Today, by contrast, the set of people who find online discussion unpleasant and believe they are being silenced – and who are willing to draw a connection between their dissatisfaction and the leaders of the far right offering to speak for them – runs into the millions.

Notes

1 B. Turner, 'Cancelled: How the Far Right Stole Free Speech,' *SW Londoner*, 18 August 2020.
2 P. Gopal, 'We Can't Talk about Racism Without Understanding Whiteness,' *Guardian*, 4 July 2020.
3 Turner, 'Cancelled.'
4 Turner, 'Cancelled.'
5 P. Gopal, 'The Dossier of White-Hot Hatred,' *Medium*, 16 July 2020.
6 D. Murray, 'Cambridge University's Very Modern Bigotry,' *UnHerd*, 26 June 2020.
7 J. Waterson, 'Daily Mail Pays £25,000 to Professor It Falsely Accused of Inciting Race War,' *Guardian*, 13 November 2020.
8 C. Butterworth, 'The Drexel Professor Who Tweeted, "All I Want for Christmas Is White Genocide" Resigned,' *Daily Pennsylvanian*, 1 October 2018.
9 D. Camfield and K. D. Griffiths, 'Why the Left Must Defend Free Speech,' *Briar Patch Magazine*, 27 April 2020.
10 J. Sparrow, *Trigger Warnings: Political Correctness and the Rise of the Right* (Melbourne: Scribe, 2018), p 28.
11 Sparrow, *Trigger Warnings*, p. 101.

13

TACTICS FOR ANTI-FASCISTS

At the heart of this book is an argument that no platform is justified only by the fascist nature of the politics at which it is addressed. The tactic loses its legitimacy when it is applied to non-fascist speakers or groups, even when they are relatively close to fascism. The further a person is from fascism on the political spectrum, the less likely it is that no platforming will be a principled or effective tactic against them.[1] Many readers of this book will feel that we have been living through a fascist moment, or something close to it. For through Donald Trump's presidency, a main plank of the Republican programme was that only he was standing in the way of what would otherwise be the inevitable victory of socialism, anarchism, and Communism. Such lurid fantasies told you almost nothing about the state of the American left; what they indicated was rather the deluded anti-Communist mind-set of the right.

When women marched on Washington to protest Trump's inauguration, they were transformed in the right-wing imagination into "the dregs of humanity," "foreign[ers]" planning "a civil war" for "tyranny."[2]

When fascists marched through Charlottesville with guns and torches, and when one of them killed Heather Heyer, Fox News explained that people who blocked the streets to stop them were "domestic terrorists ... antifa burns all it comes in contact with."[3] The right projected its own lurid fantasies onto its opponents and claimed that anti-fascists had been responsible for "the killings of multiple police officers throughout the United States," opening the path for Trump to blame the fighting on the left. On the anti-fascist side, he insisted,

> You also had troublemakers, and you see them come with the black outfits, and with the helmets, and with the baseball bats, you get a lot of bad, you get a lot of bad people in the other group ... they didn't have a permit.

From Trump's perspective, the people with guns and fascist symbols on their shields and fantasies of genocide were the ones who had come "to innocently protest," and against them were antifa who deserved every bullet that was shot at them.[4]

The accusation of extremism has been used not merely against those who would fight fascists on the streets, but even against milquetoast liberals. "You won't be safe in Joe Biden's America," Mike Pence warned.[5] As the election came closer, President Trump insisted that Joe Biden controlled an air-borne army of protesters, "People that you've never heard of. People that are in the dark shadows … People that are controlling the streets … thugs wearing these dark uniforms, black uniforms with gear."[6]

Anti-fascism had become a ghost haunting the American right, as vivid in the right-wing mind as once the spectre of Communism was. That was why Trump's answer in the first presidential debate was so disturbing. Presented with the question, "Are you willing tonight to condemn white supremacist and militia groups and to say that they need to stand down and not add to the violence?" Trump prevaricated and refused to condemn them. Finally, he answered, "I would say almost everything I see is from the left wing, not from the right wing." He said, "I'll tell you what, somebody's got to do something about antifa and the left. Because this is not a right-wing problem, this is a left-wing problem." Rather than tell his troops to go home, he told them to be ready for anything, "Proud Boys, stand back and stand by."[7]

Among the 50 percent of voters who were likely to vote Democrat, the idea that the President was a fascist was widespread. People were aware of his narcissism, his lack of attention to detail, the fundamentally personal and not political character of Trump's opinions. Others spoke of Trump as an aspirant dictator, the "ill Duce," rather than a full-formed fascist.

In the terms of this book, Donald Trump was a radical conservative rather than a fascist. His relationship to his armed base was opportunistic and, at the moment of its key test (the 2020 election), it failed to make the difference he had hoped. Whether parts of his base would in future radicalise in the direction of fascism, it is too early to say. But it is right to begin with Trump since he presents us with something that is a recurring problem in our moment. In Britain, America, or Europe, people instinctively grasp that fascism deserves a different kind of response to other forms of right-wing politics. They share the calculation which underpins no platform, that the way in which you should respond to fascism is different from the way you respond to other forms of right-wing politics. That reality places a premium on rightly characterising a politics you dislike. If the people in a community do not accept that a proposed speaker is a fascist, or that their politics threaten the rights of others, then any attempt to limit their speech rights will appear unjust. Anti-fascists need to be as accurate with our words and our analysis as we can.

Fascism

The account which follows is based on the anti-fascist writers of the 1920s and 1930s and represents an anti-fascist "minimum," i.e. a synthesis of views shared by a generation of anti-fascists. From the early 1920s onwards, the most compelling theory of fascism developed by its opponents has been to understand fascism as a specific form of reactionary mass movement. Palmiro Togliatti, writing in 1928 for a Communist audience made points which several generations of anti-fascists (socialists, anarchists, and others) would have accepted:

> If someone thinks it is reasonable to use the term "fascism" to designate every form of reaction, so be it. But I do not see the advantage we gain, except perhaps an agitational one. The actuality is something different. Fascism is a particular, specific type of reaction.[8]

For the interwar anti-fascists, fascism belongs to a wider political family, i.e. reactionary mass movements, which share the same broad dynamic as fascism, albeit that most of them were not mass movements to the same extent as fascism, and therefore lacked its capacity for repeated self-radicalisation. The most frequent points of reference were the military dictatorships of József Piłsudski in Poland, Miguel Primo de Rivera in 1920s Spain, or the rule of Admiral Miklós Horthy in Hungary.[9] These regimes were authoritarian dictatorships, practised censorship and refused free elections. However, they were unlike fascism. Their ideology owed as much to conservatism as it did to fascism. Their support drew to a much greater extent on existing pre-fascist military and business elites. Their relationship to the great mass of the people was also different. Fascism needed to raise the people up into a mass, counter-revolutionary army. The non-fascist far-right welcomed street support momentarily then demobilised it and did not return to violence.

Fascism is a distinct form of politics, recognisable through identifiable features in terms of what it believes, how it organises, and the sustained way it employs violence against its enemies, so although it is close to other reactionary mass movements it can be distinguished from them. At every stage of its development, fascism relied on violence. When fascist parties were launched, the fascists won recruits through mass demonstrations in uniform and through physical attacks on their enemies. Later, when fascist parties had been founded and were contending for power, physical force played a different role. At this point, the fascists would parade their determination to take on and defeat the existing democratic state. The fascist parties became "dual" parties, both standing in elections and threatening their rivals with violence, for which they maintained a private army. Fascism meant shaved heads alongside pin-striped suits, both ballot boxes and AK-47s. On taking power, fascist parties briefly relegated their militia. As fascism became more radical in office it employed new forms of violence: the use of military power in war, to create new forms of colonial rule, and to enact genocide against fascism's racial enemies.[10]

A specific form of reactionary mass movement

Fascism is a reactionary movement in the specific sense that, while it seeks to maintain a society dominated by the rich (i.e. a capitalist economy), it seeks to sustain production without social conflict, and it refuses to allow any opportunity for workers to organise against their employers. So, while fascism is like other reactionary political movements; one way it has repeatedly distinguished itself from other right-wing ideologies has been the enthusiasm with which it has rejected liberalism and social democracy. It argues that the present state of affairs (a capitalism marked by the revolutions of democracy and social democracy) has gone so badly wrong that a fresh revolution is required in order to reverse the effects of the politics of the past 200 years. In the words of Joseph Goebbels, the Nazi propagandist: "We will chase the parliament to the devil and found the state on the basis of German fists and German brains."[11]

Fascism's anti-liberalism is different from that of conservatism, for the latter is capable of an intermittent rhetorical enthusiasm for the goal of increased fairness. This willingness accompanies a pessimism as to whether human beings in general or any nation in its moment of impoverished finances can move towards a more equal state. So that a conservative might say that, yes, it would be better if society was fairer. But sadly, human beings are selfish, some are cleverer than others. Life does not allow us a greater amount of equality than we have now. The conservative emphasis on human nature as an impediment to reform is rejected by fascists. Fascism demands radical change. It acknowledges that our society is already unequal; it proposes to maximise inequality. It holds that supposedly natural differences based on class, race, and sex should be intensified and society can be forced into a future of military and race war.[12]

Fascism seeks to recruit millions of people with little stake in society towards its project of defeating hostile political, social, and racial groups. Both Mussolini and Hitler were early adopters of radio, cinema, propaganda posters, and amplified speech. In appealing to the people, and in rapidly adopting these new technologies to make that appeal, fascism distinguished itself from conservatism. The former needed to raise the people up to achieve a counter-revolution, the latter already possessed political power. It preferred its supporters to be the passive recipients of decisions taken always from above.[13]

In the present day, there have been racist street movements which can be seen as the possible precursors to the launch of a genuine fascist-style party (i.e. in the style of the Fasci di Combattimento, or the Freikorps whose growth preceded the electoral success of the NSDAP).[14] There have been mass electoral parties of the far right, although few of them have emulated the dual electoral and military model of the interwar fascists. There have also been individuals who have broken off from either of these formations, and taken part in acts of violence, which have then subsequently been justified by invoking the leaders of the fascist past.

None of these correspond exactly to the fascist model. The street movements are not fascist parties but are closer to the post-1918 milieu from which fascism emerged than the mass fascist parties of 1922 or 1933. The electoral parties are unlike fascism because very few of them retain an independent militia (the few that did have suffered electoral defeats while more moderate groups have grown).[15] Even the individual terrorists are new. Their urge to kill assumes that fascist parties cannot take power unaided; violence is their response to fascism's weakness.

The far right in an epoch of right-wing convergence

When speaking of fascism and the far right, these are two different kinds of words with different political meanings. Fascism is, as described above, a specific form of politics with a relatively long history and an identifiable and narrow tradition in terms of ideas and people. While different theories of fascism abound, all engage with its specificity (i.e. the ideas it holds, its organisational forms, and its use of violence). There has never been a meaningful theory of fascism which has excluded Mussolini, nor one which has included Reagan or Thatcher. By contrast, "far right" is a different kind of term. It refers simply to whatever form of politics is dominant on the centre-right at any one time, and then separates out from it the most radical forms of right-wing thought and focusses on them. Thus, in a British context, it might have been meaningful to describe the precursors to Thatcherism (i.e. Enoch Powell or Keith Joseph) as far-right Conservatives in around 1970, when they organised in opposition to Heath; it could not be persuasive to use the same language once (say) Keith Joseph was Secretary of State for Education.

Because the term far right is defined relationally – i.e. in contrast to centre-right – it is always, potentially, an extremely vague and amorphous term. And it has only become broader in recent years as different kinds of right-wing groups have emerged.

The last decade has seen a series of convergence-dynamics on the right. The political far right has been able to draw on the energy of a cultural right, i.e. a whole range of online practices ranging from expressing right-wing ideas via trolling, up to the emergence of video-blogging celebrities, sometimes with an audience of hundreds of millions of people, some of whom have used the iconography of the far right (Pepe the frog memes), retweeted far right accounts, used Nazi jokes, etc. Previous chapters have given examples of how this has boosted the political far right: for example, with online culture providing a steady stream of recruits to the offline right.

Money, speakers, styles of organising, and myths of white suffering have been rapidly shared across borders. So that parties who had a small basis in their own country, no history of electoral support, etc., could seem to have a huge army of supporters behind them. Another example is the emergence of Tommy Robinson as the local expression of a pan-European and worldwide movement for free speech against Islam. At the Free Tommy Robinson marches, speakers shared messages of support from America, Holland, Australia, and many other countries, their breadth concealing the narrowness of his domestic base.

The centre-right has borrowed ideas previously associated with the far right, with the former copying from the latter a rhetoric of racialised welfarism and agreeing to its attacks on political Islam. This has in turn made possible examples of coalition government between centre-right and far right (Italy, Austria), and instances of centre-right politicians and institutions lining up behind candidates previously seen as extremists (Brazil, France).

One of the processes which have made these alliances possible has been the way in which the leaders of the far right have distanced themselves from inter-war fascism. Tommy Robinson has tattoos of Churchill on his arm. When Steve Bannon sought to launch a far-right international, "the Movement," the most senior politician to sign up was Mischaël Modrikamen of the Belgian People's Party. Modrikamen has a huge portrait of Winston Churchill in his hall and named his dog Clemmie, after Churchill's wife.[16] The insistence on the non-fascist character of the far right has not (in contrast to, say, Britain in the 1970s) been cosmetic. Reflecting on the model of fascism which this chapter has developed, we can distinguish fascism from conservatism as follows:

- Fascism seeks a counter-revolution against the existing state and the creation of a one-party state; while conservatives will tolerate a greater range of voices, and while they might on occasion restrict speech, they do not share fascism's totalitarian ambition.
- Fascism rejects parliament and elections; conservatism eulogises them.
- Fascism employs street violence against its opponents, conservatism does not; instead, it expects the existing state to deal with its enemies in the streets.

Thinking through these distinctions, while the growing forms of far-right politics in the last decade have been poised between conservatism and fascism, for the most part they have been closer to the former than the latter. While the far right's recent success shows undoubted echoes with the past, we are not yet in a fascist moment.

The two politicians who are most often cited as proof that today's far right is fascist, Donald Trump and Jair Bolsonaro, have each threatened violence against their opponents. Running for office the first time in 2016, Trump led chants of "Lock Her Up" directed against Hillary Clinton and invited his supporters to "knock the crap" out of any hecklers.[17] Four years later, this became "Lock Him Up" for Biden. In 2020, Trump's approach to Black Lives Matter protests was similar, "When the looting starts, the shooting starts," he tweeted.[18] He promised his supporters he would support "your Second Amendment rights"; in other words, the right of the white owners of homes and businesses to aim their guns at potential black interlopers.[19]

In the run-up to elections in Brazil in 2018, Bolsonaro promised to exile or jail members of the outgoing Workers' Party government, "These red outlaws will be banished from our homeland. It will be a clean-up the likes of which has never been seen in Brazilian history."[20]

But what is striking about both governments is how hard they found it to govern as authoritarians or to introduce a 1930s-style dictatorship. In the United States, where Trump had a steady majority in the legislature and control over the

Republican Party, by summer 2020 his attempt to control the media had fallen flat and amounted to little more than bickering with journalists in press conferences. Trump's vision was not one of a fascist-style censoring of all discordant speech, but rather of a rapid aggrandisement of his own and his family's wealth and the wealth of his business allies.

The account here does not exclude the possibility of a second generation of Trumps or Bolsonaros heading in a fascist direction. There are compelling reasons to think that if the far right continues to grow its fascist component could enlarge at the expense of other far-right politics. While the concept of the far right is relative, this kind of politics does have a recurring logic and, over time, groups positioned there tend to end up adopting more or less the same positions: they oppose social reforms that tend to greater equality, and they become restless with democracy, which is criticised precisely because it allows liberals and socialists a chance to rule, etc.

Far-right parties who challenge for power find themselves having to give up the provocateur's mask. They learn that holding power gives them responsibility over their supporters' lives. They reflect on what they will do with their newfound authority. They find an increasing need for a programme for government. In order to develop its political project, and to avoid falling into the traps of patronage, incoherence, etc., the right is compelled to join up the dots between the different positions that it holds, and to argue its ideas with a greater consistency.

For the champions of the far right, fascism is a coherent ideology, which provides a series of interlocking positions which justify the adoption of violence and offer its supporters not just the excitement of military struggle and race war, but a society different enough to justify sacrifice. Nothing developed by the far right in the past decade, in the United States or in Europe, offers the same coherence. It is for that reason that the question of whether to permit fascist speech is a recurring one: for the past 70 years, the far right has been continuously discarding fascism in order to make its politics seem more acceptable, only to take up parts of its legacy again when the opportunity allows. There is every reason for this cycle to continue.

Fascist acts

From the perspective of someone who is considering whether to invoke no platform in response to a proposed fascist speech, the key questions are: objectively, is the speaker a fascist? And how might you go about persuading others that they are? When historians have addressed the first of these questions, our answers have tended to focus on one of three different aspects of fascism: its ideology (i.e. belief in the inequality of different human beings, its belief that its own nation is in crisis and requires to be reborn); its organising style (i.e. its belief in a dominant single leader, uniforms, and spectacle, its willingness to use violence against its every racial or political enemy); and its relationship to existing parties and the state (i.e. its demands for a fascist counter-revolution which would destroy both social and political democracy).

It is possible that a speaker is recognisably close to fascism in many or most but not all of these characteristics. If there is one which is most important, it is the willingness of fascists to threaten their many opponents with violence.

This is not to deny that anti-fascists, too, have employed violence, but to insist that it has been used in a different way and to different ends. For fascists, violence was the natural condition of humanity – something to be done willingly, the means to achieve the subordination of a wide variety of political opponents. Fascists employed a recurring, even monotonous, mystification of death. The very symbol of fascism, the *fasces* of the Roman *lictors*, contained an executioner's axe. A song of fascist parachutists boasted, "There are those who like to make love / There are those who like to make money / We like to make war / Face to face with death." When Enrico Vezzalini, fascist chief of the province of Novara, was captured by partisans in 1945, he wrote to his wife that nothing gave him greater pleasure than the possibility of his own execution. He would die, if that was what it took, "shouting for Italy and for fascism, Long Live Death!"[21]

When Italians joined anti-fascist groups the spirit in which the largest number of people signed up was one of resigned self-sacrifice, knowing that violence could only be defeated through force, but insisting that this choice was as unwelcome as it was necessary. The writer Italo Calvino told his brother, "We are on the side of redemption, while they are on the other side." This idea that even fascists could be changed and won back to democratic politics was a recurring theme of anti-fascist Italians, ranging from Communists with their predictions of a revolution in which the weakened but not defeated German working class would finally take revenge on its oppressors, to Catholics who spoke of praying, "For all of them. For the *others* too." In the letters home sent by captured partisans facing execution at the hands of fascist shooting squads, the partisans insisted on their innocence. "I have never killed nor had anyone killed," one wrote. A second proclaimed that he was "dying innocent and like a partisan."[22] The anti-fascist counterpart to Enrico Vezzalini's joy in self-annihilation is the 24-year-old chemist Pietro Mancuso who was hanged by German soldiers in September 1944. His last words, so strange and incomprehensible to his executioners that they made him say them twice were, "Long live a free Germany!"[23]

The case for denying a platform to a fascist speaker, in other words, depends on a rationale which is clearly articulated around key fascist characteristics, and is consistent. That position is at its strongest when the fascist has a history of violence.

When the 43 Group attacked fascist platforms, for example, their key task was to persuade the people around them that the speaker was a fascist. The words they shouted at their enemies: "Germany calling," "Go back to Belsen,"[24] were intended to generate a response of recognition. If a fascist speaker looked nervous on hearing these accusations, the point was made, people watching would understand why he was being attacked. The members of the 43 Group could then charge the platform, confident in the awareness that the people around them would accept the morality of anti-fascism. They needed to persuade their fellow Londoners that the speaker was a fascist; if that was agreed, then any limitation of the fascist's ability to speak would be accepted.

Something broadly similar played out when Richard Spencer was confronted by protesters at the time of Trump's inauguration. "Are you a neo-Nazi?" he was asked. "'No, I'm not a neo-Nazi," he answered, glaring back. "Do you like black people?" he was asked. "Why not?" he said, smiling at his own response. "Sure," he added.[25] The dishonesty of his answers was palpable: so clear that even a child could recognise it. Spencer was being filmed, as was the unnamed person who struck him, and "the punch memed around the world."[26] But without Spencer's smirks and justifications, the footage would not have received the positive reaction it did.

When campaigners demand that a fascist speech is stopped, the anti-fascists must persuade the people around them both that the speaker is a fascist and, in addition, that the restriction on their speech is justified. Given what this chapter has written about the significance of a fascist style of organising, it is likely that the most effective arguments that a certain speaker is a fascist will be the ones which focus on their adoption of fascist style. While violence is the easiest way to make this point, it is not the only possible consideration.

In the aftermath of Charlottesville, anti-fascists wanted to explain why Donald Trump was wrong to have claimed that there were "very fine people on both sides,"[27] and the most effective visual rebuttal of that argument were the photographs which showed James Alex Fields Jr, before driving the car that killed Heather Heyer, carrying a black shield emblazoned with two bundles of rods and an axe emerging from them.[28] These axes are *fasces* and are the symbol of authority from which fascism takes its name. It would be a hard task for anyone to carry a shield like that, and deny they were a fascist.

Similar criticisms of British far-right speaker Tommy Robinson, for attracting a regular crowd of supporters who routinely gave each other fascist salutes, received this unconvincing response in Robinson's memoir, *Enemy of the State*: "Anyone who has ever pointed to something above waist height can be made by the papers to be giving a Nazi salute."[29] Such passages do not reflect the reality of what it is like to watch a far-right march, and to see the participants as they clash the police or with anti-fascists, their right hand reaching out, embarrassing the leaders who still need to disassociate themselves from fascism.

If you want to identify a part of the far right as a fascist then begin with the people who join their protests, and how they dress and behave: the company they keep.

Ultimately, the best evidence of fascist intent is where a party or a speaker has a repeated history of using violence, where they have done this against a wide range of opponents (i.e. not just anti-fascists, but the speaker's other racial and political enemies), and where they make that threat within a structure which is recognisably comparable to fascism. That is the point at which its opponents can successfully label an opponent fascist and refuse them a platform.

Fascism – And those closest to it

No platform is a tactic for dealing with fascist parties and speakers. The other bodies to which it can be plausibly extended are parties and movements which stand so close to classical fascism that they are almost, as it were, standing on fascism's toes. One example is movements of an incipient fascist character. The best guide to their existence is the work of Robert Paxton, a historian of French fascism, who argues that interwar fascism went through five distinct stages: first, its creation, then fascism's rooting in a political system, next its acquisition of power, then the holding of power, and finally its radicalisation in power.[30]

What concerns us here is the first stage, when fascist parties were just being formed and as in the case of the Italian squadristi or the German Freikorps took the form of a movement rather than a party. At this point, the fascists won recruits through mass demonstrations in uniform, through physical attacks on the (racial, political, and sexual) enemies who were everywhere around them. Violence was used to demoralise the fascists' opponents. Physical force advertised the services of fascism to potential allies who shared its reactionary goals but not their mass base. A number of street movements in the last ten years have been broadly comparable to such squadristi- or Freikorps-era fascism: Pegida in Germany, the English Defence League and Democratic Football Lads Alliance, and the likes of the Proud Boys in the United States.

They have not been political parties, nor have they adopted the full fascist programme of the 1920s or 1930s. Yet the comparison with the post-1918 right is appropriate. These groups have a repeated history of using violence against a wide range of political opponents. In the case of Pegida and the English Defence League, there was a successive drift in the way that was used from an initial focus on political Islam and Muslims, to increasingly against the political left as well.

In the case of the Proud Boys and the militia movement, the shift has been from threatening liberals, socialists, and anarchists with words to physically attacking liberals, anti-racists, and those further to the left participating in Black Lives Matter protests. "Everything about them goes back again and again to violence," writes Talia Levin of this milieu, "as a hummingbird to nectar; it is what they crave, it fills them with a fleeting sense of virility and meaning."[31]

Their organisational structure has been recognisably close to fascism, with a preponderance of young and male members, and a leadership cult. Their ideology has shared with fascism a belief in the radical inferiority of racialised others. Like fascist parties and unlike conservative ones, they have promised their members a revolt against existing society. In every case these movements have been more amorphous, both organisationally and ideologically, than the parties which brought Mussolini or Hitler to power. But these protest groups are recognisably akin to the social movements within which fascism grew. For that reason, their speakers too can come within the reach of no platform.

A similar argument can be extended to those far-right splinter groups who idealise the fascist doctrine of the 1930s while arguing that the conditions are not ripe for mass fascist politics and who fill the gap between these two contradictory positions by advocating acts of individual terror. In recent years, perhaps the highest-profile advocate of terrorism on the British far right has been the group National Action, whose supporters planned such spectacles of violence as the murder of Labour MP Rosie Cooper.[32] In a strategy document, the group declared, "We have been presented with an opportunity for this project ... a doldrum period in nationalism where there is no clear nationalist project to get behind."[33] Or, as Jeff Sparrow argues in his book, *Fascists Among Us*, it is the inability of fascists to "transform online propaganda into real-world organisation" that drove events such as the 2019 Christchurch massacre.[34]

Such groups can be fitted into a history of fascism not because of the way in which they announce their praise and admiration for the likes of Hitler or other interwar fascists, or declare themselves fascists (i.e. it is relevant but not determinative that the Christchurch killer could write "I mostly agree with Sir Oswald Mosley's views"). The reason why they should be treated like fascists is that their violence fits within a cycle of behaviour which begins and ends with fascism. The practice of far-right terror begins from the insistence that fascism is right. It moves away from it, in conceding that this is a "doldrum period" and most people are not ready to vote for or join a fascist party. It proposes terror as a step in what it assumes must be an ever-escalating war between white nationalists (i.e. fascists, or people capable of becoming fascists) and their racial antagonists, one of whose intended consequences is to make fascism a viable politics for millions of people still on the side-lines. This is how one such killer, the Norwegian terrorist Anders Breivik, justified his actions, as "gruesome but necessary" in a longer project of legitimising fascism.[35]

Both the incipient fascists and the far-right terrorists come within this broader category of fascism and both deserve the sanction of no platform, not because they copy exactly the politics of the 1930s but because the end goal to which their politics tend is the recreation of a fascist party or of the popular support for fascism which would make such a group possible.

Putting this all together produces a result something like the following:

In compiling this table (Table 13.1), I am aware of how likely it is to date as the far right evolves. For example, at the time of drafting (December 2020), the far right is different to the one of 20 years ago in which by far the largest category was the third in the above list, i.e. "Euro-fascist" parties in France, Italy, and Austria. Today, by contrast, by far the largest group is the fifth row in the list, parties which may have a relationship to fascism but are not fascist.

What this analysis is trying to suggest rather, is a general approach, in which fascist parties and those pointing in a fascist direction are distinguished from those which have non-fascist origins, or which have been moving away from a fascist politics.

TABLE 13.1 Fascists whose platform can be denied

	No platform	*Platform*
Supporters of far-right terrorism	No platform	
Recognisable fascist parties and individuals (e.g. Golden Dawn, Daily Stormer)	No platform	
Parties of fascist origin (e.g. RN, FdI, Freedom Party) but of indeterminate future	Assess how far they have travelled from fascist origin, and whether they are seen as sharing a fascist style	
Right-wing street movements of non-fascist origin (DFLA, Pegida, Proud Boys)	Assess how far they have travelled down a path towards fascism, and whether they are seen as sharing a fascist style	
Far-right electoral party of non-fascist origin		Platform (but challenge: criticise, heckle, etc.)

Actions short of no platform

When thinking of how to confront a far-right speaker, for example, a mass populist party in which non-fascist and fascist elements combine but the former predominates, no platform will rarely be a wise tactic. The basic idea of suppressing the suppressor loses its credibility when faced with an opponent with no record of violence or who lacks the intention of leading a counter-revolution and prohibiting views they disagree with.

At the start of this book, no platform was characterised as a range of behaviour up to and including violent confrontations with fascist speakers. In much the same way, there are a range of tactics available to those who would allow a non-fascist speech to proceed, while challenging the speaker. At various points, this book has given examples of anti-fascists allowing a far-right group to speak, using the profile of the latter tactically, to discredit them. This happened at Olympia in 1934, when the far left broke into the meetings held by Mosley's BUF, daring the fascists to attack in order to delegitimise them. It was a desperate measure, made necessary by the reality that the main fascist party of the day had ten times more members than the largest left-wing group around which any anti-fascist alliance could be built.

Something similar could, arguably, be seen in the United States since 2016, when anti-fascists had to deal with the problem of a far right which was better funded than it was, and whose allies held positions of power in the media and the state. In those circumstances the task faced by the left was to use the right's platforms against them. As did Alexandria Ocasio-Cortez in building a social media presence by picking talking-points at which to bait the likes of Fox News.

Another example of that process is the trend for people hostile to the far right to record and share instances of violent and discriminatory behaviour. Think for example of Mark and Patricia McCloskey, the middle-aged Trump fans who pointed their guns at Black Lives Matter protesters in St Louis, Missouri in June 2020,[36] who were filmed and photographed, and whose images were shared around the world. Or of Christian Cooper, a middle-aged black birdwatcher, and Harvard graduate, who crossed paths with a white woman in Central Park in May 2020. He invited the woman to place her dog on a lead, as is required in that park. She responded by calling the police to report that there was "an African-American man … threatening me."[37] He filmed and shared their conversation, showing how far at odds with reality her speech was. In both these instances, what seemed to be at stake was whether middle-class white people were capable of using violence (either theirs or the state's), as it had been used routinely prior to the 1960s, to enforce the domination of affluent whites over their black neighbours.

In the 1970s or 1980s, you would expect the exposure of such behaviour to be the work of seasoned activists, but these days with our mobile phones everyone is potentially a citizen journalist. Such stories infuriate the right, and the left is accused of misrepresenting the people caught up in them. But they are not being silenced. Rather, their acts of verbal or threatened or actual violence are amplified for everyone to see. Not as a general rule of political engagement, and without subscribing to any fantasies about the necessity of free speech as the only means to win an argument ("sunlight is the best disinfectant"), but in the particular context of summer 2020, and with a mass movement on the streets, hearing their words exposed them.

It is possible to use combative tactics against a far-right but non-fascist speaker without preventing them from speaking at all. Fifty years ago, in the *Red Agitator* contribution to the original debate around no platform, some of those who supported the National Union of Students' no platform motion gave an example of how to disrupt but not prevent a far-right meeting. The example which they cited was the pseudo-scientist Hans Eysenck, who had given talks at various universities, insisting that black people were genetically inferior to white, incapable of intelligence, and that cities which had a large black population should be ignored by government. Such views were hateful and plainly capable of contributing to a fascist project, and yet Eysenck was not a fascist. If he had a political counterpart it was rather Enoch Powell, who had his own non-fascist but militant conservative project of banning black migration to Britain and repatriating those who had come here. In response to Eysenck, the *Red Agitator* authors argued for tactics of radical opposition that would still fall short of no platforming. To debate with Eysenck, they argued, or to treat him as a genuine scientist, would be to legitimise Powellism. That should be avoided. But his speeches should be permitted to proceed:

> This is not to say that we should go out to break up meetings which he addresses – the real threat lies in organised fascist groups – but rather that we should picket them and organise counter-meetings in order to show up the real nature of his ideas.[38]

Appropriate tactics to challenge a non-fascist speaker might include orchestrated walkouts, synchronised heckling, or turning your back on a speaker. There are an almost infinite number of ways you can show a speaker that they are unwelcome and signal that overwhelming sentiment in a room, even as the speaker talks, showing that a majority of people are opposed to them.

In the 2019 European elections, a series of candidates from the British far right, Carl Benjamin (Sargon of Akkad), Tommy Robinson, and Nigel Farage were humiliated, mid-election, when members of the public saw them and poured milkshakes over them. The purpose of the tactic was to shame, rather than to hurt. The likes of Robinson or Farage were free to stand and express their views. But a point was being made, that the majority of people disagreed with them.[39]

These examples are not given to prove the timeless superiority of the tactics of heckling or humiliating reactionaries over no platforming fascists. Rather, they are cited to insist that there may be occasions when the left should avoid no platforming its opponents, and this approach can be done, tactically, without giving up on our commitment to a different and equal world.

Notes

1 This book does not discuss the phenomenon of liberal or left-wing speakers making exaggerated claims that they have been no platformed. Examples of that phenomena are collected in A. Lentin, 'Open Letter on Peter Tatchell, Censorship, and Criticism,' *AlanaLentin.net*, 22 February 2016.
2 'Oath Keepers on Guard at Inauguration of President Donald Trump,' *Southern Poverty Law Centre*, 20 January 2017.
3 N. Ryun, 'Antifa Is a Domestic Terrorist Organization and Must Be Denounced by Democrats,' *Fox News*, 18 September 2017.
4 M. Keneally, 'Trump Lashes Out at "Alt-Left" in Charlottesville, Says "Fine People on Both Sides,"' *ABC News*, 15 August 2017.
5 B. Riley-Smith, 'Mike Pence Wars Voters: "You Won't Be Safe in Joe Biden's America,"' *Telegraph*, 27 August 2020.
6 K. Shepherd, 'Trump Blames People in "Dark Shadows" for Protest Violence, Cites Mysterious Plane Full of "Thugs" in Black,' *Washington Post*, 1 September 2020.
7 D. Renton, 'When Trump Defends Armed Right-Wing Gangs, His Rhetoric Has Echoes of Fascism,' *Guardian*, 1 October 2020.
8 P. Togliatti, 'On the Question of Fascism,' in D. Beetham, *Marxists in Face of Fascism: Writings on Fascism from the Inter-War Period* (Manchester: Manchester University Press, 1983), pp. 136–148, 137.
9 C. Zetkin, 'Fascism,' *Labour Monthly*, August 1923, pp. 69–78, 69; L. Trotsky, *The Struggle Against Fascism in Germany* (New York: Pathfinder, 1971) p. 125.
10 D. Renton, *Fascism: History and Theory* (London: Pluto, 2020), pp. 145–147.
11 B. C. Hett, *Crossing Hitler: The Man Who Put the Nazis on the Witness Stand* (Oxford: Oxford University Press, 2008), p. 93.
12 Renton, *Fascism*, pp. 147–152.
13 Renton, *Fascism*, pp. 152–157.
14 M. Davis, 'Catholics and Lumpen-Billionaires,' *London Review of Books* (podcast), 27 October 2020.
15 D. Renton, *The New Authoritarians: Convergence on the Right* (London: Pluto, 2019), pp. 46–67; D. Renton, 'The New Mainstream,' *Jacobin*, 29 May 2019.

16 P. Conradi, 'Steve Bannon Launches Right Wing Movement on the EU,' *Times*, 8 October 2018.

17 A. Mahdawi. 'The Bill Clinton Rape Shirt: What Anti-Hillary Merch Says about This Election,' *Guardian*, 20 July 2016; S. Levitsky and D. Ziblatt, *How Democracies Die* (London: Penguin, 2018), pp. 62–64.

18 D. Trump, Twitter, 29 May 2020.

19 G. Evans, 'Trump Mentioned the "Second Amendment" in His Speech about the Protests and People Are Terrified,' *Independent*, 2 June 2020.

20 T. Philipps, 'Brazil's Jair Bolsonaro Threatens Purge of Left-Wing "Outlaws,"' *Guardian*, 22 October 2018.

21 C. Pavone, *A Civil War: A History of the Italian Resistance* (London: Verso, 2013), pp. 515, 517.

22 Pavone, *A Civil War*, pp. 504, 509, 513.

23 Pavone, *A Civil War*, p. 263.

24 D. Renton, *Fascism, Anti-Fascism and Britain in the 1940s* (Houndmills: Palgrave, 2000), p. 98.

25 P. Murphy, 'White Nationalist Richard Spencer Punched during Interview,' *CNN Politics*, 21 January 2017.

26 S. Vysotsky, *American Antifa: The Tactics, Culture and Practice of Militant Anti-fascism* (London: Routledge, 2021), p. 1.

27 B. Jacobs and O. Laughland, 'Charlottesville: Trump Reverts to Blaming Both Sides Including "Violent Alt-Left,"' *Guardian*, 16 August 2017.

28 J. Wilson, 'Charlottesville: Man Charged with Murder Was Pictured at Neo-Nazi Rally,' *Guardian*, 13 August 2017; S. Hendrix, 'It's Still Hard to Look at,' *Washington Post*, 10 August 2018.

29 T. Robinson, *Enemy of the State* (Luton: The Press News, 2017), p. 105.

30 R. O. Paxton, *The Anatomy of Fascism* (London: Penguin, 2004).

31 T. Lavin, *Culture Warriors: My Journey to the Dark Web of White Supremacy* (London: Monoray, 2020), p. 5.

32 Press Association, 'Man Who Plotted MP's Murder Avoids Retrial for National Action Membership,' *Guardian*, 2 April 2019.

33 M. Hayes, *The Trouble with National Action* (London: Freedom Press, 2019), p. 17.

34 J. Sparrow, *Fascists among Us: Online Hate and the Christchurch Massacre* (London: Scribe, 2019), pp. 121–122.

35 'Anders Breivik and The Turner Diaries: How a 2011 Norwegian Massacre Echoes a 1978 American Novel,' *Foundation for Defences of Democracies*, 25 July 2011.

36 J. Lussenhop, 'Mark and Patricia McCloskey: What Really Went on in St Louis That Day,' *BBC*, 25 August 2020.

37 'America Explodes,' *London Review of Books*, 18 June 2020.

38 Red Agitator, *No Platform for Fascists* (London: LSE International Socialists, 1974).

39 'Nigel Farage and Tommy Robinson Attacks see "Milkshaking" Added to "Brexicon,"' *SkyNews*, 7 November 2019.

14

CONCLUSION

This book has argued that when faced with an enemy who can rightly be identified as fascist and a movement demanding that their event is cancelled, anti-fascists should start from an approach of no platform rather than one of hate speech. No platform teaches a scepticism in relation to authorities: social media companies, broadcasters, and universities – and is averse to granting these bodies more power unless strictly necessary. Moreover, only a part of today's far right is fascist, and no platform should only be applied to groups which are, and which behave like, fascists. The risk otherwise is of playing out a culture war on a terrain which is favourable to the far right.

Where no platform would be inappropriate (because the speaker is not a fascist or not seen as one by sufficient members of the affected community) a better starting point is to permit the speech to take place but to protest at it – rather than by seeking to prevent the speech taking place at all. In those circumstances, other tactics remain available to anti-fascists, including heckling, acts of demonstrative censure, and boycott.

The left, at its best, has had a conception of free speech in which everyone is entitled not merely to speak but to have a fair opportunity to be heard. This is a different conception of speech from that which inspires liberalism, which has to fit the question of free speech for fascism into its pre-existing model of negative liberty, in which citizens require protection from the banning instincts of an over-mighty state.

Socialists have long argued that the reason why more people's voices are not heard is not the active hostility of a censorious state but the subtler processes of class exclusion in which the children of the rich are more likely to become journalists, novelists, poets, etc. Everyone – above all poor and working-class people – should have the same ability to speak and shape society as any billionaire. We want to see more people speaking, more of the time, on a greater set of topics. We want speech to be free and diverse, chaotic, and satisfying.

Done in a way that is consistent with the left's values, no platform can be a unifying experience. Sixty years after the Battle of Cable Street, one of the rank-and-file participants in the day's events, Harold Rosen, described what it was like to have contributed to a successful protest against the rising force of British fascism:

> If you are lucky, there are moments in your life which are especially and uniquely illuminated. They stand out from the rest of your life as bright icons, huge representative symbols, which give meaning to how you have lived.[1]

There are times when no platform is the right approach, when there is a chance to close down a fascist speaker and to do so in a way that builds the strength of local campaigns and shows people that they can change their world. When you can create in a town or a city your generation's own counterpart to Cable Street – that victory is worth savouring.

That said, the end goal of left-wing politics has to be something else: not the abolition of fascism, but the satisfaction of the desire of millions to speak and be heard. The tactical opposition to the speech rights of fascists is an early part of that larger understanding, that we need more speech not less. There is no route to the collective liberation of humanity except by creating mass campaigns of hundreds of thousands of people in which competing views can be heard and properly discussed. The best of the anti-fascist movements described in this book have been like that, a cacophony of competing voices, a range of opinions with the space for participants try out competing strategies in order to establish what works. No platform is merely an initial and necessary acknowledgement that unless the oppressed can protect themselves from those who would silence them for ever, a future in which everyone can talk will never be realised.

Note

1 H. Rosen, *Are You Still Circumcised: East End Memories* (Nottingham: Five Leaves Publications, 1999), p. 108.

INDEX